13.10

THE TWILIGHT
OF ATHEISM

THE TWILIGHT OF ATHEISM

The Rise and Fall of Disbelief in the Modern World

Alister McGrath

RIDER

LONDON · SYDNEY · AUCKLAND · JOHANNESBURG

3 5 7 9 10 8 6 4

Copyright © 2004 by Alister McGrath

The right of Alister McGrath to be identified as the Author of this work has been
asserted by him in accordance with the Copyright, Designs and Patents Act, 1988.

First published in 2004 by Doubleday,
a division of Random House Inc.
Published in 2004 by Rider,
an imprint of Ebury Press, Random House,
20 Vauxhall Bridge Road, London SW1V 2SA
www.randomhouse.co.uk

Random House Australia (Pty) Limited
20 Alfred Street, Milsons Point, Sydney,
New South Wales 2061, Australia

Random House New Zealand Limited
18 Poland Road, Glenfield,
Auckland 10, New Zealand

Random House South Africa (Pty) Limited
Endulini, 5A Jubilee Road,
Parktown 2193, South Africa

The Random House Group Limited Reg. No. 954009

BOOK DESIGN BY DEBORAH KERNER / DANCING BEARS DESIGNS

Papers used by Rider are natural, recyclable products made
from wood grown in sustainable forests.

Printed by Mackays of Chatham plc, Chatham, Kent

A CIP catalogue record for this book is available from the British Library

ISBN 1844135748

CONTENTS

THE TWILIGHT
OF ATHEISM

INTRODUCTION

"THE EMPIRES OF THE FUTURE WILL BE EMPIRES OF THE mind." In speaking these words to a wartime audience at Harvard University in 1943, Winston Churchill attempted to express a transition he discerned within Western culture, with immense implications for the postwar era. The great powers of the new world would not be nation-states—as with the Roman or British empires—but ideologies. It was ideas, not nations, that would captivate and conquer in the future. The starting point for the conquest of the world would now be the human mind. Churchill may well have been thinking of the astonishing power of systems—above all, Nazism and Marxism—to capture the minds and loyalties of his own generation. It was ideas, not nations, that would be at war in the future.

The greatest such "empire of the modern mind" is atheism. It has been estimated that in 1960 half the population of the world was nominally atheist. At its height, this was a vast and diverse empire embracing many kingdoms, each with its distinct identity, yet united by a common rejection of any divinities, supernatural powers, or transcendent realities limiting the development and achievements of humanity. Atheism comes in various forms, its spectrum of possibilities extending from a rather mild absence of belief in God or any supernatural beings to a decidedly more strident and rigorous rejection of any religious belief as manipulative, false, and enslaving.

Atheism, in its modern sense, has come to mean the explicit denial of all spiritual powers and supernatural beings, or the demand for the elimination of the transcendent as an illusion. For some, it was felt, the mirage of religion might comfort. Christianity, after all, inculcated a soothing possibility of consolation in the face of life's sorrows. But increasingly it was argued that this illusion imprisoned, trapped, and deceived. By any index of its capacities, Christianity, like all religions, was held to be deficient. Intellectually, its central ideas were ridiculous and untenable; socially, it was reactionary and oppressive. The time had come to break free of its clutches, once and for all.

The idea that there is no God captured human minds and imaginations, offering intellectual liberation and spiritual inspiration to generations that saw themselves as imprisoned, mentally and often (it must be said) physically, by the religious past. It is impossible to understand the development of Western culture without coming to terms with this remarkable movement. Although some such idea has always been around, it assumed a new importance in the modern era, propelling humanity toward new visions of its power and destiny.

Yet the sun has begun to set on another empire. It is far from clear what the future of atheism will be, or what will replace it. Yet its fascinating story casts light not simply on the forces that have shaped the modern world but on the deepest longings and aspirations of humanity. It is one of the most important episodes in recent cultural and intellectual history, studded with significance for all who think about the meaning of life or the future of humanity. This book sets out to tell something of the story of the rise and fall of a great empire of the mind, and what may be learned from it. What brought it into existence? What gave it such credibility and attractiveness for so long? And why does it seem to have lost so much of its potency in recent years? Why has it faltered? What is its permanent significance?

This book is an expanded form of a speech I gave at the landmark debate on atheism in February 2002 at the Oxford Union, the world's most famous debating society. The great Debating Chamber was packed to capacity to hear four speakers argue passionately with each other—and with the huge audience—on whether it is possible to "rid the mind of God." I am immensely grateful to my three fellow speakers—Professor Peter Atkins, Dr. Susan Blackmore, and Dr. David Cook—for their partnership in a highly stimulating exchange, and their camaraderie over a memorable dinner beforehand. Oxford University has always prized debate as a means of advancing thought. Given the many questions that are now being raised about the viability of an atheist worldview in a postmodern culture, it seemed only right to extend that debate far beyond the audience that gathered in Oxford. This book will not settle anything; but at least it can further discussion of one of the greatest issues of our time.

ALISTER MCGRATH
OXFORD UNIVERSITY

THE DAWN OF
THE GOLDEN AGE OF ATHEISM

THE REMARKABLE RISE AND SUBSEQUENT DECLINE OF atheism is framed by two pivotal events, separated by precisely two hundred years: the fall of the Bastille in 1789 and that of the Berlin Wall in 1989. Two brutal physical structures, each of which served as a symbol of a worldview, were destroyed, to popular acclaim. These dramatic events crystallized massive changes in perceptions in Western culture. They frame a fascinating period in Western history, in which atheism ceased to be the slightly weird outlook of those on the fringes of polite society in the West and became instead its dominant cultural voice. The fall of the Bastille became a symbol of the viability and creativity of a godless world, just as the fall of the Berlin Wall later symbolized a growing recognition of the uninhabitability of such a place. They mark neither the beginning nor the end of atheism, simply providing the historian with convenient boundary posts for a discussion of its growth, flowering, and gradual decay.

The Bastille was a grim medieval fortress in the east of Paris, which served as a state prison for the kings of France. In the popular mind it was associated with the violence, oppression, and torture employed by the French monarchy in the final years of the *ancien régime*. Its thick walls and high towers projected the power, permanence, and security of the old system. The Bastille was a tangible assertion of the futility of any attempt to alter things. Like the laws of the Medes and Persians, the social structure of France was set in stone and could not be changed. The events of July 1789 destroyed that myth of unchange-ability. More than an ancient fortress was overthrown on that day; the harsh despotism that it had come to represent was exposed as weak and vulnerable, equally capable of rout and destruction.

On July 14, 1789, an armed mob of about one thousand men and women marched against its heavy gates. The Marquis de Launy, governor of the fortress, was confident that he could defend it with his garrison of more than one hundred heavily armed men. After all, the walls were ten feet thick and one hundred feet high. He was proved wrong; within hours, the fortress had fallen and de Launy had been lynched by the angry mob. Pieces of masonry were taken home as souvenirs of an event that had demonstrated beyond doubt the power of the people to overthrow the old order. Two days later, the National Assembly ordered the Bastille to be razed to the ground.

What the French Revolution began, the Russian Revolution continued. Soviet political and military expansion after the Second World War led to the imposition of a new order upon much of Eastern Europe and became the inspiration of Communist parties throughout Western Europe. The divided city of Berlin was a key site of the ideological conflict between East and West. Just after midnight on August 13, 1961, the East German government deployed twenty-five thousand militiamen and Vopos ("people's police") to seal the border between East and West Berlin. Barbed-wire fences were hastily erected, to be replaced by a more permanent brick wall, heavily fortified with electrified wire and machine guns. Although presented as a measure designed to defend the East from fascist invasion, the real purpose of the wall was to prevent the destabilization of the East German regime by massive emigration to the West. Within a few years, the wall had permanently divided Berlin into two cities. Its minefields, electrified fences, and automatic machine gun emplacements had become physical symbols of a deeper intellectual malaise—the bunker mentality into which the Marxist states of Eastern Europe had fallen, and their total lack of credibility to their own people. A self-styled liberator was now seen as an oppressor.

By 1989, it was evident that Marxism was locked into a state of decline throughout Eastern Europe. Enthusiasm and credibility had long since been eroded; what remained were purely physical constraints, now themselves at the point of tottering to the ground. A graffito boldly inscribed on the western side of the Berlin Wall declared that "every wall must fall sometime." On September 11, Hungary began to permit visiting East Germans to exit to the West through neighboring Austria. Pressure for reform in East Germany became irresistible. On November 9, the East Berlin authorities resigned themselves to the inevitable and threw open the crossing points to the West. Pieces of the wall were soon on sale for twenty deutsche marks, souvenirs of a hated past which could not be allowed to be forgotten.

Parts of that wall still remain intact. The machine guns and minefields are gone. Their crumbling structures are now overgrown with weeds, a potent symbol of the transience of the appeal of human ideas. Yet it is impossible to view the remains of the wall without being reminded of a not-so-distant past, and the glories of a revolution that seems to have spent its power.

This book sets out to tell the remarkable story of the rise and fall of modern atheism. Like a tidal wave crashing against the shoreline, atheism surged over the West, sweeping away its rivals, before itself gradually receding. Over a period of two centuries, atheism emerged from the shadows to conquer and captivate the imagination of an era. The reversal of the fortunes of this movement is a remarkable development in European history. While a rumor of godlessness hovered uneasily over the world of late antiquity, modern atheism possesses an intellectual pedigree and cultural sophistication that set it far apart from the modest and tentative experiments of the classical period. In its golden age, atheism emerged as an increasingly sophisticated, powerful, and influential "empire of the mind." In its modern forms, it is unquestionably one of the greatest achievements of the human intellect, capable of capturing the imagination of generations. Like all such movements, it has its saints and charlatans, its visionaries and nutcases, some of whom will feature prominently in these pages. To tell the full story of this intellectual revolution lies beyond the scope of this work, which can only hint at the massive upheavals in Western society and patterns of thought, and sketch the outlines of some of those who shook the foundations of traditional Western culture.

It is impossible to tell the full story of this highly creative and turbulent phase in Western history in a few hundred pages. What can, however, reasonably be attempted is a series of "snapshots"—explorations of specific themes and moments that cast light on the broader patterns of ideas in its history. Like an archaeologist cutting a trench across a major historical site, this work offers a series of thematic cross sections of the high noon of atheism.

Although modern atheism rose to prominence in the eighteenth century, its origins can be traced back to the dawn of Western civilization itself. Our story therefore begins in the mists of early Greek history, when a blind poet is believed to have told the epic tale of the Trojan War and its aftermath—and in doing so, began to undermine belief in the great gods of Olympus.

THE CRITICS OF THE GODS: CLASSICAL GREEK ATHEISM

The discovery of the site of ancient Troy by Heinrich Schliemann in 1870 has passed into folklore as one of the greatest archaeological achievements of the nineteenth century. In his memoirs, Schliemann recalled how, as a young child, he was taken on his father's knee and told the tales of the Greek heroes. Above all, he found himself fascinated by the story, swathed in the distant mists of history, of the for-

4

bidden love between Helen, wife of the king of Sparta, and Paris, son of Priam of Troy, and how Helen's abduction resulted in a war that destroyed a civilization. Homer's great story of the Trojan War, according to Schliemann, awoke him from his slumbers, and aroused a passion to search for archaeological confirmation of the existence of Troy and the other great civilizations of this distant age of heroes. He went into business to make his fortune so he could fund his passion to find out the truth about Troy, and confirm his original insights into its location. Armed with his knowledge of the ancient world, gained through painstaking reading of the classics, he found the original site of Troy in northwestern Turkey, and uncovered its fabulous treasures.

A close reading of Schliemann's journals makes it clear that this is largely romantic nonsense. Schliemann's discoveries were achieved largely by hijacking the work of the English archaeologist Frank Calvert. Yet however tainted its scholarship, Schliemann's work points to the deep popular fascination with the ancient world that has been such an integral aspect of Western culture. Homer's great epics the *Iliad* and the *Odyssey*, traditionally assigned to the ninth century B.C., tell the story of the Trojan War and its aftermath in such a compelling way that they have become part of the inherited tradition of the Western imagination. They are also of fundamental importance to our theme. For Homer's gods are corrupt, vain, and self-serving—exactly the kind of human invention that a later age would find childish and embarrassing.

Homer's unflattering account of the petty squabbles on Mount Olympus and their malignant impact on human history is best seen in the *Iliad*. This epic—whose name literally means "a poem about Ilion" (an ancient name for Troy)—celebrates the achievements of the Greek and Trojan heroes of this golden age, such as Agamemnon, Achilles, Hector, and Paris. The poem gives a highly dramatic account of some episodes in the war, involving the complex interplay of human heroes and the gods of Olympus. Although both the *Iliad* and the *Odyssey* make an appeal to the intervention of the gods to explain the events of human history, this tendency is especially marked in the *Iliad*. These heroes are often depicted as glory-seeking individualists, merciless and brutal by modern standards, whose moral code is dominated by the need for public demonstration of their bravery and honor.

The activities of these heroes are set against the backdrop of the constant intervention of the Olympian deities. This perpetual interference in the affairs of humanity reflects intense rivalry and bickering on the heights of Olympus itself, as the gods seek to advance the fortunes of their favorites on earth. The situation is made much more interesting through Homer's assumption that the gods are as lascivious as their mortal counterparts, and have turbocharged sexual appetites that lead them to prowl the face of the earth, copulating with desirable mortals who cross their paths. As a result, many mortal heroes have divine parents who assist and protect them. Homer regularly depicts the gods as manipulating situations to the advantage of their favorites.

The classic tale of Zeus and Europa neatly illustrates the voracious sexual appetite of the immortals and its impact on their dealings with humanity. Europa was the beautiful daughter of Agenor, king of Phoenicia. Noticing her beauty, Zeus responded as only one with Olympian levels of testosterone in his veins might: he transformed himself into a sleek and handsome bull and approached Europa and her companions as they played by the seashore. Europa was unwise enough to mount the bull, who then swam to the island of Crete. Here, Zeus revealed his true identity, and added yet another notch to his bedpost. In due course, Europa gave birth to three sons—Minos, Rhadamanthys, and Sarpedon. Each of these now had a claim to Zeus's special favors and protection, further complicating the dynamics of divine intervention in earthly affairs.

Homer is particularly scathing concerning the ethics of female deities. This can be seen in the famous incident known as the Judgment of Paris. Athene, Hera, and Aphrodite are here depicted as taking part in a beauty contest on Mount Ida, judged by the Trojan prince Paris. After what appears to be an embarrassingly thorough examination of their charms, Paris awards the victor's crown to Aphrodite. From that moment onward, Aphrodite is fiercely loyal to the Trojans. Having been so publicly humiliated by a prince of Troy, it is not surprising that Athene and Hera should set out to take revenge against the Trojans by intervening on behalf of the Greeks throughout the war.

For Homer, the gods are immortal humans, demonstrating and engaging in the same emotions, vices, and power games as their human counterparts. It soon turns out that immortalization just means the infinite extension of existence, not the infinite projection of moral qualities. There are no limits to what the gods can do, nor to how long they can do it for. Homer often refers to divine activities humorously, suggesting that they are not to be taken too seriously. Yet there is a deeper, perhaps more sinister, aspect to the *Iliad*, which is perhaps best seen from the famous scene in Book 1, in which Achilles considers whether or not to murder his rival Agamemnon. Achilles' decision not to kill Agamemnon is portrayed as the outcome of a rather whimsical personal intervention by the goddess Athene. No human ethical norm or value appears to be implicated in his decision. Obedience to the gods seems to be the foundation of human morality. And for Homer, those gods are egocentric, jealous, and petty tyrants. Who could seriously base ethics on the personal vanity of such creatures?

Homer's gods are human beings writ large, complete with vices and virtues. Far more than being morally superior to humanity, they are the immortal counterparts to human weakness. The only limits placed upon them are their specific spheres of activity—for example, Poseidon as the god of the sea, Ares as god of war, Hermes as divine messenger, and Aphrodite as the goddess of sexual desire. Each divinity is sovereign within an arc, a portion of the total circle of all things, beyond which it is powerless. Yet within that arc, the gods can act with complete impunity, subject to no external constraint or ultimate accountability. To be accountable is human; and the gods had long since liberated themselves from that tiresome limitation.

Homer's sly insinuations concerning the pillow talk of Olympus shaped growing Greek concerns over the morality of their gods. Increasingly, the Olympian gods came to be seen as something of an embarrassment, an awkward reminder of a bygone age ruled by force. When Protagoras set out the laws that would govern the city-state of Thurioi in 444 B.C., he insisted on the public accountability of its citizens on the basis of mutually agreed values. They would not be like the gods of Olympus. Who could admire such corrupt divinities, or seriously want to imitate the lifestyles they modeled? Although ancient Greece would continue to honor its classic divinities for centuries to come, their moral and intellectual credibility had been fatally eroded.

The term "atheist" now came into use. Far from meaning "one who denies the existence of supernatural beings," the Greek term *atheistos* meant something like "one who denies the traditional religion of the Athenian establishment." To deny the existence of the gods was seen as a punishable offense in Greek society, as the indictment and enforced suicide of Socrates (469–399 B.C.) makes clear. Classic Athens was far from being the center of free thinking that later writers like to make it. It was protective of its deities, believing that these enshrined its ideals. For Melitus, one of Socrates' accusers, the "atheist" philosopher had corrupted the city's youth by encouraging them not to believe in the city's gods. Yet Socrates was no atheist in the modern sense of the term.

One of the ironies of history is that the first Christians were also widely accused of being "atheists" by their pagan critics—not because they denied the existence of a god but because they challenged the validity of the pagan religious system of the late classical world, especially the cult of the Roman emperor, who increasingly came to be worshiped as a god. As the Christian apologist Justin Martyr pointed out to his Greek critics in the second century, Christians such as himself "were even called 'atheists'—which we are in relation to what you consider gods, but are most certainly not in relation to the Most True God." The Christian refusal to observe the state religious conventions marked them out as troublemakers and potential revolutionaries—something that the Roman authorities were not prepared to tolerate.

The imperial cult was so strong in the major cities of the eastern Roman Empire that it was inevitable that some form of confrontation would take place between the secular authorities and Christian "atheists." One of the most frequently cited pieces of evidence here is the letter of Pliny the Younger to Trajan, dating from about 112. In this letter, Pliny the Younger comments on the growing number of Christians who refused to worship the image of the Roman emperor. Although Pliny reports that he found nothing more sinister than "a depraved and extravagant superstition," it is clear from his letter that Christianity was suspect on account of its refusal to worship the emperor, which suggested that it was bent on overthrowing the existing social order. While the major persecution of Christians instigated at Rome under Nero does not seem to have had any direct link with the imperial cult, this became increasingly significant in the following century. "Atheism" was understood to designate a refusal to worship the official divinities of the Roman Empire—and hence potential sedition.

Yet atheism failed to have the impact on the late classical world that some feared and others secretly longed for. Roman writers such as Lucretius (c. 94–c. 50 B.C.) argued that religion merely evoked terror—as, for example, in the case of Agamemnon, whose fear of the goddess Artemis led him needlessly to sacrifice his only daughter. Atheism, Lucretius declared, eliminates such terror, and allows us to focus on the natural forces and processes at work around us. These ideas had relatively little impact on their own era. They would, however, find a new and highly receptive audience centuries later. Perhaps the world was not yet ready for the announcement of the death of the gods. Yet that day would come—with a vengeance.

THE TRANSITION TO THE
MODERN ERA

Our story now crosses the centuries of history from the classical era to Western Europe in the seventeenth century. By this stage, belief in God had become a deeply embedded aspect of Western European culture, with the institution of the church widely seen as a stabilizing influence on the region. The great Protestant Reformation of the sixteenth century brought about massive religious change. Yet belief in God was unaffected by these demands for reform. Whatever disagreements existed between Catholics and Protestants, they were united in their fundamental belief in God. As we shall see, there are some reasons for suggesting that the rise of Protestantism may have laid the foundations for the later emergence of atheism. But this important development lay some centuries in the future.

Yet the seeds of a renewed interest in atheism had been sown. The power, influence, and wealth of the church became seen as an increasingly scandalous matter, which required urgent action. There were many who believed that the power of the church needed to be curbed, and possibly even broken. It had become an agent of oppression and exploitation. However important it may have been in holding Europe together and securing an often frail peace during the chaos of the Dark Ages, the church was now holding back social, intellectual, and political progress. The institution of the church gave legitimation to an older order that was increasingly seen as incapable of coping with the pressures and concerns of a new era in the history of humanity. How could humanity be liberated from the bondage of the past, which seemed to be both perpetuated and legitimated by the church?

There were two options for dealing with this situation. The first was that adopted in the early sixteenth century by Protestant reformers such as Martin Luther (1483–1546) in northeastern Germany, Huldrych Zwingli (1484–1531) in Zurich, and John Calvin (1509–64) in Geneva. These writers argued that the church needed to rediscover its original vision—to set aside its claims to wealth, power, status, and influence, and return to the more modest and authentic models of the New Testament. The remarkable success of that movement is due to many factors, and one of them is the sense of liberation and empowerment that it brought to the emerging middle classes of Western Europe, who at last had found their champion. The story of that Reformation is fascinating in its own right, but it is not the story we shall be telling in this volume.

Our story concerns those who believed that the only way to liberate humanity from its bondage to the past was to launch an attack on the institution that was the ultimate cause of this oppression—the church. That attack was launched on many fronts, including demands for limits to be set to the power of the church, for regional devolution of its authority, and for a complete ending of military adventurism. Francis I, king of France, for example, curtailed the authority of the pope in France by the simple expedient of defeating the papal armies in battle in 1517. Henry VIII, taking advantage of England's geographical remoteness from Italy, managed to substitute his own authority for that of the pope in the 1530s without the need for military action.

Not everyone had the capacity to defeat the church on the battlefield, or in the political arena. An increasingly important alternative strategy now emerged—attacking the *ideas* on which the church was based. For an increasingly numerous and articulate group within Western culture, the best way to reduce the excessive influence of the church was to undermine the credibility of its teachings. While some saw the attraction of atheism as lying in what it proposed, most saw its appeal in its ability to weaken, perhaps even destroy, the institution of the church. Paradoxically, the historical origins of modern atheism lie primarily in an extended criticism of the power and status of the church, rather than in any asserted attractions of a godless world.

Yet as exploration of this option proceeded, atheism began to develop a philosophical and cultural sophistication that marks it out as one of the enduring monuments of the modern period. Many of the atheist ideas first developed in the classical period found a new life in the golden age that now opened up. A challenge to the fundamental religious ideas of Christianity was now about more than the exercise of intellectual freedom; it represented a highly significant and credible threat to the status quo, opening the door to revolution and transformation—in short, to the dawn of the modern period.

So where do we begin? How can we tell this fascinating story to best effect? The most obvious place to begin our exploration is the eighteenth century, widely recognized as the most creative period of atheist experimentation and reflection, which laid the intellectual foundations for the transformation of Western culture in the nineteenth and twentieth centuries.

AN AGE OF REVOLUTION: THE EIGHTEENTH CENTURY

The eighteenth century is widely regarded by historians as one of the most dynamic and exciting periods in history. It was an age of optimism, with the whiff of revolution in the air. By the end of the century, the ancient doctrine that the present was doomed to repeat the errors of the past lay in tatters. It seemed that a brave new world lay ahead, unfettered by the bonds of tradition. A rising generation could hope to enjoy a degree of freedom denied to their parents and grandparents. But they could only do so by eliminating what stood in their path. There was little doubt on the part of potential revolutionaries as to what the greatest obstacle to human progress was.

The church was seen as the enemy of progress, lending a spurious divine authority to the traditions of the past and the corrupt monarchies that depended on them for what little credibility they possessed. Perceptions of the extent of this problem varied across Europe and beyond, with France witnessing perhaps the most concerted and certainly the most influential critique of both the power of the church and the ideas on which it was ultimately based. In North America, atheism was not taken seriously as a means of social transformation. The solution there lay in radical reform of the relation of church and state—a reordering in which many see the foundations of America's rise to become the most influential Christian nation on earth. Our story, however, begins in Britain, destined to be one of the great laboratories for testing the ideas of the new worldview.

By the beginning of the eighteenth century, most British intellectuals had lost their patience with institutional religion. The English Civil War (1642–49), which had seen the temporary overthrow of the monarchy and the execution of Charles I, was widely viewed as the outcome of a very un-English religious extremism. Memories of the Puritan Commonwealth (1649–60)—the nearest thing to a theocracy England had ever seen—were bitter. There was particular resentment that it had forbidden plum pudding, one of England's relatively few culinary triumphs. One of the many merits of Charles II, who was restored in 1660, was that he was totally out of sympathy with the radical Protestantism of the Puritans, thus guaranteeing that there would be no further government-imposed religious prohibitions. Christmas was once more celebrated as a public festival (with plum pudding).

Other cultures might have been tempted to adopt atheism or a corporate agnosticism in response to the religious intolerance and bigotry of the Puritan Commonwealth. The English, however, decided to reinstate the Church of England instead, presumably believing that, to all intents and purposes, this amounted to more or less the same thing. Under Charles II, who reigned from 1660 to 1685, a decidedly docile form of Anglicanism emerged as the religion of the English establishment. The Church of England would be expected to be submissive to the expectations of the people, and keep its religious beliefs to itself, rather than impose them on others.

Charles II, however, proved far less religiously compliant than the English expected. On his deathbed in 1685, Charles confessed himself to be a Roman Catholic. This fueled a fresh religious controversy, which threatened a new civil war in England. The real difficulty was that Charles's son James, Duke of York, had become a Roman Catholic in 1670. Having just managed to extricate themselves from the excesses of Protestantism, the English Parliament was in no mood to have to deal with its diametric opposite. In 1679, in a desperate attempt to avoid engulfing England in a new religious conflict, the House of Commons declared that the Duke of York was excluded from the succession to the throne. The House of Lords, however, promptly overthrew this act. Charles II was succeeded by his son, who, as James II, promptly and openly confessed his Roman Catholic faith. James's decision to appoint his own choice of Roman Catholic favorites to prominent positions in the state, army, and universities prompted widespread concern and gave rise to furious rumors of a plot to convert England to Roman Catholicism. A new religious civil war seemed inevitable.

A characteristically English solution, however, lay to hand. James II's daughter Mary had married William III, Prince of Orange, a firmly committed Protestant with a reputation for tolerance and generosity. A secret approach was made to William by seven leading Englishmen: if he were to invade England, he could count on their total support. Initially delayed by storms, William's invasion fleet sailed for England in November 1688. After landing at Torbay in England's West Country, William's army marched on London, finally arriving in the capital late in December. By then, his steady progress had triggered widespread defections to his cause, along with riots and revolts against James's authority. It was simply a matter of time before James's cause was utterly lost. In January 1689 he left England for France. William and Mary were declared king and queen of England in February—but only after agreeing to sign a Bill of Rights that guaranteed free elections and freedom of speech. This was followed by the Act of Toleration later that year, which permitted those seeking religious alternatives to the Church of England (often referred to as Dissenters) to hold their views and religious worship within the law.

Never again did the English want to face such religious conflict. Was not the best way to prevent such crises to eliminate any notion that some specific form of religion was to be given preference, and instead to offer toleration to all and privilege to none? That, at least, was the argument set out in philosopher John Locke's *Letter Concerning Toleration* (1689). In this work, Locke set out a compelling case for the freedom of conscience and religious expression, arguing that there are clear limits to social and political incursion into the realm of personal belief or nonbelief. While encouraging rational persuasion in matters of religion, Locke was implacably opposed to the use of force in such matters. Locke does not respond to concern over the social role of religion by espousing atheism, but by setting limits to the extent to which religion can be involved in public life—an important anticipation of the American constitutional separation of church and state.

Although the period witnessed some significant criticisms of the fundamental ideas of Christianity, the eighteenth century did not see a major erosion of faith. Indeed, the Scottish philosopher David Hume (1711–76), often cited as a major influence on the rise of atheism, once commented that he had never actually met an atheist. This intriguing comment was not intended as a reflection on Hume's limited social life or the peculiarities of his circle of acquaintances, but on the absence of individuals in England who were prepared to define themselves in this way at this time. Hume would certainly meet such individuals in the sophisticated salons of Enlightenment Paris, following his appointment as secretary to the British Embassy in 1764, which led to regular visits to Baron d'Holbach's famous gatherings in the Rue Royale; in Britain, however, atheism was still seen as slightly eccentric and dangerously seditious at this time. The dramatic transition by which atheism came to be seen as the greatest achievement and proudest boast of the Enlightenment was still some decades away. But it would come, with a vengeance.

In part, the failure of atheism to gain wide support in Britain at this time reflected the quality of some Christian responses to Deist critiques of faith, most notably Bishop Butler's *Analogy of Religion* (1736). Butler showed that Deism itself rested on somewhat shaky philosophical foundations, and also set out an argument for the reliability of Christianity based on an appeal to probability, not certainty.

Atheism did not become a significant force in British life in the eighteenth century. The foundations for its dawning might well have been laid, and its seeds sown; they had yet, however, to grow and flourish. The freedom of expression resulting from the Glorious Revolution of 1688 allowed frustration with the existing social order to be expressed (and hence contained) politically. Most Britons preferred to make fun of the established church rather than systematically undermine its leading ideas. One of the most successful works of clerical satire was Laurence Sterne's *Tristram Shandy*, published over the period 1759–67. The work opens with probably the most famous coitus interruptus in English literature (relating how Tristram's mother interrupts his father in the act of conception by asking whether he has remembered to wind the clock) and moves on to chronicle—though in a remarkably gracious manner—the failings and vices of the English clergy through the person of good-hearted rustic Parson Yorick.

The tradition continued during the Victorian period. While the clergy continue to be the butt of much good-natured humor (as in Anthony Trollope's Barchester chronicles), many authors found the slightly daffy religious views of lay people much more amusing. Wilkie Collins's masterpiece *The Moonstone* (1868) introduces us to Miss Drusilla Clack, a particularly fastidious devotee of a Protestant sect with a doubtless commendable concern to convert those around her. With this end in mind, Miss Clack carries about with her a small handbag laden with suitable religious tracts to foist on her relatives, such as her aunt, Lady Verinder. Collins takes great delight in telling his readers of an especially sophisticated tract entitled *The Serpent at Home*, designed "to show how the Evil One lies in wait for us in all the most apparently innocent actions of our daily lives." Its chapters include detailed treatments of such topics as "Satan in the Hair Brush," "Satan behind the Looking Glass," and "Satan under the Tea Table." But best of all—"one continuous burst of burning eloquence!"—is the chapter dealing with "Satan among the Sofa Cushions."

The most significant factor in muting the impact of critiques of Christianity was the growth of Pietism in eighteenth-century Britain. Pietism was a Protestant religious movement originating in seventeenth-century Germany. Many German Protestants were appalled by the failure of the Lutheran church to connect up with the life experiences of ordinary Christians. Lutheran theology appeared to mimic the worst features of medieval scholasticism, indulging in theological debates about things that nobody cared about, one way or the other. Writers such as Philip Jacob Spener (1635–1705) stressed the importance of a personally selected faith—a faith that was vitally connected with the experience of the individual.

The movement was exported to Britain in the 1730s, particularly through the ministries of John and Charles Wesley, the founders of the movement generally known as Methodism. Again we find an emphasis placed on faith as an experience of the living God, who is known as a personal reality in the life of the believer. Pietism is essentially a privatized form of the Christian faith, which plays down its institutional aspects. For the Wesleys, it is the individual's free decision to repent and admit Christ into the soul that secures the hope of salvation. The human heart is the ultimate "gateway to heaven," in that the individual has the final decision as to whether she enters into the heavenly realms. The institution of the church plays no critical role in this process, however valuable it may subsequently be as a means of pastoral support and spiritual nourishment. The Church of England was unimpressed with these ideas, and did all it could to marginalize the Wesleys and their dangerous views.

Yet a movement that the established church regarded as a threat to its influence defused a potentially greater threat to its existence. Pietism made it possible to be critical of the established church as an institution, while still experiencing and valuing the faith it embodied.

The rise of "experiential religion" in Britain during the eighteenth century did much to blunt the force of the criticism of religion that developed during this period. Pietism reestablished the connection between religion and the individual subjective consciousness, ensuring that it was experienced as a living reality. People were less likely to criticize a faith that meant something to them.

In other parts of Europe, the situation was rather different—as in the critically important case of France. Pietism was a development within Protestant Christianity that sought to reconnect head and heart through a "living faith." France, however, was a Roman Catholic country, in which Pietism gained virtually no influence. Nor was there any Catholic equivalent of the movement, despite the attempts of Jansenists to promote their approach to personal religion. The success of the Jesuits in suppressing Jansenism in the late seventeenth century can be seen as laying the foundations for their own overthrow a century later, at the hands of the French Revolutionaries. The radical new ideas of the eighteenth century could flourish without any really significant opposition. The results, as we shall see, were dramatic—so dramatic, in fact, that they must be seen as marking the transition to the golden age of atheism.

PART I

THE HIGH NOON
OF ATHEISM

THE FRENCH REVOLUTION

I F ANY EVENT SIGNALS THE DAWN OF THE GOLDEN AGE of atheism in the West, it is the French Revolution of 1789. Generations of accumulated popular resentment and intellectual hostility against king and church could finally be contained no longer. The storming of the Bastille on July 14 of that year was widely seized upon as an icon of liberation, symbolizing the sweeping aside of an old order based on superstition and oppression. A brave new world lay ahead, firmly grounded in nature and reason, and equally firmly committed to the liberation of humanity from "tyranny" and "superstition." The wisdom of the day was as simple as it was powerful: eliminate God, and a new future would dawn. It was a vision that thrilled many across Europe, drawing aside a curtain from a once-forbidden world, which now seemed about to become reality.

In 1804 the young English poet William Wordsworth penned words that captured something of this contagious sense of optimism and hope amongst the youth of Europe. The French Revolution had shattered the tired old political framework of Europe, sweeping away its outdated, tradition-bound practices and beliefs, and opening the way to a bright new future. A new dawn seemed to be at hand, promising to usher in an era of hope and opportunity. "Bliss was it in that dawn to be alive, / But to be young was very heaven!" Wordsworth's feelings were echoed by many young people throughout Western Europe. Here, at long last, was something new, something *liberating*, which a repressed and disillusioned youth could embrace. The future seemed to belong to them. True, his enthusiasm and faith in human nature were dampened significantly with news of the Reign of Terror—a violent period that the literary critic and commentator William Hazlitt castigated as one of "hatred and scorn." Yet there is no doubt that many in nineteenth-century Britain believed that the French Revolution opened the way to intellectual liberation, especially in eliminating archaic and oppressive religious ideas.

Atheism suddenly became *conceivable*, and there were many across Europe who now began to explore its secret byways. Having ventured from the straight and narrow way of Christian orthodoxy, some returned, chastened and appalled by what lay beyond its well-trodden path. Yet others stayed to savor and embrace a brave new world, which they found as exciting as their elders found it shocking. This new world order would owe its origins to that French Revolution, now seen by many as marking a turning point in the history of the world.

So how did this revolution begin? And how did its association with atheism take shape? We may begin our story by considering some of the failings that led many to conclude that the violent overthrow of the past was the only way of securing the future.

Louis XVI ascended the throne of France in 1774 at the age of twenty. He inherited a financial crisis that proved uncontainable. Punitive taxation and the perception of extravagance at court caused a surge in popular anger against the monarch. Things were made much worse by growing hostility toward his queen, Marie Antoinette, who was widely portrayed as sexually rapacious and frustrated by her husband's sexual incompetence. Unlike her shy, awkward husband, Marie Antoinette was admired for her beauty, grace, and elegance. Where she led, the fashion trends of Europe followed. Yet her extravagant lifestyle and the enormous sums spent on her pleasure palace, the Petit Trianon in the park of Versailles, earned her increasing criticism. She was known as *Madame Déficit*, plundering state funds while the people starved. Her Austrian origins proved to be just as much a problem as her personal extravagances. The fact that France had been at war with Austria for much of the century did not endear her to the older families of the nation.

The unpopularity of the monarchy reached new heights in the closing months of 1788. The disastrous harvest of that year gave way to the coldest winter in living memory. France was faced with a food crisis severe enough to cause a famine, with a failed economy and a despised monarchy. By the spring it was obvious that something had to give. Things could not go on like this. In desperation, an embattled Louis XVI summoned the Estates General on May 4, 1789. It would prove his undoing.

Traditionally, French society was divided into three estates, which collectively made up the Estates General: the First Estate, consisting of the aristocracy; the Second Estate, made up of the clergy; and the Third Estate, consisting of the middle-class bourgeoisie. The church and monarchy devoted their attention to the first two estates and treated the middle classes with complete contempt. The alienation of the Third Estate was vividly highlighted in 1789, the year of the French Revolution itself, by the clergyman Abbé Sieyès (Emmanuel Joseph Sieyès, 1748–1836), when he posed his three great questions: "What is the Third Estate? *Everything!* What has it been until now at the political level? *Nothing!* What does it want? *To be something!*" An alienated middle class—the economic engine of the nation—demanded change. In the end, it obtained a more radical shake-up than it had anticipated.

Yet however much the origins of the French Revolution may owe to widespread disaffection with the monarchy within the middle classes, an equally significant groundswell of opinion was building up within the sophisticated and elegant salons of Paris—namely, that the church was an outmoded institution that rested on demonstrably false ideas. As the church lent religious support to the monarchy, a new interest in undermining its distinctive ideas would have far-reaching implications for church and state. Atheism began to emerge as a worldview capable of challenging the settled world of France.

VOLTAIRE:
CRITIC OF A CORRUPT CHURCH

A disgruntled Catholic priest, Jean Meslier (1678–1733), is usually identified as one of the first serious advocates of atheism in France. Meslier served as curé of Étrépigny and But in the Champagne region of France. On his death, Meslier's *Testament* was published. This long and rambling work vigorously denounced the church as a complete fraud, maintained only by ludicrous ideas, a totally dishonest priesthood, and a credulous people. On the pretext of helping people to get to heaven, priests and bishops cause them to have a miserable time on earth. The Old Testament is full of nonsense that only a fool would believe. Christianity is morally corrupt, degenerate, and intellectually risible.

Yet was Meslier actually an atheist? While his *Testament* consists of page after page of denunciation of Christian beliefs and practices, it does so on the assumption that Christianity is a sect that has distorted the true knowledge of God, available to every human being through nature and reason. Meslier appeals to the true God of "natural religion" to overcome the Christian perversion of the true faith of nature and reason: "I shall finish by asking God, if outraged by this sect, to see fit to recall us to natural religion, of which Christianity is the sworn enemy—to that holy religion which God has set in the hearts of all people, which requires of us to do nothing to others that we would not do for ourselves. Then the world would be made up of good citizens, righteous fathers, obedient children, and caring friends. God gave us this religion in giving us reason. May fanaticism never pervert it!"

Meslier's words are an important reminder that the terms "anti-Christian" and "atheist" are most emphatically not identical, even though the religious situation in eighteenth-century France led to a confluence of their agendas. Both, after all, were hostile toward the French church and sought to undermine its institutions and ideas. The real animus behind Meslier's hatred of Christianity is his passionate belief that it has corrupted the beautiful and sacred natural religion that God intended for all people, distorting it through false ideas and forcing it to serve the ends of a degenerate institution and its fraudulent priests.

Most radical French philosophers of the eighteenth century are actually to be categorized not as atheists but as Deists—that is, supporters of an ideal philosophical notion of God, based on reason or nature, rather than a more specifically Christian view of the matter. Denis Diderot (1713–84), Jean-Jacques Rousseau (1712–78), and Voltaire (1694–1778)—all of whom are regularly stereotyped as atheists—are clearly best regarded as Deists. Voltaire regarded atheism with about as much enthusiasm as he did the teachings of the Christian church. In the place of both he urged the reconstruction of religion on the basis of the Supreme Being disclosed in nature. As Voltaire wrote in 1768:

> *If the heavens, stripped of their noble imprint,*
> *Could ever cease to reveal Him,*
> *If God did not exist, it would be necessary to invent Him,*
> *Whom the sage proclaims, and whom kings adore.*

Many atheist apologists have fallen into the habit of only citing the third sentence of this citation, thus making Voltaire appear as a precursor of Freud's view of God as wish fulfillment. In fact, Voltaire defended the notion of a supreme being, known through intelligent reflection on the natural world, who has been hijacked and distorted by the world's religions in general and warring Christian sects in particular. This is clear from his *Letter to Uranie* (1722; published 1732), in which he offered a strong defense of the existence of a supreme being, who was inadequately and falsely represented by the great positive religions of the world, especially the French Catholic church and its leading representatives. Voltaire's criticism is directed primarily and vigorously against the French church of his day. His fighting slogan— *Écrasez l'infâme* ("Eliminate infamy!")—was directed specifically against the hierarchy, morality, and distinctive ideas of French Catholicism. He justified the belligerency of his approach by insisting that one simply could not tolerate intolerance.

Voltaire was joined in his anti-Catholic crusade by many who were atheists in the strict sense of the term—such as Julien Offroy de La Mettrie (1709–51), Paul-Henri-Dietrich d'Holbach (1723–89), and Claude-Adrien Helvétius (1715–71). Yet this must not be taken as evidence that Voltaire himself was an atheist. The political realities of the situation were such that a coalition of forces gathered to combat the power and corruption of the church, setting their disagreements over the existence of God to one side in order to focus on the task at hand. Yet, as Voltaire's celebrated article on "atheism" in the definitive *Dictionnaire raisonné des sciences, des arts et des métiers* makes unequivocally clear, he regarded atheism and French Catholicism with equal loathing. Is it any wonder, he asked, that there are atheists in the world, when the church behaves so abominably?

Voltaire's satirical masterpiece *Candide* (1759) is a witty and powerful criticism of the French Catholic church of his day. He argues that the church has added a series of degenerate notions to a true belief in God. As a result, the church hierarchy has become so busy defending these absurd ideas that it has lost sight of the fundamental belief in God that underlies true religion. Although refraining from any criticism of God in *Candide*, Voltaire has no hesitation in poking mischievous fun at the Catholic hierarchy. Thus when Candide—the naive antihero of the novel—arrives in the fabled El Dorado and discovers that the local inhabitants are very interested in talking about God, he asks to be introduced to some of their priests. He is informed that there is no need for them. In El Dorado everyone is a priest. Candide is astonished:

> "What! Do you not have any monks to teach, to argue, to rule over you, to have intrigues, and to burn people who do not agree with them?"
>
> "We would have to become fools to let that happen," replied the old man. "Here we are of the same opinion and do not understand what you mean with your monks."

Voltaire's critique of the excesses and blatant immorality of the French church of his day was certainly not intended to encourage atheism; indeed, Voltaire's constant demand, *Écrasez l'infâme*, can be seen as an attempt to remove the cause of atheism. Eliminate the immorality, power, and corruption of the church, and what reason for atheism remains? Voltaire's writings are a powerful testimony to the way in which institutional criticism of the church could easily be transposed to criticism of the ideas of the Christian faith—in other words, to atheism. Yet Voltaire, for all his many savage criticisms of the French religious establishment of his day, did not himself espouse atheism. Atheism, for Voltaire, remains an excessive reaction against a corrupt church, not a positive philosophy in its own right.

Voltaire's insight is of fundamental importance to our study of the emergence of atheism. His argument is simple: the attractiveness of atheism is directly dependent upon the corruption of Christian institutions. Reform those institutions and the plausibility of atheism is dramatically reduced. To explore the relevance of this point, we may ask a very simple question: Why did the American Revolution show no interest in atheism, when its French equivalent did?

THE AMERICAN REVOLUTION: RADICAL REFORM WITHOUT ATHEISM

One of the most remarkable features of the American Revolution was that the overthrow of British colonial power was not accompanied by any serious move toward atheism. Some of its leading representatives—including George Washington himself—were unorthodox by the religious standards of their day; others were clearly of a Deist, rather than traditional Christian, persuasion. Yet the Revolution lacked the antireligious dimension so characteristic of its later French and Russian counterparts. Why?

Perhaps the most obvious answer is also the most satisfying. Many of the settlers of the Eastern Seaboard of North America were descended from religious refugees from England, especially during the reign of Charles I. Their strong Puritan religious convictions, which were initially the cause of their eviction from England, now became the basis of their individual and corporate life in the New World. They watched with delight as their brethren in England overthrew a tyrannical monarchy opposed to their understanding of the true faith, and with horror as that monarchy was restored under Charles II. The North American colonies, especially in the Massachusetts Bay area, were strongholds of precisely those forms of Christianity that the authorities had tried to suppress in England.

The American Revolutionaries saw themselves as called to break the spiritual and temporal power of the Church of England in America. Like their forebears at the time of the English Civil War, they saw the conflict as a moment of purification, a time in which the true identity of a nation would be shaped. The battle was not between Christianity and atheism, but between a compromised state church and a pure gospel church. It would be a battle for the soul of America. While some Revolutionaries had economic and political goals, others had religious objectives—objectives that demanded the *purification* of religion, not its *elimination*. The constitutional separation of church and state can be argued to rest upon a fundamental desire to prevent any specific form of Christianity from defining the establishment, after the manner of the Church of England, which was widely regarded as corrupt and degenerate in American republican circles. Yet political republicanism was not seen as entailing atheism. Was not Calvin's Geneva, that city of God set upon a hill for all to see and imitate, itself a republic? And might not republicanism and the cause of true religion thus be united, where in England they were seen as divided?

Yet the French Revolution was fundamentally different in character. Instead of throwing off the yoke of a colonial power, the Revolutionaries saw themselves as deposing oppressive institutions within their own nation. For American republicans, Christianity—in various forms—motivated and guided their struggle. It was their ally. The French Revolutionaries saw it as their enemy, a power that gave legitimation and support to those who opposed the will of the people and that claimed divine support for the status quo. It was an institution that had to be neutralized. The great debate of the age concerned how the power of the church might be blunted. It was an old controversy. Yet a new answer now came to be taken with increasing seriousness.

THE RISE OF FRENCH ATHEISM

Voltaire, like many other French writers of the eighteenth century, was able to criticize the many failings of the church without denying the existence of its God. Others, however, were more than content to advance an atheist agenda, where Voltaire and others had held back. The real atheism of this period is to be found in the writings of La Mettrie, d'Holbach, and Helvétius. Whereas Voltaire and his Deist colleagues sought to rearrange existing understandings of the relation of the transcendent to everyday life, these more radical writers sought to eliminate the transcendent altogether.

D'Holbach's *Système de la Nature* (1770) illustrates this trend particularly well. The guiding principle underlying the work is that any attempt to understand nature must be based upon reason and experience. On applying these faculties to nature, it becomes clear that there is no reason to propose a God to explain the observed ordering of nature. Whereas Isaac Newton (1642–1727) had argued that the regularity of planetary motions was evidence of divine design and governance of the universe, d'Holbach argued that they could be accounted for on purely materialist grounds. Belief in God is the product of a misguided human imagination, not the rigorous scientific application of the senses. The rigorous application of scientific approach should therefore lead to atheism.

> An atheist is someone who destroys human chimeras in order to call people back to nature, experience and reason. He is a thinker who, having meditated on matter, its properties and ways of behaving, has no reason to imagine ideal forces, imaginary intelligences or rational beings in order to explain the phenomena of the universe or the operations of nature—which, far from making us know nature better, merely make it capricious, inexplicable and unknowable, useless for human happiness.

Science liberates humanity from false ideas of supernatural powers or beings. Ignorance of nature gave birth to the idea of God, just as a deeper knowledge of nature allows humanity to destroy this idea and the evils resulting from it. It is in this line of argument that we can discern the development of the more radical form of atheism that dominated the golden age.

THE FAILED PHILOSOPHICAL
ATTEMPTS TO DEFEND GOD

Curiously, a significant contribution to the rise of this hard-nosed atheism lay in developments within French religious philosophy during the seventeenth century. Aware of possible threats to Christianity from radical philosophical critics, writers such as Marin Marsenne (1588–1648) and René Descartes (1596–1650) set out to make belief in God invulnerable to skeptical assault. Descartes is a figure of immense importance to our study, as he is widely regarded as laying the foundations for modernity. True knowledge was universal and necessary, capable of being demonstrated with absolute certainty. Having established this criterion of truth, Descartes set out to demonstrate the existence of God with precisely this degree of certainty. To his critics, Descartes merely managed to show that, by his own criteria, God's existence seemed rather unlikely.

Convinced that the scientific discoveries of their day could be harnessed to serve the needs of the church, Descartes and his colleagues abandoned any appeal to religious experience in their defense of their faith. The secure proofs of religion lay in philosophy and the natural sciences—in the reasoning of this world rather than the intrusion of the next. Philosophy alone could establish the necessity and plausibility of the Christian faith.

With the benefit of hindsight, this was not a particularly wise strategy. The English experience suggested that nobody really doubted the existence of God until theologians tried to prove it. The very modest success of these proofs led many to wonder if God's existence was quite as self-evident as they had once thought. A well-meaning defense of God ended up persuading people that the case for God was surprisingly uncertain. Descartes's failed defense of God led to the widespread conclusion that every attempt to prove God's existence was either contradictory or unintelligible as a matter of principle, because this God simply cannot be related to the world of everyday experience.

Descartes's was a brave and bold strategy, which backfired spectacularly. Historically, it can be shown that arguments used by French atheists against religion in the late eighteenth century were borrowed from religious writers who had previously sought to eliminate atheism. This hitherto unprecedented denial of God developed out of the very strategies employed to defend Christianity a century earlier. Descartes and his colleagues proposed that a perfect divine being was the best explanation of the universe. Yet by doing so, they opened the way to the response that the universe was perfectly capable of explaining itself, and they also heightened awareness of one of the Christian faith's greatest vulnerabilities—the problem of evil. If God is supremely perfect, why do suffering and pain exist, causing such distress to humanity? One of Descartes's most significant achievements was to make what had hitherto been a practical issue of Christian spirituality (how can I cope with suffering?) into a disconfirmation of the faith. How could anyone believe in a perfect divine being, when the world was so clearly imperfect?

The situation was made even worse for faith by the breathtakingly pointless and petty arguments within the French church over the best way of refuting atheism. The pages of such popular learned journals as *Journal des Sçavans*, *Journal de Trévoux*, and *Nouvelles de la République des Lettres* were filled with articles by contentious Christian apologists, each denouncing his rivals with even greater venom than the atheism he meant to combat. The Christian faith could be vindicated in many ways; in their anxiety to demonstrate that their specific technique was the best, Christian apologists began by destroying the defenses erected by others, only to find their own torn to shreds in the next issue of *Journal des Sçavans*. The curious reader of such works gained the impression that the defenders of the faith were locked in a ferocious self-defeating vendetta, with the "atheism" that was meant to be under sustained assault actually emerging as the covert victor.

Up to this point, atheist writers had made an increasingly good case in arguing that their philosophy was probably true, and that it would undermine the power and influence of a corrupt church and monarchy. Yet might this new philosophy prove as tedious as the rather dull works of theology that it sought to replace? For at least one of its more enthusiastic advocates, atheism had the immense advantage of adding a little spice to some aspects of life that cardinals, monks, and priests were not meant to know about. D'Holbach made atheism credible; the Marquis de Sade made it interesting.

THE MARQUIS DE SADE AND THE ORIGINS OF EROTIC ATHEISM

In 1748, Julien Offroy de La Mettrie published *L'homme machine*, his best-known work. Its theme is simple: human happiness depends upon the triumph of atheism, which alone can liberate humanity from tyranny, war, and oppression—all of which have religious roots. Although La Mettrie clearly believes that there are excellent intellectual reasons for espousing an atheist worldview, the dominant argument deals with its wider consequences. One of the speakers in *L'homme machine* represents this view as follows: "If atheism were generally accepted, every form of religion would be destroyed, and cut off at its roots. There would be no more theological wars, no more soldiers of religion—such terrible soldiers! Nature, having been infected with sacred poison, would regain its rights and purity. Deaf to all other voices, tranquil mortals would follow only the spontaneous dictates of their own being, the only commands which . . . can lead us to happiness." While La Mettrie presumably had political and social emancipation in mind, one of his contemporaries was not slow to note that adopting atheism might have rather interesting consequences in another area of human activity.

As might be expected, one of the more entertaining affirmations of atheism came from the pen of Donatien-Alphonse-François de Sade (1740–1814), known simply as the Marquis de Sade. De Sade initially pursued a military career, serving during the Seven Years' War

(1756–63). A classic example of the eternal rebel, he went on to lead the life of a libertine, including sexual gratification through the infliction of pain. He was imprisoned at Vincennes, then in the infamous Bastille in Paris, and finally in the insane asylum at Charenton. During his time in prison he wrote most of his more scandalous works, setting out some of the themes of sadism.

Perhaps having concluded that most atheist propaganda of his day was worthy yet hopelessly pedestrian, de Sade decided to liven things up. His *Dialogue Between a Priest and a Dying Man* invites us to imagine a priest summoned to hear the confession of someone close to death. The priest offers to absolve this sinner, on condition that he repent. A robust theological conversation follows, in which the dying man dismisses belief in God as repressive superstition. Obedience to natural desires is what really matters. The priest has simply invented his god as a means of legitimating his own passions and suppressing those of others. The dying man regards the rejection of God as the first stage in human enlightenment, removing the only barrier that prevents humanity from really enjoying its vices.

> Your god is a machine you fabricated to serve your passions; you manipulated it so that it suited them—but the moment it interfered with mine, I kicked it out of my way, and was glad that I did so . . . Nature shaped my soul, which is the result of the dispositions she formed in me while pursuing her own ends and needs. And as she needs vices just as much as virtues, whenever she wanted to arouse me to evil, she did so, just as whenever she wanted a good deed from me, she roused in me the desire to perform one. I just did as I was instructed.

The dying man—who clearly speaks for de Sade himself—insists that abandoning faith in God is the first step to enjoying life. There is no life to come, he argues; only a life in the present, which we ought to enjoy as much as possible.

My friend, sensuality means more to me than anything else. I have idolized it all my life and my wish has been to end it in its bosom. My end draws near. But six women more beautiful than the light of day are waiting in the next room. I have reserved them for exactly this moment. Why not share in this feast with me? Why not follow my example, and embrace them instead of the empty sophistries of superstition? And let their caresses help you to forget your hypocritical beliefs for a while.

So the dying man rings a bell, and is promptly joined by the six ravishing beauties he has promised. The priest proves unequal to the task of resisting them. "After he had been a little while in their arms the preacher became one whom Nature had corrupted, all because he had not succeeded in explaining what a corrupt nature is."

In 1793 de Sade developed this theme of the sexually repressive effects of belief in God a little further. In his dialogue *Philosophy in the Bedroom* he asks his readers to imagine a fifteen-year-old nun who abandons faith in God and discovers in his place such delights as sodomy, incest, and flagellation. De Sade intersperses his erotic tableaux with speeches supporting atheism and the ideals of the French republic. The idea of God is firmly presented as an outmoded superstition that merely gets in the way of enjoying life to the full. Admittedly, some just read the book for its dirty bits and skipped the sermonizing. But the link was clear: atheism made sexual experimentation legitimate and interesting.

Yet it was the social and political aspects of atheism that attracted the attention of many French radical thinkers in the 1780s. If there was no God, then there was no limit to human action, no divinely determined social or political order that had to be respected and perpetuated. Without the restraining influence of the idea of God, anything was possible, including the creation of a new society, liberated from the oppressive rule of the Bourbon monarchy and the French church. As

Diderot commented, France would not be free until the last of its kings had been strangled with the entrails of its last priest. Atheism promised liberation and encouraged revolution. And it would not be long before promise turned to reality.

THE CRITIQUE OF CHRISTIANITY: THE FIRST PHASE

In the 1780s, just prior to the Revolution, there was immense enthusiasm in the Parisian salons for reform, as well as optimism concerning the future. Many intellectuals expected constitutional reform to emerge as a matter of course, and seem to have had no idea of the cataclysmic events that awaited them. The past could be set aside without undue difficulty, and a more positive future created without formidable obstacles. This revolutionary optimism of the immediate pre-Revolutionary period is well caught in the memoirs of Louis-Philippe Ségur (1753–1830): "Without regret for the past or anxiety for the future, we walked gaily on a carpet of flowers that concealed an abyss . . . All that was ancient seemed to us wearisome and ridiculous. The gravity of old doctrines oppressed us. The laughing philosophy of Voltaire amused and entranced us . . . We were ready to follow with enthusiasm the philosophical doctrines advanced by bold and brilliant leaders. Voltaire appealed to our intelligence, Rousseau touched our hearts."

At the religious level, there was widespread discussion of the issues. One of the more interesting aspects of the French Revolution is that some French Catholic clergy appear to have genuinely regarded it as a divine reform of their church, perhaps along the lines of the Protestant Reformation of the sixteenth century. Claude Fauchet, for example, preached a sermon at the Cathedral of Notre-Dame in Paris on February 4, 1791, in which he declared the Revolution to be a "divine work" that demonstrated the "accord of religion and liberty." There is no doubt that some clergy believed that the basic structures and beliefs of their church could be maintained; the real problems, in their view, lay in the way in which the church had failed the French people, both morally and pastorally.

Other Christian writers took quite different views. Count Joseph de Maistre (1753–1821), a strong defender of both royalism and papal authority in France, increasingly took the view that the Revolution was a divine judgment on a flawed church and corrupt nation. Like many French churchmen at the time, de Maistre was aware of—indeed, sympathetic to—the need for reform within church and monarchy, and initially welcomed the summoning of the Estates General in 1789. But he was appalled by the radical course of events. In his *Considérations sur la France* (1797), de Maistre construed the Revolution as both a divine punishment and a providentially ordained means for the regeneration of France. On the basis of this theological interpretation of the Revolution, he was able both to condemn the Revolution and the ideas it embodied, and to simultaneously view it as a necessary prelude to the restoration of the Bourbon monarchy.

In any case, Fauchet's was decidedly a minority view. Two rival viewpoints jostled for dominance in pre-Revolutionary circles. Voltaire and those around him argued that every positive religion—including Judaism, the various Islamic sects, and Christian denominations—had corrupted a pure, rational concept of God, known to every person through nature and reason. The reformation of religion might well focus on the French Catholic church, but it extended far beyond this. A new state religion was required, grounded in the worship of the Supreme Being. It can easily be argued that this radical Deist program of reform was, as a matter of historical fact, fundamentally anti-Christian. Yet the specific animus against Christianity was actually due to its historic position within France, rather than any specifically Christian belief—a matter of historical contingency, reflecting the realities of the situation.

A still more radical view, however, was rapidly gaining support. It claimed that the oppression of the French people by both the court and the church could be put down to a belief in God, including the

Supreme Being of Deist writers such as Voltaire. A genuine revolution would therefore necessitate overthrowing this fundamental belief altogether, rather than attempting to reform it. Atheism was the Promethean liberator, which alone could guarantee the initial success and subsequent triumph of the Revolution. Any notion of a transcendent God—whether deriving from Christianity or the "Religion of Nature"—was to be eliminated and replaced with a secular alternative.

At one level, this divergence of understandings was virtually invisible. During the period between the fall of the Bastille and the ending of the monarchy, Deists and atheists collaborated and campaigned for political, social, and ecclesiastical reform. For political reasons, any tensions between them were carefully underplayed. Yet the tension was there, unmistakably, between those who believed that there existed a god, known through nature and reason, who was the ultimate basis of social order and personal morality, and those who enthusiastically secularized any idea of divinity, proclaiming that the true god of the Revolution was *la patrie*—France itself.

The events of July 14, 1790, did not give any particular indication that a complete social upheaval was about to take place. The first anniversary of the fall of the Bastille was celebrated at the open-air Festival of the Federation, held on the Champ de Mars, directly in front of the École Militaire. Some 150,000 citizens gathered for the occasion. Mass was celebrated by Bishop Charles-Maurice de Talleyrand-Périgord (1754–1838), assisted by sixty Catholic priests. A placard declared the central values of the new constitutional monarchy: "nation, law, and king." Louis XVI pledged to uphold the ideals of the new republic. A series of measures, presided over by Talleyrand, led to the nationalization of the church and the public appropriation of its assets. Clergy were now required to sign the Civil Constitution, pledging obedience to the Republic.

These measures paralleled events that had taken place earlier elsewhere in Christian Europe. For example, in 1535 the city of Geneva secularized the churches and their assets, transferring them from ecclesiastical to civil control. Around that same time, Henry VIII of England suppressed various monasteries and confiscated or sold their assets, and demanded that the clergy swear obedience to him personally rather than to the pope. In neither case could such events conceivably be regarded as "atheist," even though they were unquestionably designed to undermine the influence and power of the Roman Catholic church in those regions. After all, Geneva was the city that John Calvin made his highly successful center of operations for the propagation of his form of Protestant Christianity in the 1550s and early 1560s. Even as late as early 1792, the French Revolution could still be portrayed as reforming French Christianity rather than aiming to eliminate it.

But that would soon change. Darker days lay ahead, reaching their climax during the autumn and winter of 1793–94.

INSTITUTIONAL ATHEISM?
THE PROGRAM OF DECHRISTIANIZATION

It is tempting to present the French Revolution as institutionally committed to the elimination of Christianity within France. Yet this is difficult to sustain. Studies of the first phase of the Revolution have emphasized its lack of central direction. Without any strong leadership at this early stage, the Revolutionary movement was increasingly subjected to influence by powerful interest groups. Control of the Revolution rested in a series of factions and loose associations, often given to infighting and intrigues, which prevented any centralized control of events and policies. Perhaps the most famous of these factions was the Jacobin Club—more formally, the Society of Friends of the Constitution—which held its meetings at the recently secularized Jacobin monastery in the Rue Saint-Honoré. While it is certainly true that some of the more radical members of these groups firmly supported radical, and occasionally violent, action against the church, this did not initially translate into Revolutionary policy.

Since Jules Michelet's landmark *History of the French Revolution* (1847), it has become customary to distinguish two phases in the history of the movement. Just as England had "good" and "bad" kings, so the Revolution had a "good" and a "bad" phase. For Michelet, the good phase of the Revolution was its first, when the people united in 1789 to overthrow tyranny and establish the rule of justice and equality. Its bad phase began in 1793 with the ascendancy of the radical Jacobin faction, which brought about the Reign of Terror.

There was a lingering resentment within Revolutionary circles, occasionally even hatred, toward the church, particularly the monastic orders, as "tithe collectors." This dislike was fueled by growing fears of foreign intervention and counterrevolution. Rumors of counterrevolutionary coups, plots, and conspiracies were constantly circulated in Revolutionary circles, giving rise to suspicions that even political allies were potential traitors. Mistrust and fear gave rise to a siege mentality, which demanded that any threat to the Revolution—real or imagined—be eliminated immediately. The infamous massacre of prisoners at a Paris jail by a mob in September 1792—one of the most shocking acts of collective violence—can only be understood in terms of this pervasive fear of foreign intervention. There were rumors that foreign agents were among the prison population.

Such fears were far from figments of overactive imaginations. Austria and Prussia, already concerned over events in France in 1791, became involved in military action against France the following year. At home, the first manifestation of counterrevolution occurred in the city of Nîmes as early as 1790; it was supported principally by unemployed textile workers and agricultural laborers living in the city. A series of largely Catholic and royalist insurrections against the Revolution took place in western and southeastern France, often requiring suppression with considerable violence. Popular distrust of the church within Revolutionary circles increased when it was realized that many of those supporting and fomenting counterrevolution were priests. Increasingly, the church came to be viewed as actively involved in supporting foreign intervention and domestic resistance.

There is no doubt that the church was generally hostile to the Revolution and that many of the great Catholic families of France found themselves in a difficult situation. The religious intolerance evident even in the first phase of the Revolution alienated many traditional Catholics, especially in rural areas. The action of the National Assembly in nationalizing church properties was condemned by the pope, who was still regarded as authoritative by many within France. The introduction of a new constitution, which provided for the election of clergy, was seen as offensive to traditional Catholics; their curés would now be chosen by atheists and Protestants as much as by the Catholic faithful. It was natural for France's traditional Catholics to support counterrevolution at home and welcome intervention from abroad—especially from a traditionally Catholic power, such as Austria, with which France was now at war.

The often extreme violence directed against the church and its priests mirrors a wider use of violence to enforce Revolutionary objectives throughout the Reign of Terror. After the execution of Louis XVI, events began to spiral out of control, as an increasingly radical faction gained power, then sought to retain it by the elimination of opposition. Terror became a tactic by which opposition was crushed, and was by no means limited to legally sanctioned executions. The *armées révolutionnaires* (basically a "people's army"), which forcibly dechristianized areas of France at this time, were not subject to significant central control and often acted independently or on the basis of their leaders' prejudices. The same cannot be said, however, of General Turreau's twenty-four *colonnes infernales*, which were directed to undertake a program of extermination of counterrevolutionary elements in the Vendée area in 1794. The defense of the Revolution and of the nation—the two were often conflated in Revolutionary rhetoric—was seen to override all other considerations.

Yet Robespierre and others could see that violence was not going to win the day, especially in relation to the question of religion. In *The Furies: Violence and Terror in the French and Russian Revolutions*, Arno Mayer has drawn attention to the counterproductive impact of antireligious violence: "It is difficult to imagine a more intractable and divisive issue than the abrupt desacralization and laicization of political and civil society. Eventually it engages opposing true believers as it turns into a main battleground between, on the one hand, the religion of revolution and, on the other, first the religion of the status quo and then the religions of counterrevolution and resistance."

While one strand of Revolutionary thought favored often random acts of violence against Catholicism, others preferred a more sustained and focused program of transformation. Over the period 1790–95, a series of developments shifted France from a constitutional monarchy in which the Catholic church had a continuing role to an apparently atheist republic in which the only gods acknowledged were the ideals of the Revolution and those who supported them. Two of these developments are of particular interest.

First, we may note the decision of September 1792, following the execution of Louis XVI, to mark the beginning of the French Republic by declaring this to be Year 1 of a revised calendar, accompanied by changes in the designation of the months. The traditional Western pattern of dating events from the birth of Jesus Christ was thus abandoned. Was this to be seen as a specifically atheist gesture? Perhaps. But it could equally be seen as a decision to break with every aspect of the past—a trend evident in the adoption of the metric system, devised by the brilliant scientist and social liberal Antoine-Laurent de Lavoisier. (Lavoisier was sent to the guillotine in 1794. The mathematician Joseph-Louis Lagrange remarked of this event, "It took them only an instant to cut off that head, and a hundred years may not produce another like it.")

The second development was the establishment of the Panthéon. In 1744, Louis XV had begun to construct a vast church on the Montagne

Sainte-Geneviève. Financial difficulties led to delays, with the result that the huge building was not complete until 1789, the year of the Revolution. After it was secularized by the decree of April 1791, it was designated as a *temple de la patrie*. Various names were suggested for it, including Mausoleum and Cenotaph. Yet the name finally chosen was of immense significance—the Panthéon. Like the ancient Roman temple of the same name, it would be a place dedicated to all the gods.

But what gods? For some, the answer lay in the divinization of ideas. The French people would worship such ideals as reason, liberty, and fraternity. Perhaps the most celebrated example of this was the Festival of Reason, held inside Notre-Dame Cathedral in 1793, in which celebration of these three ideals was substituted for more traditional Trinitarian forms of worship. Yet as Antoine-François Momoro pointed out at the time, "We must never become weary of telling people that liberty, reason, and truth are only abstract beings. They are not gods, for properly speaking, they are part of ourselves." We can see here an anticipation of one of the great ideas of nineteenth-century materialism: that human beings create divinities out of their deepest longings and aspirations. It is a theme that demands long and careful consideration.

Yet for many at the time of the Revolution, such antitheological abstractions were of little value. If there is no God, there must be something or someone that can act as a focus of worship or object of inspiration. The Panthéon provided this, in effect becoming a cathedral of the religion of humanity. More significantly, however, it provided a place of burial for the great heroes of the republic. Voltaire's remains were transferred to the Panthéon from their burial site at Ramilly on July 11, 1791, in an elaborate ceremony, accompanied by an estimated cortège of 100,000 people. To be "panthéonized" was virtually the secular equivalent of the canonization of a Christian saint.

Some contemporary sources went further, and used the term *apothéose*—a term that has its origins in classical Roman history, referring to the elevation of certain Roman emperors, on their death, to the status of gods. Might this be taken to imply that such Revolutionary heroes as Voltaire were now to be regarded as gods? The best evidence suggests that this was not the case. The term "apotheosis" was robbed of its transcendent elements and reinterpreted as "made immortal." In other words, an apotheosized hero was one absorbed so deeply into the Revolutionary consciousness that he could never be forgotten. In fact, we can see here one of the most interesting antireligious literary strategies of the late eighteenth century: the use of religious or supernatural language to describe individuals, objects, experiences, and ideas that are known to be purely natural, thus subverting the language of religion by directing it against itself. The attitudes of reverence and devotion that are traditionally associated with religion are thus transferred to the secular world.

A similar practice can be seen in the artistic representations of the American Revolution. For example, consider Constantino Brumidi's work *The Apotheosis of Washington* (1865), which adorns the interior of the Rotunda of the Capitol in Washington, D.C. This highly allegorical work depicts Washington sitting in majesty, flanked on his right by the Goddess of Liberty and on his left by a winged figure of Fame sounding a trumpet and holding aloft a palm frond as a symbol of victory. Thirteen female figures, representing the thirteen original states, stand in a semicircle around Washington. On the outer ring of the canopy, six allegorical groupings surround him, representing classical images of agriculture, arts and sciences, commerce, war, mechanics, and seafaring. Washington was most certainly not understood to be divinized or made an object of worship; nor could Washington conceivably be regarded as displacing the Christian God. Brumidi was simply providing a highly visual depiction of Washington's pivotal role in founding the American republic and in providing for its well-being. The painting dates from immediately after the American Civil War, when fostering a sense of national unity and identity was of paramount importance.

THE FRENCH REVOLUTION AND
ATHEISM: AN ASSESSMENT

So was the French Revolution fundamentally atheist? There is no doubt that such a view is to be found in much Christian and atheist literature on the movement. Equally, there is evidence that atheism—then seen as novel, exciting, and thoroughly Promethean—was a major driving force for some of those involved in the Revolution, especially around the period 1793–94. Yet the situation is more complex than this crude pastiche suggests. To illustrate how nuanced things were, we may consider one of the more colorful personalities of the period—Baron Anacharsis Cloots (1754–94). Cloots was at the forefront of the dechristianization movement that gathered around the militant atheist Jacques Hébert. He "debaptised" himself, setting aside his original name of Jean-Baptiste du Val-de-Grâce. For Cloots, religion was simply not to be tolerated. "We shall, in turn, see the heavenly royalty condemned by the revolutionary tribunal of victorious Reason; for the Truth, seated on the throne of Nature, is supremely intolerant. The star of the day will make meteors and all the flickering lights of the night disappear." When the light comes, the shadows must disappear—and if they do not disappear by themselves, they must be made to disappear. For Cloots, nature and reason must triumph against both genuine earthly and imaginary heavenly monarchs, both with the capacity to enslave and deceive.

Where Robespierre sought to advocate the religion of the Supreme Being, around which the French people could unite, Cloots vigorously pursued a more atheistic approach. He was an active member of the faction that successfully campaigned for the atheistic "Cult of Reason," which was officially proclaimed on November 10, 1793. On May 7, 1794, this was abandoned, being replaced by the more restrained Deist "Cult of the Supreme Being." Robespierre was worried that the program of dechristianization, actively and clumsily propagated by Cloots and Léonard Bourdon, was causing growing resentment and fueling counterrevolutionary sentiment. God required reinstatement—at least, in some modest form. The end of those insisting upon more radical measures was as inevitable as it was unpleasant. Cloots was executed in March 1794. Robespierre himself would soon fall victim to Revolutionary infighting and factionalism. Three months later he followed Cloots to the guillotine.

Inspiring and ennobling, the project of the French Revolution was at the same time brutal and repressive. The same movement that made such a powerful appeal to nature and reason for its justification ended up using systematic violence to subdue those who were unpersuaded of its merits. The movement that gave the world such noble monuments as the Declaration of the Rights of Man also gave it the Reign of Terror. To those who suggest that religion is responsible for the ills of the world, the Revolution offers an awkward anomaly. As the historian Reynald Sécher has shown, pressure from Paris to eliminate counterrevolution in the south of France led to the deployment of Turreau's *colonnes infernales* of 1794, whose wholesale destruction of villages and their inhabitants came close to genocide. The new religion of humanity mimicked both the virtues and vices of the Catholicism it hoped to depose. It might well have a new god, a new savior, and new saints. But it also had its own inquisition and began its own particular war of religion.

During the French Revolution, for the first time in modern history the possibility of an atheist state was explored. That exploration was incomplete, inconsistent, and not entirely encouraging. Within a decade, the fledgling French republic found itself overtaken by events, as Napoleon Bonaparte entered Paris and seized power. A new constitution was proclaimed on December 15, 1799, containing the sentence that marked the end of an era: "Citizens, the Revolution is established upon the principles which began it: it is over." The restoration of Catholicism soon followed.

In one sense, therefore, the Revolution was an experiment that failed. Its ten years did not establish atheism as the self-evident religion of European humanity, nor as the philosophical foundation for modern political theory. Yet the unthinkable had happened—true, only for a short period. What some had thought was a new age in the history of the world turned out to be an interlude. Yet the real significance of the French Revolution to our story lies not so much in what it accomplished in the realm of France, but on the impact it created on the minds and above all the imaginations of many alienated individuals throughout Europe. Seeds were planted, mental horizons were extended, and hopes for change ignited. Might others succeed where the Revolutionaries had failed? Might minds be changed permanently by argument, rather than temporarily by force?

Three giants emerged to lay the intellectual foundations of atheism with a rigor and permanence denied to others. The three great pillars of the golden age of atheism are Ludwig Feuerbach (1804–72), Karl Marx (1818–83), and Sigmund Freud (1856–1939), who between them turned a daring revolutionary hypothesis into the established certainty of an age, placing Christianity constantly on the defensive. In what follows we shall assess the contributions of each of these thinkers in creating the mind-set of modern atheism, exploring both their original ideas and how these were received and appropriated in the golden age.

THE INTELLECTUAL FOUNDATIONS: FEUERBACH, MARX, AND FREUD

T HE FRENCH REVOLUTION ATTEMPTED TO BRING ABOUT by force a permanent change in ways of human thinking. What had once been thought to be self-evident and unchangeable was suddenly declared to be untrue and open to change. The domination of France by king and church was not a matter of necessity; both could be swept away by Revolutionary enthusiasm, where necessary augmented by the judicious application of terror. Dr. Guillotin's excellent new invention proved a remarkably effective means of concentrating people's minds on this matter. Yet decapitating people is never the best way of proving a new idea. As Blaise Pascal (1623–62) argued, the best way of advancing any idea is to make people wish it were true, and then show them that it is indeed so.

But how could the predominantly Christian culture of the West be permanently altered? As the nineteenth century dawned, the French Revolution was already being spoken of in the past tense—an inconvenient interruption to European life, which had given way to the more predictable nationalist agenda of Napoleon Bonaparte. What was necessary for the advancement of atheism was a revolution within the collective Western mind, in which the presumption of God by Christians was displaced by an intellectual skepticism directed against their ideas, rather than a physical assault directed against their members and institutions.

A SECULAR PRIESTHOOD:
THE RISE OF THE INTELLECTUAL

Atheism needed to take root at two distinct, though related, levels: the popular and the intellectual. Although many social historians have stressed the importance of grassroots movements in the shaping of nineteenth-century culture, there is no doubt that a "trickle-down" mechanism was of decisive importance in the shaping of Western atheism. Ideas originally limited to a small elite gradually percolated downward and outward into society as a whole. Eventually, they became so accepted and familiar that it was difficult to imagine that it was ever otherwise. Popular culture was led by intellectuals, who increasingly became the shapers and movers of Western thought. As clerical power began to decline in the eighteenth century, Western society began to look to others for moral vision and intellectual inspiration. It found such leaders in the growing community of intellectuals.

The emergence of the intellectual as a recognized social type is one of the most remarkable developments of recent centuries. Intellectuals became a secular priesthood, unfettered by the dogmas of the religious past, addressing a growing audience who were becoming increasingly impatient with the moral failures and cultural unsophistication of their clergy. At some point, perhaps one that can never be determined with historical accuracy, Western society came to believe that it should look elsewhere than to its clergy for guidance. Instead, they turned to the intellectuals, who were able to portray their clerical opponents as lazy fools who could do no more than unthinkingly repeat the slogans and nostrums of an increasingly distant past. A new future lay ahead, and society needed brave new thinkers to lead them to its lush Promethean pastures.

For some, the intellectual leaders of society were poets—the "un-acknowledged legislators of mankind," as Percy Bysshe Shelley called them. The poet bore the heavy weight of articulating a moral vision for humanity, grounded in reason and nature, and inspiring a community to yearn for a new and better order—and by doing so, to reach out and embrace such a world. For Tennyson, the poet was one whose words shook the world, tousling its settled patterns and habits of thought. Others argued for the special place of the novelist in challenging the prevailing consensus and generating a desire for an alternative vision of reality, offering fictional depictions of what such a new world might look like and critiquing the world they saw around them. George Eliot's novels were of particular importance in creating a climate of suspicion toward faith in Victorian culture.

Many saw the serious writer of major treatises as the creator of new political and social orders. Had not Jean-Jacques Rousseau's *Social Contract* launched a thousand revolutionaries? Edward Gibbon's *Decline and Fall of the Roman Empire* (1776–88), while making some conventional comments on the benefits of religion, nevertheless portrays the early successes of Christianity in terms of a rather unattractive psychology of violence, fanaticism, and intolerance. Richard Knight's sensational *Discourse on the Worship of Priapus* (1786) shocked polite English society as much by its Lucretian suggestion that religion was a human invention to explain otherwise puzzling aspects of nature, as by its explicit depiction of certain aspects of nature not normally mentioned in polite conversation. Its lurid prose descriptions and illustrations of phallic cults left little to the imagination.

The idea that the gods were a human invention was a not always welcome commonplace of late classical antiquity. Lucretius's works had enjoyed a renaissance in the Restoration England of the 1660s, no doubt due to the popular revolt against the religious excesses of the Puritan period. Yet the idea that humanity invented its gods was still seen as little more than an interesting suggestion, without rigorous proof. We must now turn to see how a German intellectual managed to persuade a generation that the idea that humanity invented its gods was not just an entertaining rumor, it was the best available explanation of the evidence. The intellectual in question was Ludwig Feuerbach (1804–72).

GOD AS AN INVENTION:
LUDWIG FEUERBACH

Revolutionary sentiment simmered in early-nineteenth-century Germany. The French Revolution had heightened a sense of injustice within many levels of German society and created an appetite for radical change. Might the German states now finally throw off their outmoded princes and dukes, and replace them with something more democratic? When the news of the French Revolution reached the universities of Germany, a sense of standing on the threshold of a new era appears to have dawned. Europe had come of age. The ideas of the Enlightenment seemed about to be transformed into social and political action.

The war between Revolutionary France and the reactionary German princes of 1792 raised hopes of social transformation to unprecedented levels. No longer were children obliged to resign themselves to the weary authority structures and outlooks of their parents' generation. The age-old theme of son rebelling against father (cf. Luke 15: 11–24) assumed a new significance: in the 1790s, sons did not merely rebel against their fathers, but against the world order that their fathers' generations represented. The defeat of imperial Germany by Napoleon Bonaparte in 1806 caused expectations of change to soar.

Class barriers were beginning to break down, and major social reforms were being introduced. All around them, the Germans could see evidence of radical change. The French Revolution had overthrown the Bourbons, the Greeks were in the process of revolting against Turkish oppression, and major uprisings were taking place in Poland against the authority of the Russian czar. With the establishment of people's assemblies, liberal German politicians like Karl von Rötteck and Karl Theodor Welcker were pressing home popular demands for freedom of the press and other democratic rights. The central demand was for a liberal, unified Germany, in the place of the Deutscher Bund (German Federation), formed by thirty-five sovereign monarchs and four independent free cities at the Congress of Vienna (1814–15).

The social realities of Germany at this time were such that radical change could not be brought about by political action. The best means of securing irreversible changes in the long term was to change the way in which people thought. The battleground for reform was thus not the courts, but the universities of Germany. If the ideas on which traditional social structures were based could be overthrown or shown to be hopelessly outmoded, the collapse of those structures could not be far away. And one of the most important social institutions of the era, playing a pivotal role in underpinning the old order, was the Lutheran church.

The Lutheran church in Germany now found itself the target of a twofold critique. Given that political action against existing forms of government was a virtual impossibility, reformers directed their attention to neutralizing the privileges and influence of an institution that was widely associated with the political establishment—namely, the church itself. Yet the focus on intellectual radicalism also led to a second aspect of this critique, a concerted criticism of the ideas upon which the church was ultimately grounded. The intellectual energies and enthusiasm that British radicals directed into the political sphere was diverted, in the German context, to the sphere of the church, with the universities acting as the spearhead of the demands for radical change.

The church was thus widely seen as an agent of reaction, just as the universities were seen as agents of radical change. Student revolts broke out at several leading universities. In 1817, some five hundred students celebrated the three hundredth anniversary of the Reformation by marching to the Wartburg in Thuringia to demand constitutional changes and a united fatherland. Demands for political reform, often driven by a strongly nationalist agenda, became widespread. Instability was linked with economic difficulties, even affecting the church.

The situation was especially problematic for theological students. Having completed their education, they were finding it more and more difficult to find employment. Of the total graduate output of German universities in the 1830s, two in every five were theologians. Ecclesiastical positions of any kind became increasingly difficult to secure: despite a sharp increase in population, the number of church posts available actually decreased over the period 1815–40. Perhaps three or four theological graduates in every ten might hope to find employment of this nature.

The situation in the universities was even more bleak, with contractions, moratoria, and salary cuts becoming a regular feature of academic life. Simultaneously, however, establishment figures (such as the landed aristocracy) were given preference in obtaining positions in the civil and ecclesiastical administration, causing intense resentment among those outside this privileged section of the community. As a result, there were many disaffected and unemployed graduates who saw themselves as members of the new "intellectual proletariat," prepared to assault the civil and religious establishment. The emergence of a socially alienated, theologically literate, antiestablishment lay intelligentsia is one of the more significant phenomena of the social history of Germany in the 1830s.

Ludwig Feuerbach was born into this revolutionary cauldron in 1804. His family was politically liberal and sympathetic to the demands for modernization that were sweeping Germany at this time. Feuerbach chose to study theology at the University of Heidelberg in 1823; however, he soon moved to the great Prussian University of Berlin, which had recently gained a reputation as one of Europe's finest academic institutions. Here he was able to attend the lectures of the philosopher G. W. F. Hegel and the theologian F. D. E. Schleiermacher. Financial pressures obliged him to move his studies to the University of Erlangen, where he went on to lecture on the history of modern philosophy. His academic career ran into the sands after the publication of *Thoughts on Death and Immortality* (1830), which was seen as irreverent and potentially seditious.

The book lampooned Christianity as "some kind of insurance company." Feuerbach argued that far from correcting modern culture's propensity to ignore or deny death, Christianity colluded with this evasion of death. Its belief in individual immortality in another world, in addition to being internally inconsistent, trivializes death by diverting believers from their actual relations with other persons and with the natural world around them. The Christian belief in heaven, Feuerbach argued, thus impoverishes the one and only life we have by distracting us from its joys and concerns. The illusion of individual immortality must be abandoned if the situation is to be improved. Authentic human existence is thus godless and limited to this life. To think otherwise is delusory.

Like so many other graduates of the time, Feuerbach was unable to obtain a university teaching position. Instead, he settled down to the life of an independent scholar and writer. This luxury was made possible by his marriage in 1837 to Berta Löw, whose family owned a porcelain factory. The factory had been established in 1762 by Alexander von Ansbach and taken over in 1803 by Berta's father, Christian Friedrich Löw from Bayreuth, and the Nuremberg banker Georg Adam Späth. The good news was that the porcelain factory made money, allowing Feuerbach to forget about financial worries and live in comfort in the Löw family castle; the bad news was that it was located at Bruckberg, in the middle of nowhere. An 1856 survey records forty-eight households in the village, with a population of 490. Feuerbach thus spent many years in splendid rustic isolation, away from the intellectual and political cultural life he hoped to influence. His problems returned in 1860, when the factory went bankrupt, forcing his family to move.

During his Bruckberg period, Feuerbach developed a formidable reputation as a revolutionary thinker. This reputation was based particularly on his definitive work *The Essence of Christianity* (1841), which many regarded as the manifesto of the revolutionary movement. But why should a book which argued that Christianity was essentially a delusion have such a major *political* impact? The answer lies in the major political role played by most of the German churches during the revolutionary 1840s. Feuerbach grasped that the political power and religious credibility of the churches could be fatally undermined by demonstrating that their basic ideas were mistaken. If Christianity could be shown to rest on errors, its social authority would be severely reduced. There is no doubt that the church of this period was too much a prisoner of existing social structures, and that it often colluded with the belief that these structures were definitively grounded on Christian dogmas. It was a convenient belief, in that it safeguarded the social privileges of the churches. Yet one of the most obvious lessons of history is that atheism thrives when the church is seen to be privileged, out of touch with the people, and powerful—precisely the situation that emerged in Germany during the revolutionary years of the 1840s.

At this time, Germany seemed ripe for revolution, with the churches being one of the most important conservative social forces. In the 1840s Germany went through a series of crises, partly through the growing social deprivation caused by industrialization, which, when combined with rapid population growth, led to the formation of an urbanized working class that lived in utter poverty and misery. Many families failed to rise above the subsistence level. During an uprising in June 1844, weavers in Silesia demanded that their "starvation wages" be increased. They were bluntly told "to eat grass," and their revolt was put down harshly by the Prussian army. In 1847 widespread crop failures led to famines. Unemployment rose, and hunger riots by desperate workers demanding food were suppressed by the army. In March 1848, the French king fell and the Second Republic was proclaimed. This time the revolution spilled over into Germany, with widespread demands for constitutional government, a bill of rights, and national unification. By April 1849, however, it was clear that the revolution had failed.

Although Feuerbach was called to Heidelberg by radical student groups to give public lectures in the city from December 1848 to March 1849, he never seems to have appreciated the importance of direct political action. His contribution would be made primarily at the intellectual level, through a radical undermining of the intellectual foundations of the old order, of which the church was perhaps the most visible symbol.

Where the French Revolution aimed to replace the traditional "religion of deity" with a new "religion of humanity" by political means, Feuerbach rightly saw that something far more deep-rooted was required. A political development could be overthrown at the whim of a foreign monarch or a fickle crowd. What was required was an intellectual earthquake, comparable to the Copernican revolution of the late sixteenth century. So successful were Copernicus's arguments that no thinking person now believed that the sun orbited the earth. No king or mob could sway this judgment, which was held to be grounded in the reality of the world.

For Feuerbach, Hegel's philosophy opened up a new possibility: *demonstrating*—not merely asserting!—that humanity invented the idea of God as a consolation and distraction from the sorrow of the world. God was a human creation, over which humanity had authority and control. Where traditional religion held that the entire religious system orbited around God, Feuerbach believed that its orbit centered on humanity—and that he could prove it. In *The Essence of Christianity*, Feuerbach set out to prove that humanity was oppressed by its own invention—something that it had created, and could now in turn destroy. There was no God to whom craven human obedience was due. Humanity, which existed alone, had brought the notion of God into being as a misguided means of comforting itself during life's dark and shadowy journey. God was not someone that humanity discovered or encountered, but "a dream of the human soul," a pure invention, the product of a mind that could reject God with equal ease.

The basic idea that Feuerbach develops with such consummate skill is that of the "projection" or "objectification" of human emotions, feelings, and longings. The human mind, without being aware of what it is doing, projects its longing for immortality and meaning onto an imaginary transcendent screen, and gives the name "God" to its own creation.

Consciousness of God is human self-consciousness; knowledge of God is human self-knowledge. By the God you know the human, and conversely, by the human you know the God. The two are one. What God is to a person, that too is the spirit, the soul; and what the spirit, the soul, are to a person, that is the God. God is the revealed and explicit inner self of a human being. Religion is the ceremonial unveiling of the hidden treasures of humanity, the confession of its innermost thoughts and the open recognition of its secrets of love.

Yet religious people are blissfully unaware of this fact. They mistakenly believe that what they have created somehow exists independently of them. As Feuerbach puts it:

This does not mean that religious people are themselves immediately aware of the fact that their consciousness of God is simply their own self-consciousness. In fact, the absence of such an awareness is the distinctive mark of religion . . . Initially, people mistakenly locate their essential nature as if it were *outside* of themselves, before finally realizing that it is actually within them . . . What religion earlier took to be objective, is later recognized to be subjective; what formerly was taken to be God, and worshipped as such, is now recognized to be something human. What was earlier religion is later taken to be idolatry: humans are seen to have adored their own nature. Humans objectified themselves but failed to recognize themselves as this object.

Feuerbach thus lays the foundations for the criticism of religion by arguing that it is now possible to recognize religion for what it really is: not a God-given set of ideas but a human construction. Religion tells us nothing about God and everything about ourselves—our hopes, fears, and deepest longings.

> God is the revealed and explicit inner self of a human being. Religion is the ceremonial unveiling of the hidden treasures of humanity, the confession of its innermost thoughts, and the open recognition of its secrets of love.
>
> God, far from being our master, should be our servant. But did we really need such a servant in the first place? Can we not dispense with such an outmoded belief altogether, and realize that we ourselves are the only gods?

This dismissal of God was as slick as it was sweeping. The longings of the human heart needed no objective foundation in any external being. *Homo homini Deus est!* Man is a god to himself. To study human conceptions of God is therefore to understand more about humanity itself. Feuerbach thus laid the foundations of the discipline of religious studies as a means of deepening our knowledge of human nature. Religious beliefs and practices are like windows into the human soul, illuminating the darkest secrets and mysteries locked within. And what humanity created can subsequently be refashioned. "God" thus becomes a redefinable concept, capable of being shaped and reshaped to meet the changing context of human existence.

There were problems with Feuerbach's approach, as his critics were not slow to point out. The circularity of the argument was a particular concern: Feuerbach postulates that there is no God, then turns to the question of why anyone would *want* to believe in God. Atheism having duly been presupposed, it is not unduly demanding to make it the argument's conclusion. It was also pointed out that if belief in God was a response to a human longing for security, might it not also be argued that atheism was a response to the human desire for autonomy? Not all individuals might long for the same things, after all.

Important though these objections might be, they were swept to one side as a generation read Feuerbach assiduously and enthusiastically. *The Essence of Christianity* went through three editions in record time, and was the sensational topic of conversation in revolutionary circles throughout Germany. To his avid readers, Feuerbach had robbed religion of any external basis and refuted its claims to authority, power, and influence. The idea of God was a dream, and the church the perpetuator of this delusion. Claims to power based on an appeal to God were simply covert appeals to human self-interest. It was not God who mandated humans to behave in certain ways; it was merely certain humans who did so, improperly claiming a false divine mandate for their personal advancement.

In the English-speaking world, Feuerbach's radical approach was propagated through George Eliot's translation of *The Essence of Christianity*, published in July 1854. Yet by 1850, Feuerbach's influence was waning. The translation was neither a critical nor a commercial success. In both Britain and North America the work was regarded as philosophically allied to trends peculiar to Germany, and hence seriously out of place in England. Its explicit atheism was regarded as "freakish" and "exotic" by many. Those who found atheism a rare and refreshing philosophy preferred to read Auguste Comte (1798–1857), whose *Cours de philosophie positive* appeared in a condensed English translation in 1853.

Even writers such as Ralph Waldo Emerson were surprisingly lukewarm toward Feuerbach's ideas. Emerson's "Divinity School Address," given at Harvard University in 1838, had led some, including Theophilus Parsons, professor at Harvard Law School, to suggest that Emerson "preached a doctrine which leads man to worship his own nature and himself." This might suggest that Emerson would be broadly supportive of Feuerbach's ideas. In fact, Emerson seems to have regarded Feuerbach's "philosophical atheism" as inferior to the "scientific atheism" of Auguste Comte.

Comte had argued, through a brilliant yet highly eclectic account of intellectual history, that the development of human thought passes through three distinct stages: the theological, the metaphysical, and the scientific. In the first phase, humanity believed that it was legitimate to seek the ultimate causes of events, and located those causes in super-human personal beings known as gods. A clear progression from animism through polytheism to monotheism can be discerned within this phase of thought. In the second stage, personal deities are transformed into metaphysical abstractions, leading to the notion of God being displaced by essentially natural categories. In the third, scientific (or "positivist") phase, a more mature outlook develops, in which the human mind comes to concern itself purely with observed facts and not with the unobservable inner essences of things. According to Comte's account, Western culture had passed the threshold between the second and third phases, and was about to enter a purely scientific mode of thinking. There was no way back to earlier ways of thinking. History had passed its verdict, and there was no appeal. Who could resist the laws of inexorable historical progress?

Precisely such an idea lay behind a more radical development of Feuerbach's thought, which proved far more influential upon the shaping of the modern atheist mind. Such was Karl Marx's status in the Soviet pantheon of the 1950s that he was venerated as a secular Zeus, with Lenin and Stalin as only slightly lesser Olympians. We must therefore turn to consider Karl Marx's critique of religion.

GOD AS AN OPIATE: KARL MARX

Like all who are unwise or unfortunate enough to rise to fame, Karl Marx (1818–83) has been misrepresented by both friend and foe. In part, this arises from the historically interesting fact that Marx's ideas only became actualizable in the twentieth century, in the aftermath of the Russian Revolution. There was thus a substantial historical and cultural distance placed between the founder of communism and those who implemented his ideas, often in ways that might well have caused him to turn in his grave had not worshipful supporters placed such a massive headstone above him, which presumably would prevent such maneuvering. A further point of importance is that Marx envisaged revolution breaking out in the industrialized nations of Western Europe, having entertained particularly high hopes at the time of the French and German revolutionary movements around 1847–48. Yet history dealt Marx's successors a quite different set of cards, forcing them to put their revolutionary agendas and policies into practice in socially backward, agrarian czarist Russia.

Why is Marx so important? To gain something of an insight into his genius, we may join the little group of eleven mourners who gathered on March 17, 1883, at Highgate Cemetery, London, to pay their last respects to their master. Friedrich Engels delivered the funeral oration (in English, although only German translations now survive):

> Just as Darwin discovered the law of development of organic nature, so Marx discovered the law of development of human history: the simple fact, hitherto concealed by an overgrowth of ideology, that mankind must first of all eat, drink, have shelter and clothing, before it can pursue politics, science, art, religion, etc.; that therefore the production of the immediate material means, and consequently the degree of economic development attained by a given people or during a given epoch, form the foundation upon which the state institutions, the legal conceptions, art, and even the ideas on religion, of the people concerned have been evolved, and in the light of which they must, therefore, be explained, instead of vice versa, as had hitherto been the case.

This dense forest of prose, compressed into a single sentence, would have made perfect sense to those gathered to mourn Marx. What Engels described in the arcane language of the initiated was the principle of historical materialism—an intellectually rigorous account of the development of history, leading to an explicit understanding of what the goal of that historical process might be.

Karl Marx was born into a reasonably comfortable middle-class home in the conservative town of Trier. His father had converted from Judaism to Protestantism as a career move. He persuaded Karl to study law at the University of Bonn, where he became engaged to Jenny von Westphalen. After moving to study at the University of Berlin, young Marx fell under the influence of Hegel and joined the "Young Hegelians." This brought him into contact with radical theologians such as Bruno Bauer and David Friedrich Strauss. Unable to find an academic position, Marx settled in Paris, where he worked as a journalist and developed his emerging ideas on social alienation under a capitalist economy. These writings are now generally known as the Economic and Philosophical Manuscripts (1844), which were not published until the 1930s.

Having been expelled from Paris on account of his political activities, Marx and his new friend Friedrich Engels moved to Brussels. Here, Marx devoted himself, with Engels, to a major study and defense of a materialist approach to history, which was published posthumously as A German Ideology. The outcome of these reflections can be seen in their Communist Manifesto of 1848, published on the eve of a wave of revolutions in France and Germany. While the Manifesto reflected rather than precipitated the revolutionary fervor of its time, there is no doubt that its ideas resonated with the mood of the day, even if a little opaquely.

Marx's political views made continued life on the Continent somewhat hazardous, and led him to begin his "long, sleepless night of exile" in London. He appears to have believed that the exile would not be long; revolutionary progress could be expected to be as rapid as it was inevitable. Eking out a living as a journalist, Marx began a large-scale work on political economy. Completed in 1857, this vast and sprawling work of eight hundred pages was not published until 1941, under the title of the *Grundrisse* ("Outlines"). Thereafter he was able to focus on *Das Kapital*, the first volume of which appeared in 1867. The remainder would be published after his death. Although Marx was obliged to witness some of the dramatic events in Europe—such as the Paris Commune of 1871—from his exile in London, he was active in organizing the First International (the International Working Men's Association). He died on March 14, 1883.

The notion of materialism is fundamental to Marxism. Some eighteenth-century writers—such as Baron d'Holbach—used this term to designate the view that the world consists only of matter, without any spiritual dimensions. Marx and his followers developed this idea further, arguing that every aspect of human life and thought is determined by social and economic factors. Material needs determine the way in which people live and think. This leads Marx to one of his most fundamental assertions: ideas and values are determined by the material realities of life. In a famous analogy, he argued that material reality was the foundation on which the superstructure of ideas was erected. People's social and economic conditions determine what they think. This doctrine has highly significant implications for Marx's understanding of the origin of religious ideas. The idea of God is a human attempt to cope with the harshness of material life and the pain resulting from social and economic deprivation.

Marx now took a step of decisive importance, affirming Feuerbach's analysis of the origins of the religious notion of God and moving far beyond this. Feuerbach had argued that religion was the projection of human needs, an expression of the "uttered sorrow of the soul." Marx agreed with this interpretation, as far as it went. But his point was more radical. Religion comes into being on account of sorrow and injustice—yet these themselves arise through the *social situation* of the individual. Feuerbach, Marx argued, failed to take this social dimension of the individual seriously, tending to see individuals as detached from social structures. If social conditions determine the world of ideas, it follows that changing those conditions will have a critical effect upon the resulting ideologies. It is this insight that underlies his often quoted (yet unpublished during his lifetime) comment on Feuerbach: "the philosophers have only interpreted the world, in various ways; the point, however, is to change it."

Religion has no real independent existence, but is merely an epiphenomenon, a symptom of something more real and substantial that lies underneath it—namely, the material world. "The religious world is but the reflex of the real world." Thus Marx argues that "religion is just the imaginary sun which seems to man to revolve around him, until he realizes that he himself is the centre of his own revolution." In other words, God is simply a projection of human concerns. Human beings "look for a superhuman being in the fantasy reality of heaven, and find nothing there but their own reflection."

Having argued that religion in general, and Christianity in particular, are direct outcomes of unjust social conditions, Marx declares that religion is so thoroughly determined by economic factors that it is pointless to consider any of its doctrines or beliefs on their own terms. Their origins are socioeconomic, not intellectual. Whereas earlier generations of atheist writers had attempted to demonstrate the intellectual incoherence of some basic religious teachings, such as the divinity of Christ or the existence of God, Marx undermines them totally by insisting that they are nothing more than the creation of purely social forces. Marx's socioeconomic explanation of the origins of religion makes a detailed engagement with its specific ideas unnecessary. Religion is a human creation in response to the alienation experienced through the process of production; its specific teachings are not of particular relevance, and need not trouble the busy critic of religion.

But why should religion exist at all? If Marx is right, why should people continue to believe in such a crude illusion? Marx's answer picks up on the notion of alienation. "Humans make religion; religion does not make humans. Religion is the self-consciousness and self-esteem of people who either have not found themselves or who have already lost themselves again." Religion is the product of social and economic alienation. It is a specific consequence of that alienation, and at the same time encourages that alienation by intoxicating the masses and rendering them incapable of recognizing their situation and doing something about it. Religion is a comfort that enables people to tolerate their economic alienation. If there were no such alienation, there would be no need for religion. The division of labor and the existence of private property introduce alienation and estrangement into the economic and social orders.

Materialism affirms that events in the material world bring about corresponding changes in the intellectual world. Religion is thus the result of a certain set of social and economic conditions. Change those conditions, so that economic alienation is eliminated, and religion will cease to exist. It will no longer serve any useful function. Unjust social conditions produce religion and are in turn supported by religion. "The struggle against religion is therefore indirectly a struggle against *the world* of which religion is the spiritual fragrance." Marx thus argues that religion will continue to exist as long as it meets a need in the life of alienated people. "The religious reflex of the real world can . . . only then vanish when the practical relations of everyday life offer to man none but perfectly intelligible and reasonable relations with regard to his fellow men and to nature." In other words, a shake-up in the real world is needed to get rid of religion. Marx thus argues that when a nonalienating economic and social environment is brought about through communism, the needs that gave rise to religion will vanish. And with the elimination of those material needs, spiritual hunger will also vanish.

At this point, we may focus on one of Marx's most quoted phrases. In his *Contribution to the Critique of Hegel's Philosophy of Law* (1843–44), Marx drew the following conclusion: "*Religious* distress is at the same time an *expression* of real distress and a *protest* against real distress. Religion is the sigh of the oppressed creature, the heart of a heartless world, just as it is the spirit of a spiritless situation. It is the *opium* of the people" (Marx's emphasis).

Religion thus dulls the pain of an unjust world, enabling the downtrodden people to cope with its sorrow and distress, and indirectly encouraging them to collude with the existing order. By numbing their pain, it blinds them to the need and possibility of radical social change, which they are in a position to bring about by revolutionary mass action. "The abolition of religion as the *illusory* happiness of the people is required for their *real* happiness. The demand to give up the illusion about its condition is the *demand to give up a condition which needs illusions*" (Marx's emphasis).

Religion thus eases pain by creating a dream world, especially "the fantasy of a supernatural world where all sorrows cease"—a clear reference to the biblical vision of the New Jerusalem, in which there will be no pain, suffering, or weeping (Revelation 21:4). Feuerbach had already argued that religion was a consoling illusion; Marx now argues that the abolition of a social condition that condemns people to live by illusions will remove the causes of religious belief in the first place. A communist revolution will thus eliminate the social basis of religion, so that belief in God will wither away. Atheism is the natural ideology of a communist society.

Marx thus concludes that the historical function of religion has been to offer a divine justification for the status quo—that is, to lend the establishment a spurious religious authority that lies beyond challenge. Christianity, he argues, taught the necessity of a ruling and an oppressed class, and declared all acts of the oppressors against the oppressed to be the just punishment of original sin and other sins. In its place, Marx proposes a society in which alienation is abolished by a radical reshaping of the process of production, which leads to the natural death of religion (which no longer has any social function) and the cultivation of more humanist forms of pursuit. Marx's depiction of this in *The German Ideology* offers an intriguing vision of the paradise that may be expected to result from this social upheaval: "Where nobody has one exclusive sphere of activity but each can become accomplished in any branch he wishes, society regulates the general production and thus makes it possible for me to do one thing to-day and another to-morrow, to hunt in the morning, fish in the afternoon, rear cattle in the evening, criticize after dinner, just as I have a mind, without ever becoming hunter, fisherman, shepherd or critic."

Although Marx's extensive correspondence suggests that he thoroughly detested life in small-town rural Germany, his vision of a communist paradise seems to idealize predominantly rural pursuits.

Marx's critique of religion is the most radical that the nineteenth century would produce, and was destined to exercise a major influence on the development of atheism in the twentieth century. Yet the advancement of atheism in that century was not merely the outcome of a political and military process that led to something like one-half of the world's population living under atheist regimes from about 1950 to 1990. Although the origins of that development lay in the West, its actualization lay in Eastern Europe and Asia, supremely China. But in the West, a new criticism of theistic belief arose, destined to shape the perceptions of a rising generation and raise new questions about the origins and cultural viability of the notion of God.

GOD AS ILLUSION: SIGMUND FREUD

Sigismund Schlomo Freud was born on May 6, 1856, in the little town of Freiberg (now Príbor, Czech Republic). He grew up in a Jewish household in which religion was taken very seriously. In 1860 the family moved to Vienna. The city of Vienna had long been noted as one of Europe's great centers of creativity, experiencing a cultural golden age between about 1750 and the outbreak of the First World War. It was home to some of the world's most brilliant composers—such as Haydn, Mozart, Beethoven, Brahms, and Mahler—not to mention its many novelists, architects, and playwrights. Freud arrived in the city at the height of its cultural influence, and in turn would add further to its reputation. He entered the University of Vienna in 1873, taking the opportunity to change his somewhat cumbersome forename to Sigmund.

Although his primary concern was the study of medicine, Freud demonstrated a deep interest in religious and philosophical matters. Initially, he found himself intrigued by the Catholic philosopher Franz Brentano, even allowing himself the speculation that "the science of all things seems to demand the existence of God." Yet such positive comments concerning theism are rare; Freud's correspondence of this period shows him to be a confirmed atheist throughout his university years. For Freud, it is natural for humanity not to believe in God. If this is so, it is religion that requires an explanation, not atheism, in that religion marks a departure from the natural state of belief of humanity. But what explanation might be offered for this irrational and unnecessary belief? In 1875 he finally discovered the philosopher who would place his atheism on a more rigorous intellectual foundation. In a letter to Eduard Silberstein of 1875, Freud wrote: "Feuerbach is the one whom I revere and admire above all other philosophers."

Earlier we explored Ludwig Feuerbach's radical idea that the concept of God was fundamentally a human construction, based on the "projection" of fundamental human longings and desires. Although these ideas achieved wide currency in the 1840s, they were rapidly displaced by alternatives, including Auguste Comte's positivism and Karl Marx's sociological account of the origins of religion. Feuerbach's basic ideas were now taken over and given a new sense of direction in Freud's writings. "All I have done—and this is the only thing that is new in my exposition—is to add some psychological foundation to the criticisms of my great predecessors." In fact, it is probably fair to say that Feuerbach's projection or wish-fulfillment theory is best known today in its Freudian form rather than in Feuerbach's original version. "Religion is an illusion and it derives its strength from the fact that it falls in with our instinctual desires."

The most powerful statement of Freud's approach can be found in *The Future of an Illusion* (1927), which develops a strongly reductionist approach to religion. For Freud, religious ideas are "illusions, fulfillments of the oldest, strongest and most urgent wishes of mankind." "We shall tell ourselves that it would be very nice if there were a God who created the world and was a benevolent Providence, and if there were a moral order in the universe and an afterlife; but it is a very striking fact that all this is exactly as we are bound to wish it to be. And it would be more remarkable still if our wretched, ignorant, and downtrodden ancestors had succeeded in solving all these difficult riddles of the universe."

The parallels with Feuerbach are evident; yet Freud went on to develop a radical and original explanation of religion, grounded in the insights of the newly emerging discipline of psychoanalysis, which took Feuerbach's critique of religion to new heights. Illusions are not deliberate deceptions; they are simply ideas that arise from within the human unconscious, as it seeks to fulfill its deepest yearnings and longings. For Marx, those longings were the tragic outcome of social alienation, requiring social transformation for their elimination. For Freud, their origins lie not in society but in the human unconscious.

It was the widely reported clinical success of Freud's psychoanalysis that established his credentials as the supreme interpreter of the human unconscious. In 1902 Freud was finally appointed to a professorship in Vienna, despite a disturbing amount of academic anti-Semitism. He gradually began to gather disciples at home and abroad, especially in North America. Out of this grew the Vienna Psychoanalytical Society (1908) and the International Psychoanalytic Association (1910), which included Alfred Adler and Carl Jung. A series of spectacular therapeutic triumphs clinched his reputation as a healer of the troubled human mind. "Anna O." (Bertha Pappenheim), whom Josef Breuer treated for hysteria in 1882–84, demonstrated to Freud that hysterical symptoms are the consequence of buried memories that must be retrieved through a "cathartic" program. The case histories of the Rat Man, Wolf Man, Dora, and Little Hans created a surge of interest throughout the West, especially in North America. Although Freud only visited the United States once—he lectured at Clark University, Worcester, Massachusetts, in 1909—the impact of that visit was enormous, leading to an exponential growth of interest in his ideas in America.

Before turning to explore the complex, shifting amalgam of ideas that constitutes Freud's massive critique of religion, it is important to note that Freud's atheism was the presupposition, not the outcome, of his theories. Freud's theory of the psychogenesis of religion predates his study of religions. He had, in effect, already decided on his theory before beginning to engage with the literature relating to the field. His writings use religious texts and ideas in a haphazard and highly selective manner, as best suited to the needs of his theories. Ernest Jones, one of Freud's most distinguished and perceptive biographers, draws attention to a letter in which Freud grumbles about having to read his way through a great many tedious tomes relating to religion. It is rather pointless, he comments, as he already instinctively knows the answer to his question about the origin of religion.

While it is a historical truism that Freud was a confirmed atheist long before he became a psychoanalyst, it is important to note that he became a psychoanalyst precisely *because* he was an atheist. His indefatigable harrying of religion reflects his fundamental belief that religion is dangerous, not least because it constitutes a threat to the advance of the Enlightenment and the natural sciences. Freud's approach to religion rests upon the perceived need to explain why anyone would wish to take the extraordinary step of believing in God, when there is obviously no God to believe in. At the logical level, Freud thus proceeds relentlessly from his preconceived starting point to his predetermined conclusion. What he proposes in between these milestones is of considerable interest, however, and merits close attention.

The first major statement of Freud's views on the origin, or "psychogenesis," of religion can be found in *Totem and Taboo* (1913). Developing his earlier observation that religious rites are similar to the obsessive actions of his neurotic patients, Freud declared that religion was basically a distorted form of an obsessional neurosis. The key elements in all religions, he argues, are the veneration of a father figure (such as God or Jesus Christ), faith in the power of spirits, and a concern for proper rituals. These can be explained at both the historical and the psychological levels. Although Freud's account of the historical origins of religion is now generally regarded as totally unreliable, it merits close attention before we pass on to his more influential views on its psychological roots.

In *Totem and Taboo* and *Moses and Monotheism* (1938), Freud traces the historical origins of religion to a series of specific, identifiable historical events that have left "ineradicable traces in the history of humanity." Freud was decisively influenced in his thinking by writings such as W. Robertson Smith's *Lectures on the Religion of the Semites* (1898), which argued that the essence of religion was not so much beliefs or doctrines but sacred acts, rites, or cults. It must be remembered that Freud was writing at a time when the ethnographic explanation of religion was taken very seriously, and seemed to possess impeccable scientific credentials. The situation, however, has radically changed since then, with such simplistic and reductionist theories being generally abandoned as unworkable. But in Freud's day, they seemed to point the way ahead. In effect, Freud had aligned himself with a scholarly theory which, though significant in its own time, is no longer taken with any great seriousness.

Religion, according to Freud's historical account, arises through inner psychological pressures, which reflect the complex evolutionary history of humanity.

> While the different religions wrangle with one another as to which of
> them is in possession of the truth, in our view the truth of religion
> may be altogether disregarded. Religion is an attempt to get control

over the sensory world, in which we are placed, by means of the wish-world, which we have developed inside us as a result of biological and psychological necessities. But it cannot achieve its end. Its doctrines carry with them the stamp of the times in which they originated, the ignorant childhood days of the human race.

Freud thus makes an appeal to the evolution of humanity from its immature religious days of childhood to its mature atheistic state. "If one attempts to assign to religion its place in man's evolution, it seems not so much to be a lasting acquisition, as a parallel to the neurosis which the civilized individual must pass through on his way from childhood to maturity."

Yet the theory of evolution that guides Freud's thinking at this point and others throughout both *Totem and Taboo* and *Moses and Monotheism* is Lamarckian rather than Darwinian. Jean-Baptiste Lamarck (1744–1829) had developed a theory of evolution which held that living things contain within themselves an urge to become better adapted. If an animal happens to acquire some useful adaptation during its lifetime—such as a giraffe stretching its neck to reach high tree branches—this acquired characteristic could be passed on to its offspring. Living creatures are understood to have a built-in desire to perfect themselves. Freud thus tends to treat religion as an acquired characteristic in response to certain specific events—above all, his wildly speculative ideas concerning the place of the Oedipus complex in the psychogenesis of religion.

At some point in the history of the human race, Freud argues, the father figure had exclusive sexual rights over females in his tribe. The sons, unhappy at this state of affairs, overthrew the father figure and killed him. Thereafter they were haunted by this secret and its guilt. Religion has its origins in this prehistorical event, has guilt as its major motivating force, and attempts to expiate this guilt through various rituals. Moses was thus murdered by his Jewish followers as a reenactment of the primal murder of the father. In his *Autobiography*, Freud set out this notion in terms of the murder and ritual devouring of the father figure:

> The father of the primal horde, since he was an unlimited despot, had seized all the women for himself; his sons, being dangerous to him as rivals, had been killed or driven away. One day, however, the sons came together and united to overwhelm, kill and devour their father, who had been their enemy but also their ideal. After the deed they were unable to take over their heritage since they stood in one another's way. Under the influence of failure and regret they learned to come to an agreement among themselves, they banded into a clan of brothers . . . and they jointly undertook to forgo the possession of the women on whose account they had killed their father. They were then driven to finding strange women.

Many of Freud's supporters have found such historical overstatements and simplistic generalizations embarrassing and irritating, not least on account of their erosion of Freud's reputation as a serious scholar and scientist. Freud, it must be remembered, was not concerned to develop a theory of the origins of religion on the basis of a rigorous analysis of history. He already knew how religion came into being; all that he required was a convenient (if largely fictional) historical framework to illustrate the theory in action.

In fairness to Freud, we shall pass over the overwhelming historical objections that make his account of the origins of religion of interest only to his more unreflective admirers. Professional anthropologists and sociologists of religion have generally passed over his historical accounts of the origins of religion, regarding them as amateurish conjectures not worth taking seriously. His genius is generally regarded as lying in the *psychological* explanation he offered for the origins of religion, to which we now turn. In his essay *Leonardo da Vinci and a*

Memory of His Childhood (1910), Freud sets out his explanation of individual religion. "Psychoanalysis has made us familiar with the intimate connection between the father-complex and belief in God; it has shown us that a personal God is, psychologically, nothing other than an exalted father, and it brings us evidence every day of how young people lose their religious beliefs as soon as their father's authority breaks down. Thus we recognize that the roots of the need for religion are in the parental complex." The veneration of the father figure has its origins in childhood. When going through its oedipal phase, Freud argues, the child has to deal with anxiety over the possibility of being punished by the father. The child's response to this threat is to venerate the father, to identify with him, and to project what it knows of the father's will in the form of the superego.

Freud further explored the origins of this projection of an ideal father figure in *The Future of an Illusion*. Religion represents the perpetuation of a piece of infantile behavior in adult life. Religion is an immature response to the awareness of helplessness, involving regression to childhood experiences of paternal care: "My father will protect me; he is in control." Belief in a personal God is thus little more than an infantile delusion. Religion is wishful thinking, an illusion. The psychological origins of human belief in God are thus to be found in a projection of the intense, unconscious desires of humanity. God is to be seen as a wish fulfillment, arising from repressed, unconscious infantile longings for protection and security. "Religious ideas have arisen from the same needs as have all the other achievements of civilization: from the necessity of defending oneself against the crushing superior force of nature." Therefore, religious beliefs owe their origins to a childlike feeling of helplessness, which arises in response to external dangers, internal impulses, and a fear of death. Just as children look to their parents to protect them from danger, so this infantile pattern is transferred to adulthood, in that adults create gods for themselves precisely because they had similar "gods" in their homes while they were growing up. Religious beliefs are thus to be recognized as "illusions, fulfillments of the oldest, strongest and most urgent wishes of mankind . . . As we already know, the terrifying impression of helplessness in childhood aroused the need for protection—for protection through love—which was provided by the father . . . Thus the benevolent rule of a divine Providence allays our fear of the danger of life."

The role of the father in developing religious belief has some important implications. One curious and slightly disturbing feature of Freud's critique of religion is the way in which it is interlocked with his thoroughly misogynist theory of gender, not least his notion of women as *hommes manqués*. Thus Freud's criticism of religion in *The Future of an Illusion* (in which religion is unfavorably compared with science) and his criticism of Christianity in *Moses and Monotheism* (in which Christianity is seen as regressive and for that reason inferior to Judaism) are both animated by his theory of gender. Christianity is Freud's feminine, and therefore inferior, form of religion; Judaism is Freud's masculine, and therefore superior, form; and the postreligious, atheistic, scientific spirit is Freud's "ideal masculinity," the mental attitude of the genuinely healthy human being. Wish fulfillment, narcissism, illusion, sensuality, femininity, and Christianity are linked together as deficient; they are opposed by the renunciation of narcissism and illusion, abstract thought, masculinity, and science, which are held up as ideals to be pursued with enthusiasm.

There is another aspect of Freud's emphasis on the role of the father that merits close attention. In *Totem and Taboo*, Freud argues that the individual's concept of God is determined by his relationship with his own father: "Psychoanalysis of individual human beings . . . teaches us with quite special insistence that the god of each of them is formed in the likeness of his father, that his personal relation to God depends on the relation to his father in the flesh and oscillates and changes along with that relation, and that at bottom God is nothing other than an exalted father." So what of Freud's relationship with his own father?

Was the concept of God that Sigmund Freud so vigorously rejected in some way determined by his relation to Jacob Freud? And thus his atheism determined by the specifics of that relationship, rather than the alleged universalities of human nature?

The cultural impact of Freud's approach has been immense, especially in North America. It is fair to say that, from about 1920, Freud's account of religion gained the ascendancy within the American intelligentsia, attracting a following exceeding that of any other modernist or postmodernist thinker. Freud set the cultural agenda of his day and for a generation beyond in a way that justifies W. H. Auden's description of him as "not a person, but a whole climate of opinion." Freudian concepts such as the ego, id, superego, and Oedipus complex began to permeate Western culture, causing many cultural analysts to nominate him as "the central imagination of our age" (Harold Bloom). The 1956 movie *Forbidden Planet* can be seen as a Freudian adaptation of Shakespeare's *The Tempest*, with Freud's id replacing Caliban. Countless writers—such as Graham Greene and William Golding—have incorporated Freudian themes into their novels. Freud was regarded as having scientifically unlocked the hidden, repressed secrets of the human mind, thus enabling humanity to face its future with confidence and hope—and without religion.

The powerful criticism of religious belief initiated by Feuerbach and developed by Marx and Freud has had a formative impact on twentieth-century Western culture. The credibility of these criticisms rested on the widespread belief that they were fundamentally scientific in character—in other words, that the origins of religious belief could be explained in terms of socioeconomic factors or human psychology in just the same way as physics explained the movement of the planets or the optics of the rainbow. There were regional variations within Western culture over the merits of the approaches; Americans might adopt Freud where Europeans preferred Marx. Yet the cumulative impact of these critiques was decisive. Belief in God was widely seen as a construct of the consolation-seeking human mind, which would evaporate with further scientific advance. And there was no shortage of such scientific advance, as we shall see presently.

The cumulative impact of the criticism of religion was immense. Earlier generations had regarded the existence of God as one of the most natural and fundamental beliefs of humanity, and took the view that atheism was puzzling. Why would anyone want to deny what was self-evidently true? Many now took the diametrically opposed view. Atheism was the natural philosophy of humanity. It was the beliefs of religious people that required rational explanation. God was the product of social and psychological factors, which led humanity to yearn for a supernatural being. It was but a small step to turn a wistful longing into a view of reality. The idea of God was an entirely understandable invention, which might even be useful in consoling weaker and foolish souls who were naive enough to believe in it. Yet it was nothing more than an illusion, created by fearful human minds to console themselves in the face of the immensity and meaninglessness of the universe.

The rational challenge to belief in God mounted by the Enlightenment was now complete. The self-confidence of faith had been broken. Philosophical and scientific progress had conclusively eliminated God from the world, with any vestiges of faith in God being seen as little more than the remnants of old superstitions or psychological defense mechanisms to cope with a perplexing world. Feuerbach, Marx, and Freud all offered "scientific" explanations of the origins of religious belief that subverted any idea that they were to be regarded as privileged or authoritative pronouncements on the nature of things. A major cultural shift began, in which Western culture decisively moved its trust from the dogmas of religion to the theories of science. The transition is neatly summarized in the words that Sir Richard Gregory (1864–1952), one of Britain's leading scientists, proposed as his epitaph:

My grandfather preached the gospel of Christ;
My father preached the gospel of socialism;
I preach the gospel of science.

In what follows, we shall explore the impact of this transition on the fortunes of atheism.

4

WARFARE:
THE NATURAL SCIENCES AND
THE ADVANCEMENT OF ATHEISM

NE OF THE MOST REMARKABLE DEVELOPMENTS OF THE
nineteenth and early twentieth centuries has been the relentless advance of the perception that there exists a permanent, essential
conflict between the natural sciences and religion. Science is at war
with religion—and that war can only lead to the elimination of religious belief as a relic of a superstitious age that is now long behind us.
Science proves things, whereas religion depends on the authoritarian
imposition of its dogmas, which fly in the face of evidence. To take the
idea of God seriously is to commit intellectual suicide. Scientists are
the Promethean liberators of humanity from their bondage to religious
tradition and superstition.

That, in a nutshell, is the understanding of the relation between science and religion that has come to dominate the corporate consciousness of Western culture. It has always been like this, and this is the way
it must be until religion has finally been eliminated. Religion has been
the implacable opponent of scientific progress. Religion was violently
opposed, for utterly stupid and self-serving reasons, to Copernicus's
theory of the solar system in the sixteenth century and to Darwin's theory of evolution in the nineteenth. Two historical vignettes have been

widely cited in the popular literature as illustrating this religious obscurantism: John Calvin's criticism of the heliocentric ideas of Copernicus and Bishop Wilberforce's dismissal of the Darwinian ideas of T. H. Huxley. As both also illustrate a somewhat different point, we may consider them in a little detail.

In his *History of Western Philosophy*, the great British atheist philosopher Bertrand Russell set out a popularized account of the complex evolution of modern Western philosophy, and the various obstacles it faced as it developed. One such major obstacle, in Russell's view, was Christianity. Russell illustrated the "bigoted" nature of Christian theology with a racy account of the early fortunes of the Copernican theory of the solar system, and singled out John Calvin's critique of the theory for special criticism. Did not the Bible say that the sun went round the earth? Well, that, according to Calvin, was the end of the matter. "Calvin," wrote Russell, "demolished Copernicus with the text: 'The world also is stablished, that it cannot be moved' (Psa. xciii.I), and exclaimed: 'Who will venture to place the authority of Copernicus above that of the Holy Spirit?' " John Calvin emerges from this episode as an arrogant religious fool, typical of the kind of person who gets in the way of scientific progress. With the coming of atheism, such obscurantist ravings against advances in our knowledge could be silenced.

Even worse was the arrogance shown by the bishop of Oxford, Samuel Wilberforce, toward Darwin's ally Thomas H. Huxley during the meeting of the British Association at Oxford on June 30, 1860, at which the theory of evolution was being discussed. After Wilberforce had delivered a typically arrogant and uninformed tirade against Darwin's theory, he delivered what he thought would be a knockout blow—inquiring of Huxley whether it was "through his grandfather or grandmother that he claimed his descent from a monkey?" Huxley replied with great dignity that if he had a choice between having "a miserable ape for a grandfather" or a talented man who uses his gifts for "the mere purpose of introducing ridicule into a grave scientific discussion," he would choose the ape any day.

Both stories demonstrate the utter stupidity of religious thinkers, and the intellectual and moral superiority of their scientific peers. Yet both stories have something else in common. Both have been known to be completely false since about 1970, and are now viewed by historians as the urban myths of journalists too lazy to check their sources, perhaps telling us more about what certain people would like to believe than what actually happened.

Take the Calvin myth. The intellectual authority of the great atheist writer Bertrand Russell was such that few bothered to check out his assertions. Russell did not source his citation from Calvin, forcing others to work out where he got it from. The noted historian of science Thomas S. Kuhn attempted to track it down when studying early responses to Copernicus's theory. Yet neither Kuhn nor anyone else could find anything like the quotation attributed to Calvin in any of his published writings. It did, however, feature prominently in the pages of Andrew Dickson White's *History of the Warfare of Science with Theology in Christendom* (1896): "Calvin took the lead, in his *Commentary on Genesis*, by condemning all who asserted that the earth is not at the center of the universe. He clinched the matter by the usual reference to the first verse of the ninety-third Psalm, and asked, 'Who will venture to place the authority of Copernicus above that of the Holy Spirit?' " Although White referred to a specific work by Calvin, at no point in that work—or anywhere else—did Calvin state anything even remotely resembling the words or thoughts attributed to him. So where did White get his quotation from? In a remarkable piece of literary detective work, Edward Rosen showed that the quotation could be traced back, not to any work of Calvin, but to a work published in 1886 by F. W. Farrer. Once more, no source was provided for the citation. The trail fizzled out at that point. Farrer was a cleric at Westminster Abbey in London who perhaps lacked the will and resources to check his facts. The remark attributed to Calvin thus had to be dismissed as pure invention.

The legend of the 1860 Wilberforce-Huxley exchange dates from the 1890s. As detailed studies of this event have made clear, contemporary accounts of that meeting of the British Association make no recognizable reference to this encounter, let alone to the ludicrous question that a later generation gleefully put into Wilberforce's mouth, or the damning retort of Huxley. Both are journalistic inventions from thirty years later. As J. R. Lucas remarks of the legend of the Wilberforce-Huxley encounter, having surveyed the credibility of the primary sources upon which it was grounded: "About what actually happened in Oxford on 30 June 1860 it tells us very little; but about currents of thought in the latter part of the century, it tells us a lot."

The 1890 account depicts Wilberforce as an ignorant cleric trying to score cheap points off Huxley, then being silenced and shamed. In fact, Wilberforce was thoroughly familiar with Darwin's views, having written an extended review of *Origin of Species* five weeks prior to the 1860 meeting, which he summarized in his speech. Darwin himself granted that the review was "uncommonly clever" and that it pointed out "with skill all the most conjectural parts" of the book, identifying some serious weaknesses that he needed to address in a future work. Darwin's 1868 book *The Variation of Animals and Plants under Domestication* can be seen as a response to the specific criticisms made by Wilberforce. Yet the 1890s legend lives on, gracing the pages of even the most recent publications in this field. It is just as false yet just as widely believed as the legend of Darwin's deathbed conversion to Christianity, which Lady Elizabeth Hope started in 1915. It all goes to confirm what Karl Marx once pointed out: if you say something often enough, people begin to believe that it is true.

The historical interaction of the natural sciences and religion is, as might be expected, far more complex and interesting than the wooden stereotypes of either atheist or religious propagandists might suggest. The really interesting question is *why* the antagonism between science and religion developed during the golden age of atheism, and whether it is likely to continue. The real issue is actually not so much what the natural sciences themselves teach, as the cultural evaluation of the sci-

entific enterprise as a whole. The Calvin and Wilberforce myths are excellent examples of cultural stereotypes of science and religion, both
disclosing and strengthening the dominant perception of this period—
that an outmoded, arrogant, and discredited religion is in full retreat
before a triumphant scientific advance. This take on things was brilliantly summarized in the words of Huxley himself (1860): "Extin-
guished theologians lie about the cradle of every science as the
strangled snakes beside that of Hercules; and history records that
wherever science and orthodoxy have been fairly opposed, the latter
have been forced to retire from the lists, bleeding and crushed if not
annihilated; scotched if not slain."

The complex and fascinating place of the natural sciences in the rise
of atheism is best understood not by analyzing the many debates and
publications of the period in a strictly chronological order, but by exploring three major aspects of the growing cultural acceptance of the
sciences throughout most of the nineteenth and twentieth centuries.
These cultural understandings of the importance of the natural sciences are:

1. The belief that the natural sciences are Promethean figures of
   liberation from bondage to a superstitious and oppressive
   past, which are locked in a mortal combat that can only end
   with the final elimination of religion from the scene.
2. The belief that the natural sciences conclusively prove all their
   theories, in contrast to the religious retreat into irrationality
   and mystery in the face of the evidence.
3. The pervasive notion that the Darwinian theory of evolution
   has made belief in God impossible, thus necessitating atheism
   on scientific grounds.

Each of these is an important element in underpinning an atheist
worldview. In what follows, we shall trace their emergence and comment on their importance.

THE ORIGINS OF THE WARFARE OF
SCIENCE AND RELIGION

There has always been a sense in which the natural sciences are opposed to authoritarianism of any kind. As Freeman Dyson points out in his important essay "The Scientist as Rebel," a common element of most visions of science is that of "rebellion against the restrictions imposed by the local prevailing culture." Science is thus a subversive activity, almost by definition—a point famously stated in a lecture delivered to the Society of Heretics at Cambridge by the biologist J. B. S. Haldane in February 1923. For the Arab mathematician and astronomer Omar Khayyám, science was a rebellion against the intellectual constraints of Islam; for nineteenth-century Japanese scientists, science was a rebellion against the lingering feudalism of their culture; for the great Indian physicists of the twentieth century, their discipline was a powerful intellectual force directed against the fatalistic ethic of Hinduism (not to mention British imperialism, which was then dominant in the region). And in Western Europe, scientific advance inevitably involved confrontation with the culture of the day—including its political, social, and religious elements. Inasmuch as the West has been dominated by Christianity, it is unsurprising that the tension between science and Western culture could be seen specifically as a confrontation between science and Christianity.

Most historians regard religion as having had a generally benign and constructive relationship with the natural sciences in the West. There were periods of tension and conflict, such as the Galileo controversy. Yet on closer examination, these often turn out to have had more to do with papal politics, ecclesiastical power struggles, and personality issues than with any fundamental tensions between faith and science. As leading historians of science regularly point out, the interaction of science and religion is determined primarily by historical circumstances and only secondarily by their respective subject matters. There is no universal paradigm for the relation of science and religion, either theoretically or historically. The case of Christian attitudes to evolutionary theory in the late nineteenth century makes this point particularly evident. As the Irish scientist and historian David Living-stone makes clear in a groundbreaking study of the reception of Darwinism in two very different contexts—Belfast and Princeton—local issues and personalities were often of decisive importance in determining the outcome.

In the eighteenth century, a remarkable synergy developed between religion and the sciences in England. Newton's "celestial mechanics" was widely regarded as at worst consistent with, and at best a glorious confirmation of, the Christian view of God as creator of a harmonious universe. Many members of the Royal Society of London—founded to advance scientific understanding and research—were strongly religious in their outlook, and saw this as enhancing their commitment to scientific advancement.

Yet all this changed in the second half of the nineteenth century. The general tone of the late-nineteenth-century encounter between religion (especially Christianity) and the natural sciences was set by two works: John William Draper's *History of the Conflict between Religion and Science* (1874) and Andrew Dickson White's *History of the Warfare of Science with Theology in Christendom* (1876). Both works reflect a strongly positivist view of history and a determination to settle old scores with organized religion. This contrasts sharply with the much more positive and settled relationship between the two typical in both North America and Great Britain up to around 1830, reflected in works such as William Paley's *Natural Theology*.

For John William Draper, the natural sciences were Promethean liberators of humanity from the oppression of traditional religious thought and structures, particularly Roman Catholicism. "The history of science is not a mere record of isolated discoveries; it is a narrative of the conflict of two contending powers, the expansive force of the human intellect on one side, and the compression arising from traditionary faith and human interests on the other." Draper was particularly offended by developments within the Roman Catholic church, which he regarded as pretentious, oppressive, and tyrannical. The rise of science (and especially Darwinian theory) was, for Draper, the most significant means of "endangering her position," and was thus to be encouraged by all means available. Like many polemical works, *History of the Conflict* is notable more for the stridency of its assertions than for the substance of its arguments; nevertheless, the general tone of its approach would help create a mind-set.

The origins of Andrew Dickson White's *History of the Warfare of Science with Theology in Christendom* lie in the heated debates surrounding the foundation of Cornell University. Many denominational schools felt threatened by the establishment of the new university, and encouraged attacks on the fledgling school and White, its first president, accusing both of atheism. Angered by this unfair treatment, White decided to launch an offensive against his critics in a lecture delivered in New York on December 18, 1869, entitled "The Battle-Fields of Science." Once more science was portrayed as a liberator in the quest for academic freedom. The lecture was gradually expanded until it was published in 1876 as *The Warfare of Science*. This book was supplemented by a further series of "New Chapters in the Warfare of Science," published as articles in the *Popular Science Monthly* over the period 1885–92. The two-volume book of 1896 basically consists of the material found in the 1876 book, to which this additional material was appended.

White himself declared that the "most mistaken of mistaken ideas" was that "religion and science are enemies." Nevertheless, this was precisely the impression created by his work, whether he himself intended it or not. The crystallization of the warfare metaphor in the popular mind was unquestionably catalyzed by White's vigorously polemical writing. The widespread late-nineteenth-century interpretation of the Darwinian theory in terms of "the survival of the fittest" also lent weight to the imagery of conflict; was this not how nature itself determined matters? Was not nature itself a spectacular battle-field, on which the war of biological survival was fought? Was it not therefore to be expected that the same battle for survival might take place between religious and scientific worldviews, with the victor sweeping the vanquished from existence, the latter never to appear again in the relentless evolutionary development of human thought and knowledge?

The idea that science and religion are in perpetual conflict is no longer taken seriously by any major historian of science, despite its popularity in the late nineteenth century. One of the last remaining bastions of atheism survives only at the popular level—namely, the myth that an atheistic, fact-based science is permanently at war with a faith-based religion. Not only is this caricature clearly untrue in the present day, but historical scholarship has now determined it to be mis-leading and inaccurate in the past. Yet the myth still lives on in popu-lar atheist writings, undisturbed by the findings of scholars. At least in the minds of some atheist propagandists, science is the supreme cham-pion of atheism.

As a generation of historians has now pointed out, the notion of an endemic conflict between science and religion, so persuasively set out by White and Draper, is itself a social construction, created in the lengthening shadows of hostility toward individual clergy and church institutions. The interaction of science and religion is determined far more by their social circumstances than their specific ideas. The Vic-torian period itself gave rise to the social pressures and tensions that engendered the myth of permanent warfare between science and reli-gion, and especially the Roman Catholic church as the "damnable per-verter of mankind" (Thomas Huxley).

A significant social shift can be discerned behind the emergence of this conflict model. From a sociological perspective, scientific knowl-edge was advocated by particular social groups to advance their own specific goals and interests. There was growing competition between two specific groups within British society in the nineteenth century: the clergy and the scientific professionals. The clergy were widely regarded as an elite at the beginning of the century, with the "scientific parson" a well-established social stereotype. Among these we may number Gilbert White (1720–93), author of the classic *Natural History of Selborne* (1789).

With the appearance of the professional scientist, however, a struggle for supremacy began, to determine who would gain the cultural ascendancy within British culture in the second half of the nineteenth century. The conflict model has its origins in the specific conditions of the Victorian era, in which an emerging professional intellectual group sought to displace a group that had hitherto occupied the place of honor. The rise of Darwinian theory appeared to give added scientific justification to this model: it was a struggle for the survival of the intellectually fittest. In the early nineteenth century, the British Association (a professional organization devoted to the advancement of science) had many members who were clergy; by the end of the century, the clergy tended to be portrayed as the enemies of science—and hence of social and intellectual progress. As a result, there was much sympathy for a model of the interaction of the sciences and religion that portrayed religion and its representatives in uncomplimentary and disparaging terms.

The conflict model of science and religion thus came to prominence at a time when professional scientists wished to distance themselves from their amateur colleagues, and when changing patterns in academic culture necessitated demonstrating its independence from the church and other bastions of the establishment. Academic freedom demanded a break with the church; to achieve this break it became expedient to depict the church as the opponent of learning and scientific advance and the natural sciences as their strongest advocates. The golden age of atheism witnessed the relentless advance of the sciences and the equally relentless retreat of faith from the public to the private domain. The cultural space within which religion was permitted to operate was gradually whittled down to private beliefs, which had no relevance to public policy.

Today, this stereotype of the warfare of science and religion lingers on in the backwaters of Western culture. Yet it has largely lost its credibility. The surging interest in the spiritual aspects of the natural sciences has been complemented by a new interest in the positive interaction of science and religion, evident in course titles such as "Science and the Spiritual Quest." The growing realization that even many scientists who are Nobel laureates are interested in issues of faith has severely dented the case for a necessary link between science and atheism, or for the outdated stereotype of the perpetual war of science and faith. The simple fact is that there is no *necessary* connection between them: some scientists are religious and some are not.

ATHEISM AS A SCIENCE: THE DEMAND FOR RELIGIOUS PROOF

One of the most important scientific writers of the nineteenth century was William Kingdon Clifford (1845–79), who was appointed professor of mathematics at University College, London, in 1871. A year earlier, an expedition to observe a solar eclipse came close to costing him his life, when his ship sank off the coast of Sicily. Although a very devout and fastidious Anglo-Catholic in his youth, Clifford's perilous experience at sea appears to have convinced him of the improbability and immorality of Christian belief. From 1871 onward, he appears to have become obsessed with the idea that human progress could only be achieved through the systematic elimination of religious belief. He reserved a particular contempt for Christianity, especially in its Anglo-Catholic forms, which he regarded as no better than the pagan abominations he read about in his Old Testament.

Clifford clearly saw himself as being in the vanguard of a great advance in the fortunes of humanity, which, guided by reason and science, would rise above and finally transcend every previous achievement of civilization. Religion and its evidentially deficient allies of magic and superstition would simply fade away, overwhelmed by the new knowledge of the world:

> The dim and shadowy outlines of the superhuman deity fade slowly away from us; and as the mist of his presence floats aside, we perceive with greater and greater clearness the shape of a yet grander and nobler figure—of Him who made all Gods and shall unmake them. From the dim dawn of history, and from the inmost depth of every soul, the face of our father Man looks out upon us with the fire of eternal youth in his eyes, and says, "Before Jehovah was, I am."

But how could religious belief be eliminated? In his highly influential *Ethics of Belief* (1871), Clifford developed a line of argument that has had a deep and lasting impact on discussions of the relation of science and religion: "it is wrong always, everywhere, and for anyone, to believe anything upon insufficient evidence." A refusal to engage in a critical evaluation of every belief, however daunting and distressing this may be, is an unforgiveable sin: "If a man, holding a belief which he was taught in childhood or persuaded of afterward, keeps down and pushes away any doubts which arise about it in his mind, purposely avoids the reading of books and the company of men that call into question or discuss it, and regards as impious those questions which cannot easily be asked without disturbing it—the life of that man is one long sin against mankind."

Whatever the belief may be—whether scientific, religious, or moral—we are under an absolute obligation to believe only what may be rigorously demonstrated by the strictest criteria of truth. Clifford opens his discussion of these questions with an analogy that presumably evoked some painful memories—a shipwreck.

A shipowner was about to send to sea an emigrant-ship. He knew that she was old, and not overwell built at the first; that she had seen many seas and climes, and often had needed repairs. Doubts had been suggested to him that possibly she was not seaworthy. These doubts preyed upon his mind, and made him unhappy; he thought that perhaps he ought to have her thoroughly overhauled and refitted, even though this should put him at great expense. Before the ship sailed, however, he succeeded in overcoming these melancholy reflections. He said to himself that she had gone safely through so many voyages and weathered so many storms that it was idle to suppose she would not come safely home from this trip also. He would put his trust in Providence, which could hardly fail to protect all these unhappy families that were leaving their fatherland to seek for better times elsewhere. He would dismiss from his mind all ungenerous suspicions about the honesty of builders and contractors. In such ways he acquired a sincere and comfortable conviction that his vessel was thoroughly safe and seaworthy; he watched her departure with a light heart, and benevolent wishes for the success of the exiles in their strange new home that was to be; and he got his insurance-money when she went down in mid-ocean and told no tales.

The fundamental point is as moral as it is intellectual: beliefs must be warranted. The shipowner was a scoundrel. His belief may have been sincere, but it was utterly immoral to entertain such a belief when he had failed to investigate it thoroughly. "He did sincerely believe in the soundness of his ship; but the sincerity of his conviction can in no wise help him, because *he had no right to believe on such evidence as was before him.* He had acquired his belief not by honestly earning it in patient investigation, but by stifling his doubts."

Clifford had no doubt that this rigorously evidential approach would undermine the claims of Christianity, especially its claims to supernatural knowledge of God through revelation and miraculous events. Nature was uniform; how could anyone legitimately believe such clear violations of the natural order.

No evidence, therefore, can justify us in believing the truth of a statement which is contrary to, or outside of, the uniformity of nature. If our experience is such that it cannot be filled up consistently with uniformity, all we have a right to conclude is that there is something wrong somewhere; but the possibility of inference is taken away; we must rest in our experience, and not go beyond it at all. If an event really happened which was not a part of the uniformity of nature, it would have two properties: no evidence could give the right to believe it to any except those whose actual experience it was; and no inference worthy of belief could be founded upon it at all.

This relentless and persistent demand for verification of all beliefs anticipates some themes that came to prominence in the great debate over logical positivism in the 1950s, and is prone to many of the same difficulties. Yet the force of Clifford's point was perceived as moral rather than intellectual. An absolute moral demand is placed on all human beings to prove what they believe. It was not long before religion was, once more, in headlong retreat. It was simply incapable of providing the evidential basis of belief that Clifford and others demanded.

Yet paradoxically, so was atheism. To conform to Clifford's demands for evidential rigor, atheism must be demonstrated to be more than intellectually plausible, conceptually economical, or culturally attractive—it must be demonstrated to be true. Clifford had turned "Lockean caution about the nature of propositions into a straitjacket" (A. N. Wilson). Clifford's legacy has been the provision of an ideal of rational justification that it has proved impossible to attain. A means of investigating reality had become the determinant of what was actually real in the first place.

Atheist writers of the nineteenth century often defined their position in terms of an absence—rather than a denial—of a belief in God, and argued that the burden of proof lay with those who had faith. A good example of this approach can be found in the writings of the socialist and women's rights activist Annie Besant (1847–1933), especially in her *Why I Do Not Believe in God* (1887):

> If my interlocutor desires to convince me that Jupiter has inhabitants, and that his description of them is accurate, it is for him to bring forward evidence in support of his contention. The burden of proof evidently lies on him; it is not for me to prove that no such beings exist before my non-belief is justified, but for him to prove that they do exist before my belief can be fairly claimed. Similarly, it is for the affirmer of God's existence to bring evidence in support of his affirmation; the burden of proof lies on him.

While there were many on both sides of the argument who preferred to overlook the point, the simple fact is that both atheism and Christian belief were found to lie beyond the available evidence. The burden of proof is equally distributed between the two. Both could be proposed; both could be defended; neither could be proved. As Alfred, Lord Tennyson (1809–92) pointed out in his *Ancient Sage*, the paradox was that nothing that was actually worth believing could be proved in the way Clifford demanded:

> *Thou canst not prove thou art immortal, no,*
> *Nor yet that thou art mortal—nay my son,*
> *Thou canst not prove that I, who speak with thee,*
> *Am not thyself in converse with thyself,*
> *For nothing worthy proving can be proven,*
> *Nor yet disproven: wherefore thou be wise,*
> *Cleave ever to the sunnier side of doubt.*

No wonder Thomas Huxley coined the term "agnostic" in 1869 to designate someone who recognized that the great questions of life lay beyond demonstration. As Huxley wrote in 1880: "Some twenty years ago, or thereabouts, I invented the word 'Agnostic' to denote people who, like myself, confess themselves to be hopelessly ignorant concerning a variety of matters, about which metaphysicians and theologians, both orthodox and heterodox, dogmatise with utmost confidence." Huxley's hostility was directed against both theist and atheist who thundered their dogmatic judgments without adequate foundations; in his view, it was impossible to arrive at any degree of metaphysical certainty in these matters. Religious and atheist might *assert* their beliefs with passion and power—yet their rhetoric had become detached from what could actually be proved. In such situations, the only moral response was to declare that the existence or nonexistence of God lay beyond true human knowledge—in effect, beyond meaningful adjudication. To do otherwise was to confuse "a conjecture with a certainty." This piece of metaphysical diplomacy merely irritated all sides to the argument, who believed that Huxley was simply dodging the issues.

Despite these cautionary words, the belief that the natural sciences have conclusively settled the debate between faith and atheism has been developed by many scientific writers subsequently, perhaps most notably by the Oxford zoologist Richard Dawkins. In a series of recent works—including *The Blind Watchmaker* (1986) and *A Devil's Chaplain* (2003)—Dawkins has argued consistently and vigorously for an atheistic worldview through an appeal to the natural sciences, especially evolutionary biology. Science, Dawkins asserts, proves things; it establishes its theories with certainty. The contrast with theology could not be more dramatic: "What has theology ever said that is of the smallest use to anybody? When has theology ever said anything that is demonstrably true and is not obvious? I have listened to theologians, read them, debated against them. I have never heard any of them ever say anything of the smallest use, anything that was not either platitudinously obvious or downright false." While science proves things through evidence, religion deliberately asserts falsehoods that mislead, seduce, and oppress people.

As Dawkins went on to argue, "a case can be made that faith is one of the world's great evils, comparable to the smallpox virus but harder to eradicate. Faith, being belief that isn't based on evidence, is the principal vice of any religion." He is quite clear: science "is free of the main vice of religion, which is faith." Really? The history of science shows a steady progression from one theory that was believed to be right in its day to another that replaces it—for example, the ether theory of light. As Michael Polanyi (1891–1976), a chemist and noted philosopher of science, pointed out, natural scientists find themselves having to believe some things that they know will later be shown to be wrong—but not being sure *which* of their present beliefs will turn out to be erroneous. How can Dawkins be so sure that his current beliefs are true, when history shows a persistent pattern of the abandonment of scientific theories as better approaches emerge? What historian of science can fail to note that what was once regarded as secure knowledge was eroded through the passage of time? Conveniently enough, Dawkins turns a blind eye to history.

He also turns another blind eye (how many does he have?) to the philosophy of science. It is certainly true that the natural sciences aim to offer the best possible explanation of the world, and that they have had considerable successes in doing so. But there are limits to this. The scientist regularly has to propose certain ideas that certainly fit in with experimental evidence, but that cannot be proved, and are thus taken on trust. I notice a firm recognition of this point in Dawkins's hero, Charles Darwin himself. In his *Origin of Species* (1859), Darwin points out that his theory of natural selection has not been proven, and that all kinds of objections could reasonably be raised against it. But he still believes it was true, and that these difficulties will eventually be resolved. "A crowd of difficulties will have occurred to the reader. Some of them are so grave that to this day I can never reflect on them without being staggered; but, to the best of my judgement, the greater number are only apparent, and those that are real are not, I think, fatal to my theory." This does not sit easily with Dawkins's simplistic mantra "science proves things." The reality—as just about everyone else is perfectly happy to admit—is that the natural sciences offer what they believe to be the best possible explanation of things, but are perfectly prepared to abandon or modify this in the light of additional information.

The same issue emerged with Einstein's theory of relativity, set out in November 1915, where certain confirming evidence was not available until nearly fifty years later. Einstein's general theory of relativity was one of the most ambitious and exciting intellectual developments of the first decades of the twentieth century. If it was correct, Einstein declared, it predicted three important and observable consequences. First, it offered a highly accurate explanation of what is usually known as the anomalous precession of the planet Mercury. This had been observed since about 1865, but had never been accounted for. Second, it predicted that a beam of light would be deflected by the gravitational mass of the sun. The extent of this deflection could be very accurately calculated, and within ten years it was shown that Einstein's theory corresponded superbly with the latest experimental findings.

There was, however, a third prediction. Einstein argued that the gravity of the sun would have an impact on the light it emitted. This "gravitational redshift" was due to the reduction of the velocity of light by the mass of the sun. But the extent of this reduction was infinitesimally small—just over two parts in a million. So minute was this effect that it simply could not be detected by any available means in the 1920s.

So what was to be done? Einstein's theory seemed elegant, and it was impressively successful in explaining certain phenomena. But one of its predictions could not be confirmed. Perhaps Einstein was wrong, and his theory would have to be abandoned. Yet most did not think so. They believed that his theory was sufficiently persuasive to allow them to trust that, at some point in the distant future, final confirmation of its predictions would take place. In the meantime, they were perfectly prepared to live with this unresolved tension. They lived and thought as if Einstein's theory was true, even though they knew that only a future generation could learn whether this was warranted or not. What they knew seemed good enough to them. They would trust that Einstein was right, and allow a future generation the luxury of knowing that he was.

In the event, the third prediction was finally confirmed in the 1960s, two generations later, when a new spectroscopic technique became available capable of observing the predicted effect. Yet nobody was entirely surprised. Nobody seems to have suspended belief in Einstein's theory of relativity until this final confirmation came through.

So what is the relevance of this famous incident in the history of science to our reflections on Dawkins's attitude to science? It shows that we can put our trust in a theory without having final confirmation of its truth. A theory can be plausible enough to gain our trust, even though some of its predictions and promises lie in the future. In short: it is about faith—a point long appreciated by Polanyi and other philosophers of science. So when Dawkins speaks of "proof," he actually means something rather weaker, such as "good reasons for believing that something is right," while realizing that it cannot actually be proved at present.

This is not a radical or controversial statement, but simply an accurate summary of the difficulties faced by the natural sciences as they seek to offer the best account of what we know about the world. It is simply not true that scientists believe theories because they have been "proved." They believe them because they represent the best explanation of what may be observed. Dawkins's overstatement here can be appreciated by considering two case studies, based on material we have just considered.

It is the year 1870. Charles Darwin holds that, with some necessary modifications, the ideas set out in his *Origin of Species* offer an excellent and deeply compelling account of the diversity of life-forms on the earth. Yet there is a serious difficulty. The very title of the book points to an explanation of how different species come into existence. Yet speciation—the formation of a new species by the accumulation of mutations—has never been demonstrated in real life or under laboratory conditions. Yet he holds on to the theory, believing that its explanatory ability and coherence are sufficient to justify it, and that the difficulty will one day be resolved. His theory has not been proved. Yet he believes it to be the best available. It can be trusted now, even though its final proof will lie some considerable distance in the future.

It is now the year 1930. Albert Einstein is passionately committed to his general theory of relativity, which has much to commend it. Yet he knows that one of its core predictions has not been observed. In the strict sense of the term, it has not been proved. Einstein, however, feels able to hold on to the theory, believing that its explanatory ability and coherence are sufficient to justify it, and that the difficulty will one day be resolved. While it cannot be proved correct now, he has faith that it will be confirmed in the future—and that he is justified in believing it now on the basis of its partial confirmation.

As Michael Polanyi insisted, there is always going to be an element of faith or trust in the natural sciences, precisely because so much cannot be proven. And when it comes to the question of God, as we shall see, nothing can be proven at all—despite the interesting exaggerations of those who tell us otherwise, on both sides of the argument.

THE BLIND WATCHMAKER: DARWIN AND A GODLESS UNIVERSE

There is no doubt that Charles Darwin's theory of evolution caused the smoldering crisis of faith in Victorian England to burst into flames. If any scientific development can be said to have converted the Western world to atheism, it is the theory originally proposed in Darwin's *Origin of Species* and subsequently developed by Darwin and others into a full-blown account of the origins of biological life, including human beings. For Thomas Huxley, who had a particular animus against Roman Catholicism, Darwin's theory of evolution was especially useful. "It occupies a position of complete and irreconcilable antagonism toward that vigorous and consistent enemy of the highest intellectual, moral and social life of mankind—the Catholic Church."

The reaction in North America was similar. For the great American atheist Robert Green Ingersoll (1833–99), Darwin had destroyed the credibility of Christianity. It was only a matter of time before it would be swept away as an increasingly scientific culture recognized it as ignorant superstition. As he put it in *Orthodoxy* (1880), a scathing attack on the intellectual shallowness of Christian preachers:

> This century will be called Darwin's century. He was one of the greatest men who ever touched this globe. He has explained more of the phenomena of life than all of the religious teachers. Write the name of Charles Darwin on the one hand and the name of every theologian who ever lived on the other, and from that name has come more light to the world than from all of those. His doctrine of evolution, his doctrine of the survival of the fittest, his doctrine of the origin of species, has removed in every thinking mind the last vestige of orthodox Christianity.

Yet it is not at all obvious why Darwinism should lead to atheism. To understand why it was understood in this way, we need to explore the specific cultural context within which the theory developed.

As has often been pointed out, the term "atheism" is intellectually derivative. While some interpret the term very loosely—"there are no spiritual beings"—the term is correctly, and more generally, understood to entail a denial of a specific conception of God. If "God" were defined as a supernatural being whose untroubled existence was invariably limited to the undefined (yet presumably remote) heavenly places—which is one influential way of reading both Aristotle and

Plato—then Darwin's theory would have no bearing whatsoever on whether God exists or not. In order for Darwin's theory of evolution to have significance to the debate over atheism, a concept of God must be proposed that is demonstrably in conflict with Darwin at this point. Precisely such a conception of God emerged within British Protestantism in the nineteenth century, achieving cultural dominance. If the Darwinian theories were to have triggered a crisis of faith anywhere, it would have been in Victorian England.

The explanation of this remarkable fact lies in a highly influential group of publications that appeared around the end of the eighteenth century, including the *Bridgewater Treatises* and William Paley's *A View of the Evidence of Christianity* (1794) and *Natural Theology* (1802). These were written against the background of a growing skepticism about traditional arguments for God's existence, that actually seemed to end up making God redundant. William Paley (1743–1805) hit on a new way of defending God's existence that proved a huge popular success. Paley argued that every aspect of the world pointed to evidence of intelligent design.

The influence of these works was immense. Undergraduates at Cambridge University throughout the nineteenth century were required to read Paley. As Aileen Fyfe has shown in a splendid study, Paley's ideas were widely accepted by natural scientists in the first half of the nineteenth century at Cambridge University. Charles Darwin, himself an undergraduate at Christ's College in this distinguished university, was no exception: "I was charmed and convinced of the long line of argumentation," he later recalled. And well he might have been. Paley produced an immense array of observations, from the intricacy of the human eye to the arrangements of the seasons, which pointed to the entire biological world's having been planned by a benevolent deity. Each aspect of the natural world seems to have been designed for its specific purpose. More than that; they interlocked with one another, as if the entire assembly—as opposed to its individual parts—appeared to have been put together with a definite purpose in mind.

With all these factors in mind, Paley presented an analogy that seemed to him to offer an admirable representation of the complexities he had observed: the watch. How could anyone look at a watch, with its complex system of interlocking wheels, springs, and other moving parts, and fail to see that it had been designed—not only that it had been deliberately constructed, but created with some specific purpose in mind? "[It] is inevitable, that the watch must have had a maker—that there must have existed, at some time and at some place or other, an artificer or artificers who formed it for the purpose which we find it actually to answer, who comprehended its construction and designed its use." How could anyone think otherwise? And nature displayed precisely the same evidences of design and interlocking of its constituent parts, forcing any unbiased observer to the conclusion that it, too, had been designed.

One of Paley's most significant arguments is that mechanism implies what he terms "contrivance"—that is, design and construction for a specific purpose. Writing against the backdrop of the emerging industrial revolution, Paley sought to exploit the apologetic potential of the growing interest in machinery—such as "watches, telescopes, stocking-mills, and steam engines"—within England's literate classes. Paley argues that only someone who is mad would suggest that such complex mechanical technology came into being by purposeless chance. Mechanism presupposes contrivance—that is to say, a sense of purpose and an ability to design and fabricate. Both the human body in particular and the world in general could be seen as mechanisms designed and constructed in such a manner as to achieve harmony of both means and ends. It must be stressed that Paley is not suggesting that there exists an analogy between human mechanical devices and nature. The force of his argument ultimately rests on an identity: nature *is* a mechanism, and hence was intelligently designed.

Paley's arguments were regarded by many as irrefutable. Every aspect of the created world was designed and assigned to its special place by a benevolent creator at the beginning of the world. It was as if every natural creature seemed to shout: "We have been designed! We have a purpose!" In his haste to present a compelling argument from nature to God, Paley made some assumptions that were theologically incorrect, and—as events proved—apologetically disastrous. God was assumed to have created all species of plants and animals in their present forms. There had never been any change or development, nor need there have been. Many of his readers disagreed. Charles Kingsley's novel *The Water Babies* (1863) argued that Paley's notion of an artisan god and manual creation were far from the only way of interpreting Christian understandings of the issue. Kingsley insisted that the most distinctive aspect of the Christian doctrine of creation was that God made things to make themselves.

Yet Paley's idea of "special creation" continued to be widely accepted, even into the 1850s. His case seemed unanswerable. Did not God create all things good, and hence requiring no modification? Might not the Book of Genesis be read literally as history, since every aspect of nature seemed to confirm this? Paley was a functionary of the established church, not a theologian; and in his desire to construct a simple and visualizable account of creation, he sowed the seeds of its ultimate destruction at the unwilling hands of Charles Darwin (1809–82).

Darwin's five-year voyage of exploration on the *Beagle* initially involved travel to the South Seas and the mysterious lands of the Pacific Ocean; they eventually led to a new understanding of how biological life came into existence. As a young man, Darwin found Paley's account of nature compelling, and saw little reason to challenge it. However, the mass of biological information that he accrued, both during his voyage on the *Beagle* and subsequently, seemed to him to raise serious difficulties for Paley's belief that God made the world more or less as we now know it. A number of observations raised doubts in his mind about Paley's account.

1. The fossil record suggested that some species had died out. But why should this be, on the basis of Paley's account? How

could the extinction of supposedly well-adapted and successful species be explained? It is known that Darwin's consideration of Thomas Malthus's theories on population growth had
a significant impact on his thinking on this issue.

2. The uneven geographical distribution of life-forms throughout
the world. Darwin's personal research trips on the *Beagle* convinced him of the importance of developing a theory that
could explain the peculiarities of island populations.

3. Vestigial structures—such as the nipples of male mammals—
were difficult to accommodate on the basis of the concept of
special creation, in that they appeared to be redundant and
serve no apparent purpose. Why should God have created
such structures ready-made, when they were pointless? Did
this not contradict Paley's notion of "contrivance"?

Darwin's task was to develop an explanation that would account for
these and other observations more satisfactorily than the alternatives
that were then available. Although the historical account of how he arrived at his theory has perhaps been subject to a degree of romantic
embellishment, it is clear that the driving force behind his reflections
was the belief that the observational evidence could be most convinc-
ingly accounted for by a single theory of natural selection. He himself
was quite clear that his explanation of the biological evidence was not
the only one that could be adduced. He did, however, believe that it
possessed greater explanatory power than its rivals, such as Paley's doctrine of special creation. "Light has been shown on several facts, which
on the theory of special creation are utterly obscure."

It was clear to Darwin, as it was to his many readers, that the foundations of Paley's arguments for the existence of God had been shattered. As Darwin wrote in his *Autobiography*: "The old argument of
design in nature, as given by Paley, which formerly seemed to me so
conclusive, fails, now that the law of natural selection has been discovered. We can no longer argue that, for instance, the beautiful hinge of

a bivalve shell must have been made by an intelligent being, like the hinge of a door by man." Darwin, often presented as an atheist by antireligious propagandists, is best regarded as an agnostic, in Huxley's sense of the word: one who ultimately believes that certain things simply cannot be known. "The mystery of the beginning of all things is insoluble to us; and I for one must be content to remain an Agnostic." As Frank Burch Brown concluded after a careful study of Darwin's writings, his religious views were complex and not readily categorized.

> His beliefs concerning the possible existence of some sort of God never entirely ceased to ebb and flow, nor did his evaluation of the merit of such beliefs. At low tide, so to speak, he was essentially an undogmatic atheist; at high tide he was a tentative theist; the rest of the time he was basically agnostic—in sympathy with theism but unable or unwilling to commit himself on such imponderable questions. Overall his thought regarding theological matters could best be described as being in what he himself termed a "muddle."

Yet a close reading of Darwin's writings shows that the main reason for his doubting the Christian concept of God had little to do with his theory of evolution. Darwin's animus was primarily his visceral distaste for the "damnable doctrine" of eternal punishment for nonbelievers, which was popular in evangelical circles at the time (although his deep grief over the death of his daughter must also be noted here). As Geoffrey Rowell demonstrated some years ago, unease about this notion was widespread in the Victorian era, and had led many to reject this aspect of evangelical teaching. Perhaps surprisingly, Darwin's rejection of God actually has little to do with the specifics of evolution, and much more to do with a general cultural dislike of some of the more noxious aspects of the hell-and-brimstone preaching of certain Victorian evangelicals, which came under increasing public criticism in the 1860s. So sensitive to this criticism was the great American evangelist Dwight L. Moody (1837–99)—the Billy Graham of his age—that he chose not to mention the idea in his revivalist preaching campaigns. He knew that an increasingly sophisticated culture simply would not accept such an idea. Darwin here echoes the concerns of his age—yet on moral, not scientific, grounds.

While Darwin was certainly not an atheist in the sense of someone who denies the existence of a divine being, he had clearly given up any belief in a God who remotely resembled Archdeacon Paley's watchmaker. There was no watch, and hence there could be no watchmaker. In place of Paley's carefully ordered natural world, in which each species was created already adapted to its unchanging environment, Darwin proposed a battlefield, in which emerging species fought for existence in a desperate struggle for survival—and subsequently for their place in posterity. The evidence, in his view, allowed him to reach no other conclusion. The tragic death of his daughter Annie wrecked his belief in divine providence. His moral sense revolted against the popular religious idea that God condemned unbelievers to hell. But other concepts of God lay readily to hand. It was not surprising that many chose to adopt them.

The most obvious was adopted by many, both in England and the United States. Evolution was to be seen as the means by which God guided his creation to its present state. Paley was quite wrong to suggest that Christianity taught that things were created as we now find them. There was no difficulty in seeing Darwin's theories as clarifying the means by which God providentially directed the evolutionary process. In 1884, Frederick Temple, who later became archbishop of Canterbury, argued that God did something rather more splendid than just make the world; he made the world *make itself*.

And the scientific doctrine of Evolution, which at first seemed to take away the force of this argument [the argument from design], is found on examination to confirm it and expand it. The doctrine of Evolution shows that with whatever design the world was formed, that design was entertained at the very beginning and impressed on every particle of created matter, and that the appearances of failure are not only to be accounted for by the limitation of our knowledge, but also by the fact that we are contemplating the work before it has been completed.

God bestowed a genuine autonomy upon creation, and has, as it were, woven creation from the bottom upward: with matter giving rise to life and life giving rise to conscious reflective existence in humanity. Charles Kingsley found that it was "just as noble a conception of Deity, to believe that He created primal forms capable of self development . . . as to believe that He required a fresh act of intervention to supply the lacunas which He Himself had made." The distinguished American botanist Asa Gray (1810–88) believed it was perfectly possible to reconcile evolutionary theory with faith. Instead of seeing God as the creator of fixed species, Gray pictured God as the designing power behind evolutionary change. Indeed, Gray went so far as to claim that "a theistic view of Nature" is implied in Darwin's writings.

Especially in North America, a persistent and vocal minority has continued to insist that one must choose between Darwin and the Bible, even taking the debate to the law courts. In 1925, John Scopes, a biology teacher in one of Tennessee's public schools, was accused of breaking a local law prohibiting the teaching of evolution. The Scopes trial, which took place in Dayton, Tennessee, in July 1925, was billed as a "duel to the death" between Christianity and atheism by prosecutor William Jennings Bryan (1860–1925), three-time candidate for the presidency of the United States. The defense was led by the celebrated agnostic Clarence Darrow (1857–1938), one of America's greatest attorneys. During the trial, Darrow was disallowed from using scientific testimony in his defense of Scopes. He hit upon a brilliant alternative.

The legal move was simple, yet had devastating consequences. Darrow called Bryan to the stand as a witness for the defense, and interrogated him concerning his views on evolution. Bryan was forced to admit that he had no knowledge of geology, comparative religions, or ancient civilizations, and showed himself to have hopelessly naive religious views. In the end, Bryan succeeded in winning the trial in the courtroom; Scopes was fined one hundred dollars. But the judgment of history has been with Darrow. The intelligentsia of North America, aided to no small extent by the journalist and literary critic H. L. Mencken (to whom Sinclair Lewis later dedicated *Elmer Gantry*), successfully portrayed those who opposed evolution on the basis of the Book of Genesis as intolerant, backward, and ignorant dolts who stood outside the mainstream of American culture. That perception remains firmly implanted in the Western soul.

Some works dating from the second half of the twentieth century did much to crystallize the growing popular perception that the idea of evolution necessarily entailed atheism. Jacques Monod's *Chance and Necessity* (1971) set out the fundamental creed of the molecular biologists: change arises by chance and is propagated by necessity. It is utterly impossible to speak of "purpose" within the biological world. Evolutionary theory demands that we realize that our own existence is an accident, and come to terms with this disturbing thought. "We would like to think ourselves necessary, inevitable, ordained from all eternity. All religions, nearly all philosophies, and even a part of science testify to the unwearying, heroic effort of mankind desperately denying its own contingency."

Monod argues that the natural sciences disclose a purposeless world, within which we must create our own values and beliefs. Nature itself has nothing to offer us as a guide. "The ancient covenant is in pieces; man knows at last that he is alone in the universe's unfeeling immensity, out of which he emerged only by chance. His destiny is nowhere spelled out, nor is his duty. The kingdom above or the darkness below; it is for him to choose." *Chance and Necessity*, steeped in French philosophy and literature, was not the easiest work for an English-language audience to appreciate. Two popularizers stepped into the gap, offering highly readable accounts of the significance of Darwinism for culture.

Richard Dawkins's *The Blind Watchmaker* set out with brilliance and lucidity, perhaps for the first time at a popular level, the basics of modern evolutionary biology and their implications, not least for belief in God. One of Dawkins's most important arguments is that the "appearance of design" can arise naturally within the evolutionary process. "Biology is the study of complicated things that give the appearance of having been designed for a purpose." Dawkins pays a compliment to Paley, noting the plausibility of his ideas in a preevolutionary world. How could Paley be expected to know, in advance of his time, that what seemed to him to be evidence of "contrivance" was simply the outcome of a long, blind, and purposeless process of development? "Natural selection is the blind watchmaker, blind because it does not see ahead, does not plan consequences, has no purpose in view. Yet the living results of natural selection overwhelmingly impress us with the appearance of design as if by a master watchmaker, impress us with the illusion of design and planning." Any argument from design must now be abandoned, as the very notion of design has been discarded on evolutionary grounds. Evolutionary theory leads inexorably to a godless, purposeless world. Dawkins does not regard this as a problem, seeing plenty of excellent things in nature to excite and console him.

Others, however, have been puzzled, not so much by Dawkins's atheism as by his insistence that this atheism is demanded by evolutionary theory. To them, Dawkins has shifted from popularizer to propagandist. To appreciate the importance of this point, we may turn to our second immensely successful evolutionary popularizer, Stephen Jay Gould (1941–2002).

Gould followed Monod in setting out the implications for humanity of evolutionary theory. His major study *Wonderful Life* concludes with this sentence: "We are the offspring of history, and must establish our own paths in this most diverse and interesting of conceivable universes—one indifferent to our suffering, and therefore offering us maximum freedom to thrive, or to fail, in our own chosen way." Gould's own account of evolution makes it clear that there is no need to propose such ideas as design or purpose in accounting for the way things are; in fact, they are rendered redundant. Everything can be explained by the purely natural process of natural selection.

But is Darwinism atheistic? Here, Gould makes it clear that he is a natural scientist, not a religious pundit. In a 1992 critique of an antievolutionary work which posited that Darwinism was necessarily atheistic, Gould invoked the memory of Mrs. McInerney, his third-grade teacher, who was in the habit of rapping young knuckles when their owners said or did particularly stupid things:

> To say it for all my colleagues and for the umpteenth million time (from college bull sessions to learned treatises): science simply cannot (by its legitimate methods) adjudicate the issue of God's possible superintendence of nature. We neither affirm nor deny it; we simply can't comment on it as scientists. If some of our crowd have made untoward statements claiming that Darwinism disproves God, then I will find Mrs. McInerney and have their knuckles rapped for it (as long as she can equally treat those members of our crowd who have argued that Darwinism must be God's method of action).

Gould rightly insists that science can work only with naturalistic explanations; it can neither affirm nor deny the existence of God.

The empirical evidence is of critical importance here. As Gould stresses, this shows that some Darwinians are theists and others not. There is simply no valid means of settling this issue on scientific grounds. The suggestion that the Darwinian theory of evolution is *necessarily* atheistic goes way beyond the competency of the natural sciences and strays into territory where the scientific method cannot be applied. If it is applied, it is *mis*applied. Thus Gould points out that Charles Darwin was agnostic (having lost his religious beliefs upon the tragic death of his favorite daughter), whereas the great American botanist Asa Gray, who advocated natural selection and wrote a book entitled *Darwiniana*, was a devout Christian. More recently, he notes,

Charles D. Walcott, the discoverer of the Burgess Shale fossils, was a convinced Darwinian and an equally firm Christian, who believed that God had ordained natural selection to construct a history of life according to His plans and purposes. More recently still, the "two greatest evolutionists of our generation" show radically different attitudes to the existence of God: G. G. Simpson was a humanist agnostic, Theodosius Dobzhansky a believing Russian Orthodox. As Gould concludes, "Either half my colleagues are enormously stupid, or else the science of Darwinism is fully compatible with conventional religious beliefs—and equally compatible with atheism."

Although Gould regarded himself as an agnostic inclined toward atheism, his admirably fair summary of the situation favors neither atheist nor religious believer. At the personal level, he considered atheism to be "more of a suspicion" than a rigorously documented conclusion. The bottom line for Gould is that Darwinism actually has no bearing on the existence or nature of God. If Darwinians choose to pontificate on matters of religion, they stray beyond the straight and narrow way of the scientific method, and end up in the philosophical badlands. Either a conclusion cannot be reached on such matters or it is to be reached on other grounds, whether rational or emotional.

Gould's analysis is borne out by a remarkable piece of empirical research, which blatantly contradicts both those who insist that the sciences inevitably lead to atheism and those who insist that they throw people into the arms of God. The natural sciences may lead some away from God and others to God. But to say that they must do one or the other is to move beyond the legitimate scope of the scientific method, and to smuggle in religious or antireligious claims under a pseudo-scientific smokescreen.

Two major surveys of the religious beliefs of scientists, carried out at the beginning and end of the twentieth century, bear witness to a highly significant trend. One of the most widely held beliefs within atheist circles has been that as the beliefs and practices of the "scientific" worldview became increasingly accepted within Western culture, the number of practicing scientists with any form of religious beliefs would dwindle to the point of insignificance. A survey of the religious views of scientists, undertaken in 1916, showed that about 40 percent of scientists had some form of personal religious beliefs. At the time, this was regarded as shocking, even scandalous. The survey was repeated in 1996, and showed no significant reduction in the proportion of scientists holding such beliefs, seriously challenging the popular notion of the relentless erosion of religious faith within the profession. The survey cuts the ground from under those who argued that the natural sciences are necessarily atheistic. Of those questioned, 40 percent had active religious beliefs, 40 percent had none (and can thus legitimately be regarded as atheist), and 20 percent were agnostic.

The stereotype of the necessarily atheist scientist lingers on in Western culture at the dawn of the third millennium. It has its uses, and continues to surface in the rehashed myths of the intellectual superiority of atheism over its rivals. The truth, as might be expected, is far more complex and considerably more interesting.

5

A Failure of the Religious Imagination: The Victorian Crisis of Faith

WORLDVIEWS THAT CAPTURE THE HUMAN IMAGINA-
tion never entirely fade away; those that make no such appeal
can expect to make little progress. Yet what of a worldview that once
captivated and nourished the imagination of the West, yet slowly saw
that power fade? It is of the utmost significance that those who were in
the forefront of the revolt against God in Victorian England were poets
and novelists, whose imaginative constructions of reality increasingly
came to rest on secular, rather than religious, foundations. The wells of
divine artistic inspiration seemed to them to have run dry; it was necessary to find new sources of inspiration elsewhere.

Christian ideas and images, previously seen as an imaginative resource and stimulus, were now held to be deficient. The imaginative
quarry that had guided and nourished the poetry of George Herbert,
John Donne, and John Milton was now regarded as exhausted. New
mineshafts needed to be sunk and new ideas explored. God increasingly became an absence in the popular imagination, no longer able to
resonate with the creative energy of the day. Victorian culture came
increasingly to prefer to explore the imaginative potential of a world
without God.

So why did this failure of the religious imagination develop within Victorian culture? There is no doubt that growing concerns over the intellectual credibility of Christianity were a major contribution to its fading appeal. The growing influence of biblical criticism, a persistent failure on the part of clergy to engage with the troubling issues of the day, and the rise of Darwinism all undermined the potency of faith. Perhaps the erosion of the Christian faith in later Victorian Britain is attributable not to its diminished appeal to human reason but to its failure to capture the *imagination* of its culture. Yet the origins of intentional atheism—as opposed to mere cultural indifference to religion—rest primarily on rational, rather than imaginative, concerns.

THE BIRTH OF INTENTIONAL ATHEISM IN BRITAIN

Historians date the birth of "avowed" or "intentional" atheism in Britain to around the year 1782, when William Hamilton drew attention to a recent incident in his *Answer to Dr Priestley's Letters to a Philosophical Unbeliever*: "Be it therefore for the future remembered, that in London in the kingdom of England, in the year of our Lord one thousand seven hundred and eighty-one, a man has publickly declared himself an atheist." The tone of surprise, even outrage, at such an outlandish view is significant: Hamilton clearly expects his readers to share his astonishment that anyone should hold such a strange idea, let alone be so vulgar as to mention it in public. Such matters were best reserved for the privacy of the boudoirs and salons of Paris. Yet while atheism may have become *conceivable* to British minds of the 1790s, it was still very far from being *fashionable*. A series of influential writings, supremely Edmund Burke's *Reflections on the Revolution in France* (1790), created the firm impression among political conservatives that atheism and republicanism were two sides of the same coin.

Others soon entered the fray, hiding their identities in order to advance their ideas. The unidentified "Scepticus Britannicus" who published *An Investigation of the Essence of the Deity* (1797) insisted that, far from being repressive, atheism was a liberator. "An atheist is a man who destroyeth chimeras prejudicial to the human species." Thomas Paine had pointed to the role of religious institutions in perpetuating such servility some years earlier, in his *Age of Reason* (1794): "All national institutions of religion, whether Jewish, Christian or Turkish, appear to me no other than human inventions set up to terrify and enslave mankind, and monopolize power and profit."

But credit for the serious advancement of atheism on the eve of the Victorian era is most due to William Godwin (1758–1836), one of the more colorful figures of the Romantic period in England. Like many, he regarded the French Revolution as having irreversibly changed the cultural face of the West. A new era had dawned, in which the advancement of human reason would lead to the elimination of governments, diseases, and death. Godwin's somewhat extravagant ideas rested on a firm belief in the ultimate triumph of reason, which the French Revolution had championed. The corruption of government would be eliminated, in that people would make right decisions for themselves without the need for consultation or coercion; disease and death would be overcome through the final triumph of mind over matter. And for Godwin, the idea of God was an outmoded superstition that had no place in this new rationalist paradise on earth.

The atheism of Godwin's *Political Justice* (1793) exercised a fascination over many during the 1790s, when his star shone brilliantly in the British intellectual firmament. Its radical—and, to many, profoundly attractive—social vision rested on the assumption of the perfectibility of humanity through reason. This notion, which arguably lay behind both the political and religious views of the French Revolution, swept to one side such notions as the authority of the past, a divine revelation entrusted to the church for interpretation, or any mysterious and dark force of destiny that governed the fate of humanity. Reason held the key to the moral transformation of humanity.

Godwinism was a philosophy that attracted many, as the young Wordsworth recalled. As he suggested in *The Prelude*, the attractiveness of its ideas to "young minds" lay in the fact that it

> *Was flattering to the young ingenious mind*
> *Pleased with extremes, and not the least with that*
> *Which makes the human reason's naked self*
> *The object of its fervour.*

Yet however firm its rational foundations or radical its social implications, the new philosophy failed to excite the imagination. As William Hazlitt pointed out in his *Spirit of the Age* (1825), it proved to be "of such short life" precisely because it represented "reason without passion." Like a setting sun, Hazlitt suggested, Godwin had "sunk below the horizon, and enjoys the serene twilight of a doubtful immortality."

To deny God is one thing; but the outcome of such a denial, for many in the early nineteenth century, was a dull rationalism that failed to excite—that singularly lacked the ability to provoke a sense of wonder on the part of its beholder. A cold and dry rational account of nature might well satisfy the human reason, but it left the imaginative and emotional faculties untouched. For Samuel Taylor Coleridge and his circle, Godwin suffered from an imaginative deficit. He failed to appreciate the importance of the emotions and imagination.

If atheism was to take hold of British culture, it had to seize its imagination—something that Godwin's dull and dry prose signally failed to achieve. A rational case for a godless world might have been made; the attractions of such a world remained, however, obscure. To polite British culture of the period, atheism was like a distant island in the tropics—a remote and faintly exotic place in which no cultured person would want to live. The great experiment of the Victorian age was to explore how such an uninhabitable island might become a paradise. One of the most promising early approaches lay in making an appeal to nature as a gateway to the transcendent.

NATURE: AFFIRMING
THE TRANSCENDENT WITHOUT GOD

Convinced that the human imagination and emotions needed something to inspire them, many writers of the first decades of the nineteenth century now found themselves in something of a quandary.
Caught up in the enthusiasm evoked by the radical ideas of the French
Revolution, they were more than willing to jettison any lingering at-
tachment to organized religion and its notions of divinity. Yet the explicit atheism of Godwin and others left them with nothing to which
they could meaningfully anchor their sense of transcendence. If God
was being irreversibly relegated to the margins of British culture, to be
replaced by the more predictable and unimaginative enterprise of
merely attending church, they would have to find something else to
which to attach their longing for the transcendent. They found what
they were looking for in nature itself.

Initially, this seemed a very unpromising approach. The rise of the
mechanical worldview—a way of conceiving the world, faithful to Isaac
Newton's discoveries of the regularities of planetary motions and his
explanation of the colors of the rainbow—led many to think of nature
as a vast mechanical device. This posed serious difficulties for Samuel
Taylor Coleridge and his circle; who would feel uplifted or thrilled at
the thought that nature was merely a giant clock? For some British
writers of the period, this was an excellent and highly instructive analogy. In his *Natural Theology; or Evidences of the Existence and Attri-
butes of the Deity, Collected from the Appearances of Nature* (1802),
William Paley argued that the "contrivance" (that is, the design and
construction) of the universe pointed necessarily to God as its designer.
Yet the images of God as a watchmaker and nature as a machine both
seemed unspeakably dull and uninspiring, prompting William Blake to
write scathingly of nature as "sheath'd in dismal steel." If nature was to
serve as the basis of a new worldview, independent of God, it would
have to be reconceived and reimagined.

This process of the reenchantment of nature began in earnest from about 1790. An early example of the reconception of the natural world can be found in the writings of Mary Robinson, a former actress who became the mistress of a member of Britain's royal family. After this liaison had ended, Robinson turned to writing poetry to make ends meet. Her *Ode to the Infant Son of S. T. Coleridge* (1800) makes a powerful appeal to nature as the ultimate ground of human aesthetic and moral judgments. Whereas for many writers of the period nature was regarded as something that God had created, Robinson foreshadows a growing trend to regard the beauty of the natural order as a thoroughly satisfying alternative to God. Nature was emancipated from being God's creation, and became a divinity in its own right.

William Wordsworth, Percy Bysshe Shelley, and John Keats attached the category of the transcendent to nature in somewhat different ways. For Wordsworth, nature is best seen as an agent that imparts moral and spiritual insights through elevation of the human senses—an idea expressed in his lines from "The Tables Turned" (1798):

> *One impulse from a vernal wood*
> *May teach you more of man,*
> *Of moral evil and of good,*
> *Than all the sages can.*

In his later works, Wordsworth develops the theme of the ability of the natural world to evoke an aching sense of longing for something that ultimately lies beyond it—as in "Tintern Abbey," which uses the poet's experience of a natural landscape to evoke deeper questions about the mystery of human nature and destiny. It seemed as if there was an ecstatic desire for union with nature, or some "sweet melancholy" that seems to have no rational cause, yet is saturated with spiritual meaning.

> *The sounding cataract*
> *Haunted me like a passion: the tall rock,*

The mountain, and the deep and gloomy wood,
Their colours and their forms, were then to me
An appetite: a feeling and a love.

There is a strong sense of the loss of connectedness here, a deep and passionate feeling that individuals have become alienated, not merely from nature, but from their true destiny, which nature somehow has the capacity to declare—at least in part. The Romantic poets knew a sense of melancholy, wonder, and yearning, which they believed has its basis in the fundamental human displacement or alienation from its true objects of desire. Humanity had become disconnected from its true transcendent goals and longings, and needed to be reconnected. Yet this process of restoration was not understood to involve God, being envisaged primarily in terms of the achievement of an individual's true human potential.

Shelley politicized the notion of nature, arguing that it served as the inspirational basis for revolutionary notions of liberty and equality, encouraging a revolt against king and priest, God and religion. Keats regarded nature as something that accentuates the human hunger for sensuous and aesthetic experience. Declining to adopt Shelley's more revolutionary political ideas, Keats held that nature was capable of disclosing truth and beauty through an engagement with the imagination. Yet despite these different readings of nature, each of these three poets believes that the fundamental human emotions are inadequately served by a denial of the transcendent. If God is to be removed, there must remain some corresponding metaphysical category to which human emotions and imagination may be linked.

Keats is thus especially scathing over Isaac Newton's scientific explanation of the rainbow. In "Lamia" (1820), he complains of the effect of reducing the beautiful and awesome phenomena of nature to the basics of scientific theory. The theory may help us understand them, but somehow it seems to deprive them of their glory. Keats here expressed a widely held concern: that reducing nature to scientific theories empties nature of its beauty and mystery and reduces it to something cold, clinical, and abstract.

> Do not all charms fly
> At the mere touch of cold philosophy?
> There was an awful rainbow once in heaven:
> We know her woof, her texture; she is given
> In the dull catalogue of common things.
> Philosophy will clip an Angel's wings.

The poet uses the idea of "unweaving the rainbow" to express his concern. Does not the scientific explanation of the colors of the rainbow in terms of refraction of sunlight through raindrops somehow destroy any sense of awe or amazement at this arc in the sky? Newton's reduction of the rainbow to a generalized optical effect uncouples any link between this natural phenomenon and the world of the transcendent. The intuitive link between the rainbow and a sense of wonder points, for Keats, to the joyful romantic longing for beauty that only finds its goal beyond the physical world.

Keats did not expect to find much help in this quest for transcendent beauty from the established church. His sonnet "Written in Disgust of Vulgar Superstition" (1816) depicts conventional British religion as casting a "black spell" over its congregations. The sound of church bells seemed to him to mark the passing of such a corrupt religion, to be displaced by new growth, new ideas, and a new future:

> Still, still they toll, and I should feel a damp,—
> A chill as from a tomb, did I not know
> That they are dying like an outburnt lamp;
> That 'tis their sighing, wailing ere they go
> Into oblivion; —that fresh flowers will grow,
> And many glories of immortal stamp.

In his 1818 sonnet "To Percy Shelley, on the Degrading Notions of Deity," Keats argues that the established church created its peculiar notion of God out of fear, passion, vested interests, and downright bigotry. But what could replace it? For Keats, the answer lies in a return to the "old golden age"—a clear allusion to the period of classical Greece—in which the beauty of nature inspired humanity to worship more worthy divinities.

> *What wonder, Percy, that with jealous rage,*
> *Men should defame the kindly and the wise,*
> *When in the midst of the all-beauteous skies,*
> *And all this lovely world, that should engage*
> *Their mutual search for the old golden age,*
> *They seat a phantom, swelled into grim size,*
> *Out of their passions and bigotries.*

Keats's most thorough exploration of the potential of classical Greek natural religion is to be found in *Endymion*, which explores how the "clear religion of heaven" arises from an imaginative encounter with "symbols of immensity." The work is notable for its articulation of the Platonic notion of ascent to heavenly realities through the contemplation of their earthly symbols and types. We rise on a Platonic ladder from contemplation of mortality to immortality; from sensuous experience of love, beauty, and joy to their ultimate origin and final goal.

> *Feel we these things?—that moment have we stept*
> *Into a sort of oneness, and our state*
> *Is like a floating spirit's. But there are*
> *Richer entanglements, enthralments far*
> *More self-destroying, leading, by degrees,*
> *To the chief intensity: the crown of these*
> *Is made of love and friendship, and sits high*
> *Upon the forehead of humanity.*

Wordsworth found *Endymion* puzzling, dubbing it "a very pretty piece of Paganism." This judgment is open to question; what is clear is that Keats, distressed by traditional Christian understandings of God, sought to find an alternative vision of divinity in the ancient world. This is clearly not atheism in the traditional sense of the term; if anything, it is a quest for alternative conceptions of deity, or for an alternative metaphysical foundation for the human quest for transcendence that might have the power to "make men's being mortal, immortal."

To the socially conservative, these ideas were subversive and seditious. To a cultural and literary avant-garde, they were like pure oxygen in a stale room, fueling controversy, exploration, and the advancement of discourse. Atheism was something sensational, whose exploration broke social taboos. This is not to say, of course, that all those who explored unorthodox ideas, by the standards of the time, were atheists. Some were like Samuel Taylor Coleridge, who was obsessed with atheistic ideas without actually commiting himself to them. An engagement with atheists was a convenient means of developing his own distinctive ideas. Others found alternatives to traditional Christian belief, particularly through the neoclassical revival, which encouraged an imaginative preference for the pantheon of classical antiquity over its Christian rival.

One of the most interesting features of British literary culture throughout the nineteenth century is that a growing interest in atheism did not entail abandoning belief in the transcendent. Reductionist forms of atheism, especially those which held that nature and humanity were essentially physical or biological mechanisms, were resisted as cold and mechanical. While poets such as Keats affirmed a transcendent dimension to human existence, they did not see this as necessarily entailing a belief in divinity, whether in the general or specifically Christian sense of the term. If the good, the true, and the beautiful were Keats's masters, he made no attempt to attach these absolutes to the concept of God.

To further our exploration of this fascinating aspect of atheism, we may consider Percy Bysshe Shelley's vigorous affirmation of atheism in the early nineteenth century.

SHELLEY AND THE NECESSITY OF ATHEISM

In 1811, the young Shelley was expelled from University College, Oxford, for having published a brief essay entitled "The Necessity of Atheism." The essay sets out a critique of belief in God that parallels earlier such arguments in the writings of G. E. Lessing and Denis Diderot. Shelley argues that, since compelling evidence for the existence of God is lacking, there is no intellectual obligation to believe in God. The essay actually makes a case for a practical agnosticism—or perhaps a skeptical empiricism—rather than atheism, in that Shelley's argument leads only to the conclusion that an informed mind cannot reach a reliable conclusion on the existence of God on the basis of the available evidence.

Without in any way wishing to call the reliability of Shelley's judgment on such matters into question, it is very difficult to avoid the conclusion that his essay "The Necessity of Atheism" does little more than make a point already familiar to generations of Christian theologians—that the existence of God cannot be proved and is ultimately a matter of faith. Like Aquinas before him, Shelley merely makes the point that, on the basis of the empirical evidence of the world and the rational resources at his disposal, belief in God is not a necessary conclusion. There can be little doubt that Shelley's thoughts on this matter may well have been catalyzed by at least a passing knowledge of the arguments of philosophers such as John Locke and David Hume. The title of the treatise simply does not represent its contents; nor do its contents entail what the title proclaims. Yet it presaged more radical views that were waiting in the wings for their moment to take center stage.

In his *Queen Mab* (1813), Shelley puts explicitly atheistic sentiments into the mouth of the poem's fairy queen, who offers the following account of the true state of the universe: "There is no God! / Nature confirms the faith his death-groan sealed." The queen seems to speak for Shelley himself in exulting in the abandonment of belief. The death of God is to be applauded, not mourned, in that this god has been allowed to sanction all kinds of atrocities and crimes. To reject God is to reject the tyranny that religious belief brings in its wake.

> *The name of God*
> *Has fenced about all crime with holiness,*
> *Himself the creature of his worshippers,*
> *Whose names and attributes and passions change,*
> *Seeva, Buddh, Foh, Jehovah, God, or Lord,*
> *Even with the human dupes who build his shrines,*
> *Still serving o'er the war-polluted world.*

Religion is thus destructive and deceitful. The traditional Christian understanding of the fall of humanity holds that the first representative humans were expelled from paradise for seeking to be like gods. *Queen Mab* points to an alternative rendering of the fall of humanity: it is organized religion that caused us to defect from the true worship of nature, and our true natural goal.

> *Look on yonder earth:*
> *The golden harvests spring; the unfailing sun*
> *Sheds light and life; the fruits, the flowers, the trees,*
> *Arise in due succession; all things speak*
> *Peace, harmony, and love. The universe*
> *In nature's silent eloquence, declares*
> *That all fulfil the works of love and joy,—*
> *All but the outcast man. He fabricates*
> *The sword, which stabs his peace; he cherisheth*

The snakes that gnaw his heart: he raiseth up
The tyrant, whose delight is in his woe,
Whose sport is in his agony.

The reattachment of humanity to nature is the essential prerequisite for the regaining of paradise, for the restoration of a lost Eden. Yet God has no place in such an Eden, in that religion is seen as the corrupting influence that led to the degeneration of human nature and the origin of strife and conflict. It is not nature but belief in God that destroys and degrades human innocence and joy.

Nature!—no!
Kings, priests and statesmen, blast the human flower
Even in its tender bud; their influence darts
Like subtle poison through the bloodless veins
Of desolate society. The child
Ere he can lisp his mother's sacred name,
Swells with the unnatural pride of crime, and lifts
His baby-sword even in a hero's mood.

Although these ideas were slow to take root, they had become the received wisdom of the age by the end of the nineteenth century. An important witness to this trend is to be found in Mathilde Blind's short, privately published essay "Shelley's View of Nature contrasted with Darwin's," which appeared in 1886. For Blind, Shelley liberated Britain from the "gloomy and cruel superstitions" of the Christian religion. In its place the poet promoted a religion of nature and reason, in which humanity would seek inspiration and vision from contemplation of the glories of the world, instead of the superstitions of religion. "The human heart turning thirstily toward a rehabilitated nature, saw that she was fair, and felt a thrill of delight at the beauty of moonlight on still waters, at the radiance of snow-crowned Alps, at the sublimity of seas in storm or calm." Blind is clear that Shelley was of central importance to this major shift in attitude toward nature, and lauded his achievement with the overexcited enthusiasm of the amateur. Get rid of kings and priests, and return to nature—and all will be well.

Shelley, above all, was profoundly and permanently swayed by this fervid feeling. In his youth, as is testified by Queen Mab, *and the notes appended to it, he had been vitally influenced by the study of Rousseau's writings and those of the other philosophical precursors of the French Revolution. From them he had to a great extent imbibed the firm conviction that if you could only rid society of kings and priests we should immediately enter on the Golden Age, and instead of discord, war, and wretchedness, the earth would become the abode of love and harmony.*

Religion corrupts nature by forcing people to contemplate and capitulate to its irrational absurdities, when the natural study of humanity is nature itself.

This is all splendid stuff, and represents an important witness to the way in which Shelley was understood and appropriated within more radical and skeptical circles in the 1880s and beyond. Yet Shelley himself, I think it is important to note, does not explicitly deny the existence of a God in general, or any specific conception of that God— even the much-maligned God worshiped by members of the established Church of England on Sundays (although what happened during the rest of the week is very much open to question). In his remarkable "Essay on Christianity" (1815), Shelley launches a sustained attack on institutional religion, not least because its preoccupation with power and status corrupts its vision of God. "An established religion turns to deathlike apathy the sublimest ebullitions of most exalted genius, and the spirit-stirring truths of a mind inflamed with the desire of benefiting mankind."

Yet the ultimate basis of the existence of Christianity—namely, a belief in God—is not challenged; rather, it is identified as a "Power" that saturates the world and evokes human attempts to capture the beauty of things. God is not eliminated; He is merely renamed. "We live and move and think; but we are not the creators of our own origin and existence. We are not the arbiters of every motion of our own complicated nature; we are not the masters of our own imaginations and moods of mental being. There is a Power by which we are surrounded, like the atmosphere in which some motionless lyre is suspended, which visits with its breath our silent chords at will."

Hints of this can be seen in Shelley's "Hymn to Intellectual Beauty," which posits the idea of an intuited higher power, which saturates nature with its presence and beauty—a power which, as we have seen, he clearly associates (while avoiding outright identification) with the Christian God.

> The awful shadow of some unseen Power
> Floats though unseen among us,—visiting
> This various world with as inconstant wing
> As summer winds that creep from flower to flower.

The human experience of this beauty may be sporadic rather than continual; it is, nevertheless, an integral aspect of the phenomenon of nature. Nature is not simply to be investigated and understood as "the other" by detached observers; it is to be encountered and allowed to evoke wonder at its sheer beauty. Nature thus elicits the memory or knowledge of "some unseen power," whose shadow or reflection can be discerned within its order and structures. Shelley's skeptical inclinations rule out any direct equation of this intuited transcendent reality with any specific God, particularly the rather troubling possibility that this might turn out to be the God of the established church.

On closer examination, Shelley's atheism thus proves somewhat problematic. *Queen Mab* sets out a radical atheist vision, which seems to be modified in Shelley's later writings. Making sense of such inconsistencies is not unduly demanding: Shelley may have deliberately wanted to shock what he regarded as a complacent establishment, or simply to assert the right to argue about some of the most fundamental and seemingly settled questions of his day, the existence of God being a case in point. As Robert M. Ryan has pointed out, the most radical poets of this era were not averse to returning to orthodoxy in their later works, their protests having been made and noted.

We may now move on to explore some further aspects of the Victorian crisis of faith by turning to the writings of one of the most important atheists of the period: the novelist George Eliot.

THE UNCONVERT: GEORGE ELIOT

Those who are converted to a creed often prove its most effective ambassadors. The story we are about to tell is how a devout but rather shy evangelical Christian came to be one of atheism's most important advocates in Victorian England. Mary Ann Evans (1819–80)—who later assumed the pen name George Eliot—was born on South Farm, part of the estate of Arbury Hall, Nuneaton, Warwickshire, on November 22, 1819. She was the daughter of a farmer, Robert Evans, who was also land agent at Arbury. When she was four months old the family moved to Griff House on the edge of the estate. Mary Ann attended church with her family at Chilvers Coton and was educated at boarding schools in Nuneaton before going to school in Coventry between the ages of thirteen and sixteen. After her mother's death in 1836 she came home to Griff House to help run the household. She continued to educate herself, however, being allowed free use of the library at Arbury Hall. She learned Italian and German with the help of a tutor in 1840. While Robert Evans raised his daughter as a conventional member of the Church of England, Mary Ann encountered more enthusiastic forms of Christianity while attending local "ladies' seminaries."

The form of Christianity that so shaped Eliot's early life was evangelicalism, a growing presence in early-nineteenth-century England.

Various hints in her personal correspondence suggest that her early religious beliefs corresponded to those that were gaining momentum within the Church of England in the 1830s. In an 1860 letter to a colleague in Geneva, Eliot spoke of "the strong hold evangelical Christianity had on me from the age of fifteen to two and twenty." While earlier forms of evangelicalism had been theologically generous, laying emphasis upon personal devotion to Jesus rather than fidelity to theological dogmas, a new stridency within the movement around this time led to a hardening of attitudes. The quality of a person's faith was now judged by doctrinal correctness rather than a love for Christ. The warmheartedness of earlier versions of evangelicalism now gave way to increasingly dogmatic and impersonal construals of the Christian faith, which repelled as many as it attracted. One of those who was permanently alienated from God in this manner was Eliot herself.

On January 2, 1842, Eliot informed her father that she no longer intended to go to church. A certain coolness descended upon their relationship, which was never entirely removed by the healing passage of time. His refusal to even discuss the matter with her forced Eliot to write to him, setting out her reasons for withdrawing from church life in this dramatic manner.

I wish entirely to remove from your mind the false notion that I am inclined visibly to unite myself with any Christian community, or that I have any affinity of opinion with the Unitarians more than with any other classes of believers in the Divine authority of the books containing the Jewish and Christian Scriptures. I regard these writings as histories consisting of mingled truth and fiction, and while I admire and cherish much of what I believe to have been the moral teaching of Jesus himself, I consider the system of doctrines built upon the facts of his life and drawn as to its materials from Jewish notions to be most dishonourable to God and most pernicious on individual and social happiness.

There is little doubt as to the cause of her alienation from faith. Some of Eliot's concerns were peculiar to specifically evangelical doctrine; others were more general, pertaining to Christianity in its most basic form. Her reading of Charles Hennell's *An Inquiry concerning the Origin of Christianity* (1838) raised questions over the supernatural aspects of faith. Eliot's personal copy of Hennell's *Origin of Christianity* has a highly significant date inscribed in its flyleaf: January 1, 1842, the day before she ceased attending church.

Was not, Hennell asked, Christianity a purely natural set of ideas, spread by purely natural means? "The true accounts of the life of Jesus Christ, and the spread of his religion, would be found to contain no deviation from the known laws of nature, nor require, for their explanation, more than the operation of human motives and feelings, acted upon by the peculiar circumstances of the age and country whence the religion originated." Jesus Christ was a religious teacher with aspirations to reclaim the throne of David. Having failed in this effort, he suffered martyrdom. Nicodemus and Joseph of Arimathea removed his body as a precautionary measure. The early church mistakenly interpreted the empty tomb as evidence of a resurrection, and thus initiated a relentlessly inflationary understanding of Jesus's identity that transformed him from a Jewish teacher to the Son of God incarnate. Yet Hennell had no doubts that something might be salvaged from this mess. "Christianity thus regarded as a system of elevated thought and feeling, will not be injured by being freed from those fables, and those views of local or temporary interest, which hung around its origin."

Eliot was not prepared to leave matters there. Making good use of her knowledge of German, she set about translating one of the most radical works of German New Testament scholarship—David Friedrich Strauss's *Life of Jesus*, which caused a sensation on its publication in Germany in 1835, partly on account of its appeal to socially and religiously alienated progressive elements, who recognized it as a useful propaganda weapon in their concerted attack on each and every aspect of the German establishment—above all, the church.

Strauss's interpretation of the events recorded in the Gospels reflects the rationalist criticism of orthodox Christianity resulting from the Enlightenment. In the face of growing skepticism concerning biblical miracles, Strauss set out to explain how Christians came to believe when there was no objective historical basis for their faith. Taking the Resurrection as the key article of faith, Strauss concluded that religion was ultimately an expression of the human mind's ability to generate myths in the first place, and then to interpret them as truths revealed by God.

Many of Eliot's misgivings about Christianity in general are best seen as a specific response to the ideas of evangelicalism. In an article in the *Westminster Review* for October 1855, Eliot offered a sustained criticism of a popular London evangelical preacher, John Cumming. She took particular exception to Cumming's insistence that only actions directed toward the glory of God might be deemed to be good.

> Dr. Cumming's theory . . . is that actions are good or evil according as they are prompted or not prompted by an exclusive reference to the "glory of God." God, then, in Dr. Cumming's conception, is a being who has no pleasure in the exercise of love and truthfulness and justice, considered as effecting the well-being of His creatures; he has satisfaction in us only in so far as we exhaust our motives and dispositions of all relation to our fellow-beings, and replace sympathy with men by anxiety for the "glory of God."

Eliot deems this to be a rather harsh and unattractive God, who "instead of sharing and aiding our human sympathies is directly in collision with them; who instead of strengthening the bond between man and man, by encouraging the sense that they are both alike the objects of His love and care, thrusts himself between them and forbids them to feel for each other except as they have relation to Him."

We can see here a leading theme of the Victorian crisis of faith: a growing moral revolt against Christianity on account of its leading ideas. Writers such as J. A. Froude, Matthew Arnold, and F. W. Newman abandoned their faith on account of a growing sense of the immorality of such doctrines as original sin, predestination, and substitutionary atonement. Theological terms and slogans that had been the proud watchwords of an earlier generation of Protestant writers now became embarrassments that could no longer be tolerated. Where Puritans had exulted in the thought of a sovereign God who could deal unaccountably with his creatures in any way he liked, many Victorians found this deeply disturbing and in open conflict with their increasingly developed sense of morality and justice.

Eliot, like many others, therefore turned to a "religion of human sympathy" in place of this rather dark and dismal conception of God. Similar patterns of alienation from conventional religion are found thoughout her novels, from *Adam Bede* through to *Middlemarch*. The moral aspects of faith could, she believed, be maintained without the metaphysical basis of Christianity. We can be good without God. Indeed, belief in the Christian God can be a significant obstacle to the achievement of "individual and social happiness." These views became the received wisdom of the age, shaping the emerging late Victorian consensus on the ability of humanity to shape its own destiny. While some—Thomas Hardy comes to mind—were more pessimistic than Eliot about humanity's ability to construct morality without God, they were a distinguished minority in this discussion.

Yet when all is said and done, there is a remarkable tameness about Eliot's critique of Christianity. None of her skeptical arguments against God gets out of hand. They are on a tight leash, like domesticated animals being taken out for a gentle stroll, rather than the more ferocious beasts found elsewhere in Europe at this time. Thus the German philosopher Friedrich Nietzsche (1844–1900) saw Eliot's position as a typically moribund English compromise. She wanted to have Christian morality but not Christian belief—as if the two could be separated. As he commented in *Twilight of the Idols*: "They are rid of the Christian God and now believe all the more firmly that they must cling to Christian morality. That is an *English* consistency; we do not wish to hold it against little moralistic females à la Eliot. In England one must rehabilitate oneself after every little emancipation from theology by showing in a veritably awe-inspiring manner what a moral fanatic one is. That is the *penance* they pay there." Nietzsche was quite clear: this was a fundamental inconsistency that superior German logic simply would not permit.

> When one gives up the Christian faith, one pulls the *right* to Christian morality out from under one's feet. This morality is by no means self-evident: this point has to be exhibited again and again, despite the English flatheads. Christianity is a system, a *whole* view of things thought out together. By breaking one main concept out of it, the faith in God, one breaks the whole: nothing necessary remains in one's hands. Christianity presupposes that man does not know, *cannot* know, what is good for him, what evil: he believes in God, who alone knows it. Christian morality is a command; its origin is transcendent; it is beyond all criticism, all right to criticism; it has truth only if God is the truth—it stands and falls with faith in God.

George Eliot's novels undermined the plausibility of God in a number of ways. Yet in her later years, she seems to have lost any sense of animus against Christianity, increasingly regarding it as playing an important cultural role. As she wrote in a letter of 1860, "I no longer have any antagonism toward any faith in which human sorrow and human longing for purity have expressed themselves." In a letter to Madame Bonichon, written two years later, Eliot made clear that she had no interest in undermining belief in God:

> Don't ever ask me to rob a man of his religious belief, as if you thought my mind tended to such robbery. I have too profound a con-

viction of the efficacy which underlies all sincere faith, and the blight that comes with no-faith, to have any negative propagandism in me. In fact I have very little sympathy with Freethinkers as a class, and have lost all interest in mere antagonisms to religious doctrines. I care to know, if possible, the lasting meaning which lies in all religious doctrines from the beginning until now.

Others, however, were prepared to complete the job that they believed Eliot had abandoned. One of the most imaginative and influential of these more radical writers was Algernon Charles Swinburne (1837–1909).

A. C. SWINBURNE: THE IMAGINATIVE APPEAL OF THE PROFANE

The Victorians, it seems, tended to think of God in imagery borrowed from their cultural context. Whatever the rich reservoir of biblical imagery might offer by way of visual depictions of the deity, many less reflective Victorians tended to think of God as a stern old man—rather like the headmaster of one of England's famed public schools, such as Eton. Although the New Testament spoke of God's mercy at least as much as his justice, the harsh discipline of such an authority figure revolted many in an increasingly egalitarian age. Who wanted anything to do with a God who could be compared with a taskmaster who preferred flogging to caring, thrashing to loving?

Swinburne might come to mind here. His celebrated addiction to masochism, especially flagellation, probably began when he was a schoolboy at Eton. In later life he was a regular at 7 Circus Road—"a lovely little villa, presided over by a well-educated lady, well-versed in the birchen mysteries." He also frequented Verbena Lodge, the flagellant brothel in St. John's Wood. Swinburne's extensive body of erotic writings shows a fascination with the infliction of pain. *The Whippingham Papers* is a case in point.

Oh, hold his shirt up, Algernon,
Hold the boy's shirt up high;
Let us all have a view of his bottom, Hugh,
Oh, doesn't the pain make him cry, by Jove!

The Victorian interest in flagellation has been carefully studied by Stephen Marcus in *The Other Victorians*, and at somewhat greater length by Ian Gibson in *The English Vice*. Both scholars point out that the appeal of this particular form of erotica was largely confined to the upper classes. Those whose taste for flagellation led them to write or read such works as George Colman's *Rodiad*, or to patronize flagellation brothels, are probably best seen as victims of their culture, which offered relatively few outlets for open sexual activity. Paradoxically, the most ardent flagellomaniacs—such as Swinburne himself and Richard Burton—were those who "felt themselves to be in rebellion against the Establishment of the day in matters of sexual morality, and greatly disliked its hypocrisy and puritanism" (Gibson); that rebellion, however, often took the form of an adolescent indulgence in their childhood sexual experiences at public school. Yet Gibson goes further, arguing that Swinburne's deep loathing of Christianity is grounded in his sadomasochism.

Swinburne is thus to be seen as a rebel, reacting against the prudery of his day at an intellectual as well as sexual level. Swinburne raised attention-seeking to the status of a new art form, deliberately attempting to outrage, shock, and intrigue the prudish culture around him. When rumors of his homosexual antics began to circulate, Swinburne supplemented them with what everyone hoped was invention (but nobody could really be sure)—such as his passionate declaration that he had brought an evening of sexual depravity with a monkey to its climax by eating it. His immense distaste for the Church of England led him to pen undignified Trollopian sketches featuring such characters as the Reverend Simplicius Pricksmall of Little Pissing.

The Victorian upper classes might well visualize God as a birch-wielding tyrant. While many would find this image distasteful, it was not without its attractions to Swinburne. Yet it was tainted by the realization that the Christian God, in creating a desire for pleasure, had caused it to be seen as a thing of shame. God was a sadist, the "lord of love and loathing and of strife," who "gives a star and takes a sun away"; who

> *makes desire, and slays desire with shame;*
> *Who shakes the heaven as ashes in his hand;*
> *Who, seeing the light and shadow for the same,*
> *Bids day waste night as fire devours a brand,*
> *Smites without sword, and scourges without rod;*
> *The supreme evil, God.*

Religion takes away a sun and offers a mere star in its place. God was the great oppressor of the human soul, creating a sense of overwhelming desire within humanity, yet offering nothing by which that longing might be satisfied—except things that were declared to be immoral. Having created such desires in the first place, God now condemned humanity to a wretched and miserable life of frustration and dissatisfaction. Using arguments that parallel those of the Marquis de Sade, Swinburne argued that only a rejection of God could open the way for human self-fulfillment.

For Swinburne's imagination had been seized by something beyond the delights of Verbena Lodge: a godless world, in which man was king. The religious stifling of the human imagination would be overwhelmed by the thought of a world from which such nonsense has been banished, and man raised to his rightful place as lord over all. God must die that man may live. In February 1870, he penned a note to Dante Gabriel Rossetti, setting out his fundamental belief in the death of Christianity:

I expect you will see shortly in the papers, "Suicide of an elderly pauper lunatic, formerly an unlicenced pawnbroker and receiver of stolen goods. His linen was marked JAH. A young man of dissipated appearance and a Jewish cast of feature who announced himself as the son of the deceased is more than suspected of being the same person who was sentenced to the gallows some time since for a nameless offence and taken down before the proper time, and restored to life after undergoing the extreme penalty of the law. Since then, he has been known to the police under a variety of aliases, and among his companions of infamous notoriety, by the slang term of "Lamb."

Swinburne had no regrets about the passing of this divinity. The death of God is simply the precondition for the divinization of man. It was no accident that Swinburne should choose to reconstruct polemically the great Christian hymn "Glory to God in the Highest" in a manner that satisfied his personal taste and the mood of the age: "Glory to man in the highest! / For man is the master of things." The Christian God is dead, and another has taken his place. As Swinburne put it in his "Hymn to Man," "O fools, he was God and is dead."

Swinburne set out his views with particular clarity in a letter written to William Rossetti, stressing the need to break free from that most corrupting and enslaving of all human inventions, the idea of God: "I feel it my mission as an evangelist and apostle (whenever necessary) to atheize the republicans and republicanize the atheists of my acquaintance. I have in my head a sort of hymn for this Congress—as it were a 'Te Hominem laudamus,'[1] to sing the human triumph over 'things'— the opposing forces of life and nature—and over the God of his own creation, till he attain truth, self-sufficiency and freedom."

To a twenty-first-century reader, much of Swinburne's critique of Christianity seems to reflect the rather uncritical evolutionary opti-

---

[1] *"We praise you, O Man," a polemical reworking of the traditional Christian hymn "Te Deum laudamus," "We praise you, O God."*

mism of his age, and to be phrased in excessively alliterative language that is flamboyant and pretentious by today's standards. Many readers view Swinburne's preoccupation with the more painful pleasures of the flesh—such as his fantasies concerning "fierce and luxurious Dolores, our Lady of Pain"—as an embarrassment, and prefer to concentrate on his imaginative engagement with issues of religion. Yet Swinburne's highly rhetorical criticism of religion shaped the manner in which many of his contemporaries viewed the world, and must be regarded as a landmark in the history of atheism.

The key to Swinburne's vital importance lies in a line from what is widely regarded as one of his greatest poems, the "Hymn to Prosperpine": "Thou has conquered, O pale Galilean; the world has grown grey from thy breath."[2] These words point to Swinburne's fundamental conviction of the imaginative deficit of the Christianity he knew and so thoroughly detested. What was there in the pallid Christ of popular devotion that could enrich the imagination of his day? The Victorian Christ might make the world meek and mild; he would never capture its allegiance through an appeal to beauty or joy. Christianity triumphed by impoverishing culture and diminishing humanity's delight in itself. Perhaps most significantly of all, there was no link between Christ and the transcendent—no reason to suppose that, in encountering and wrestling with the person of Jesus Christ, one was stepping over the threshold of a mystery, and passing into the presence of something (or someone) of compelling beauty or delight.

To understand Swinburne further, we must move on to consider the impact of the Life of Jesus movement of the early nineteenth century, which had such a devastating impact on the literary imagination of that era.

---

[2] *This unusual way of referring to Christ is based on the dying words of the Roman emperor Julian the Apostate in 363: "vicisti, Galileae." Julian attempted to reverse the gains of Christianity throughout the Roman Empire by reintroducing paganism.*

THE LIFE OF JESUS MOVEMENT

Even a cursory glance at one of the great icons of Byzantine basilicas reveals the definitive place of Christ in Eastern Orthodoxy. The risen Christ reigns triumphant over the forces that oppress humanity; he may be relied upon to deliver those who put their trust in him. As God incarnate, he offers a window into the transcendent. As John of Damascus, the great Syrian theologian of the sixth century, put it: "Previously there was absolutely no way in which God, who has neither a body nor a face, could be represented by any image. But now that he has made himself visible in the flesh and has lived with people, I can make an image of what I have seen of God . . . and contemplate the glory of the Lord, his face having been unveiled." Christ is the means by which we may experience "heaven in ordinary" (George Herbert), gaining access to the mysterious world of the heavenly places while we sojourn on earth. The imaginative potential of this conception of Christ can only be overstated with some difficulty. If God was indeed the true goal of humanity, contemplation of Christ was the means by which this goal could be visualized, and hence undertaken more boldly. Generations of theologians, philosophers, poets, and writers found this incarnational framework to be of central importance to their reflections on the hidden transcendent world, and the true destiny of humanity.

By the middle of the nineteenth century, this understanding of the person of Christ had been demolished for many Western writers. Jesus was a distant moral sage, useful for moral guidance—especially as a role model for young children. How many Victorian parents must have nodded appreciatively at the words of Mrs. Cecil F. Alexander from *Once in Royal David's City*, penned in 1848: "Christian children all must be, / Mild, obedient, good as he." But when it came to anything more than that, Christ had nothing more to tell us or show us than any educated person. Traditionally, Christianity anchored its grasp of the transcendent to Christ through the concept of the Incarnation, a notion that rationalism found unconvincing and unpersuasive. For many, the hitherto presumed connection between Christ and the divine had been dismantled and discarded. It is no accident that many turned to the contemplation of nature and the history of human culture in searching for the meaning of life. Christ had been systematically decoupled from the ultimate questions of existence.

The origins of this development can be traced back to a seminal essay by the German rationalist thinker G. E. Lessing (1721–89). Stressing the historical distance of Christ from the present, Lessing argued that this remote and largely unknown figure could not give or guarantee access to an absolute world of truth. "The contingent truths of history can never become the proof of the necessary truths of reason." Lessing and other Enlightenment thinkers dismantled the supernatural structure that generations of Christian theologians had erected around Christ, arguing that no rational justification could be offered for such developments. They were metaphysically inflationary and rationally impossible. In place of these elevated understandings of Christ, the Englightenment proposed a naturalist reading of his significance, as a religious teacher and moral educator.

Two publications were of special importance in the English-speaking world. David Friedrich Strauss, whose *Life of Jesus* was translated by George Eliot, argued that the church had transposed Christ into a myth. Much more importantly, Ernest Renan (1823–92) wrote a life of Jesus that was entirely naturalist in its approach, depicting Jesus as a human figure with an exaggerated sense of his own importance. It was hard work being the Son of God, and hence understandable that he suffered intermittent lapses in his responsibilities. So accessible was the English translation of this work that it scandalized much of British society rather than merely its intellectual elite.

By the 1870s the cheerleaders of Victorian culture were coming to the view that Christ had nothing distinctive to say, other than to encourage people to behave themselves properly. If Christ echoed the prevailing assumptions of Western culture, that was well and good. But he could not add to these, nor could he challenge them, by proposing radical alternatives. While many continued to view Jesus in mystical categories, as through a softly focused Romantic haze, others had concluded that he lacked the ability to captivate the imagination of their culture. Jesus was a moral teacher, the Great Prohibitor. And who now wanted to make a glorified Sunday school teacher into a cultural icon?

The Roman Catholic scholar George Tyrrell (1861–1909) was appalled by this evacuation of Christ's significance. The nineteenth century, he wrote scathingly in *Christianity at the Cross-Roads* (1909), had accommodated Jesus Christ to its own ideas as to what was proper and decent, finding "a moralist in a visionary; a professor in a prophet; the nineteenth century in the first; the natural in the supernatural. Christ was the ideal man; the Kingdom of Heaven, the ideal humanity. As the rationalistic presupposition had strained out, as spurious, the miraculous elements of the Gospel, so the moralistic presupposition strained out everything but modern morality. That alone was the substance, the essence, of Christianity." As Tyrrell knew only too well, the Christ that the nineteenth century came to invent and admire was nothing more than a pale reflection of its own ideas, incapable of exciting the human imagination or offering a gateway to the transcendent.

Admittedly, the rationalist "lives of Jesus" were far from what they appeared to be. While offering to liberate their readers from dogmatic views of Christ, they nevertheless assumed, often with equally great dogmatism, that the church could *not* have got Jesus right. The distinguished German scholar Martin Kähler, writing in the 1890s, argued that the new understandings of Jesus that entranced and scandalized the nineteenth century were just as arbitrary, dogmatic, and problematic as those they displaced.

> The historical Jesus of modern writers conceals the living Christ from us. The Jesus of the "life of Jesus" movement is merely a modern example of a brain-child of the human imagination, no better than the notorious dogmatic Christ of Byzantine Christology. They are both equally far removed from the real Christ. In this respect, historicism

is just as arbitrary, just as humanly arrogant, just as speculative and "faithlessly Gnostic," as that dogmatism which was itself considered modern in its own day.

But Kähler's protests went unnoticed in Victorian culture. They were never translated from their original German in time to be appreciated.

And so the late Victorian period came to see in its Christ nothing more than its own pallid reflection, and chose to look no further. The magnificent Byzantine Christ, *pantokrator* of the universe, had been torn down, and replaced with a more modest construction, more tempered to the spirit of the age. This metaphysically adjusted Christ posed no real difficulties to the reason, but failed to engage the imagination. The outcome was perhaps inevitable: the Christ who had once been the bright polestar of British culture now found itself in eclipse. His metaphysical brilliance had been diminished on the one hand by the dark glass of rationalism, and on the other by the rise of rival luminaries in the late Victorian firmament.

A CULTURE IN CRISIS: THE LOSS OF FAITH

One of the many merits of *God's Funeral*, A. N. Wilson's study of the rise of atheism in Victorian Britain, is his careful documentation of the ambivalence felt within late-nineteenth-century England over its loss of faith. The secular enterprise, begun with great enthusiasm, had achieved substantial successes by the end of the century. Politically and socially, Christianity remained highly significant in national life, and would remain so until after the First World War. Yet its ideas were increasingly seen as discredited, unattractive, and outdated by its novelists, poets, and artists. Christianity had been tried and tested at the imaginative and rational levels, and found wanting on both counts. Although it might be thought that this grand retreat from faith would have been greeted with delight and celebration, Wilson brings out the

deep sense of emotional loss and confusion that the inexorable elimination of God brought in its wake.

The Victorian era is widely regarded as undergoing major changes
from about 1870 to 1900, which can be seen as ultimately subverting
the values and beliefs of its earlier phases. Many writers of the period
were conscious of standing at the threshold of a new age, uncertain of
what it might bring, yet suspecting that the old ways of thinking were
on their way out. In his *Stanzas from the Grand Chartreuse*, written
around this time, Matthew Arnold (1822–88) speaks of being caught
"Between two worlds, one dead, / The other powerless to be born, /
With nowhere to lay my head." Arnold's journey through the Alps is the
backdrop against which he explores his sense of displacement, focusing
especially on the erosion of faith in his culture—and perhaps even in
himself. His once-robust faith, he comments, more than a little wist-
fully, now seems "but a dead time's exploded dream." Arnold expresses
a sense of melancholy and sadness over his nation's loss of faith, which
he had seen pathetically mirrored in the ebbing of the tide on Dover
Beach:

> *The Sea of Faith*
> *Was once, too, at the full, and round earth's shore*
> *Lay like the folds of a bright girdle furl'd.*
> *But now I only hear*
> *Its melancholy, long, withdrawing roar,*
> *Retreating, to the breath*
> *Of the night-wind, down the vast edges drear*
> *And naked shingles of the world.*

That tide was now ebbing, and Arnold never expected to see it return.
It is impossible to read his poem "Dover Beach" without glimpsing
something of his pain and bewilderment over his nation's willing loss of
its religious soul.

Arnold's sadness was shared by others, who might have been expected to be rather more positive about the nation's loss of faith. There is something almost tender in Thomas Hardy's marking the end of the era of faith, as he envisages God's funeral procession: "I did not forget / That what was mourned for, I, too, long had prized."

The more radical elements of the French Revolution believed, with a passion and depth that seems slightly misplaced today, that the elimination of God would lead to public rejoicing and the end of craven submission to the crass ideologies of the past. In the event, the fading of God, like a slow but inevitable sunset, was marked by a sense of loss, of bereavement, that earlier generations would have found difficult to comprehend. Suddenly it became meaningful to speak of the death of God in Western culture. God had ceased to be a living presence; what other metaphor could be employed to describe this development? This naturally led to an intriguing inquiry into the cause of death. Did God simply perish, or was he killed off? These are themes that demand more detailed exploration in the chapter that follows.

6

THE DEATH OF GOD:
THE DREAM OF
A GODLESS CULTURE

O N OCTOBER 22, 1965, *TIME* MAGAZINE RAN A COVER
story that stopped America in its tracks. Emblazoned on an all-
black cover were three huge red words: "Is God dead?" Although the
article focused primarily on a few relatively unknown theologians who
had launched a theology that everyone suspected was stillborn and was
going precisely nowhere, it raised broader issues. Had God been
sucked out of American culture? Was America entering a new secular
era, in which God would merely be a memory of an increasingly distant past?

The headline writers had a feast. What had once been spoken in
whispers was increasingly stated openly: God had ceased to be a living
reality in Western culture—even in one of its most openly religious nations. The new religionless and godless era that the French Revolution
initiated would now finally come to pass, marking a turning point in
the history of the world. The death of President John F. Kennedy had
made headlines two years earlier. The death of God would be the
scoop of the millennium.

So how did the rumor that God was dead come about? As we shall
see, many streams converged to form this torrent. We can only hint at

the many developments that created an impatience with traditional religious belief, and led many to conclude that God had died or been put to death. The public atheism that had taken its first faltering steps in the eighteenth century had finally come of age.

So where should we begin to tell this tale of the loss of any sense of the presence of God in the West? For many scholars, the most obvious place is the massive protest registered against God in one of the great novels of the nineteenth century, Dostoyevsky's *The Brothers Karamazov*.

DOSTOYEVSKY AND THE REVOLT AGAINST GOD

Two interrelated questions can be identified throughout the writings of Dostoyevsky, especially *The Brothers Karamazov* and *The Possessed*: Is atheism a credible worldview, and if so, what kind of world does it envisage and sustain? There is no doubt that Dostoyevsky was well aware of the arguments of many Russian bourgeois liberals around this time, to the effect that the espousal of atheism would heal Russia's wounds and lead to her social and political regeneration. Vissarion Belinsky and others in the Russian Utopian Socialist group in the late 1840s had argued for precisely such an approach, holding that revolution must begin with atheism, above all the overthrow of Christianity.

Dostoyevsky's novels can be read as an implicit critique of such revolutionary optimism, exploring both the grounds of such a belief and its implications. In effect, he pictures certain of his characters as already inhabiting an atheist worldview, and uses them as a way of exploring its strengths and weaknesses. Although careful to note the clear attractions of a godless world, especially during a particularly repressive period of Russian history, Dostoyevsky is clearly determined to highlight some of its more troubling features. Against the facile argument that atheism will liberate Russia from its backwardness and authoritarianism, he argues that it could open the door to unprecedented brutality and oppression, precisely because it removes any divine limitation to human actions.

The Brothers Karamazov (1880) is the last and perhaps the greatest of Dostoyevsky's novels. Set against the social fragmentation of Russia in the 1870s, it explores the intense intellectual and physical rivalry among three brothers. One of its great themes is the tension between belief and atheism. Dostoyevsky splendidly presents the two sides of the question of God, one believing and the other doubting, in two of the brothers: Alyosha and Ivan. The one submits, the other rebels. Ivan Karamazov acts as a spokesperson for those who question the coherence of traditional Christian belief. Ivan's criticisms are directed not so much against God as against the world that God is alleged to have created. How can one believe in God, when the created order itself seems riddled with injustice and contradiction?

Ivan's polemic against God has become a classic instance of "protest atheism"—a revolt against God on moral grounds. A refusal to believe in God (a mutiny, to use Ivan's language) is the appropriate principled response to the inequities of the world, and the God who is alleged to have brought it into being, yet such a response seems curiously distant from the world's sorrow and pain. Raging against injustice, Ivan asks Alyosha to imagine a shocking scene. An eight-year-old child accidentally bruises the leg of a general's favorite beagle. Outraged, the general sets a pack of dogs upon the child, who is torn to pieces in front of his mother. What's the justice in that, asks Ivan? How can anyone sing, "You are just and true, O God, for your ways are made clear"? Ivan continues: "I hasten to return my entry ticket. And if I am at all an honest man, I am obliged to return it as soon as possible. That is what I am doing. It isn't God I don't accept, Alyosha. It's just his ticket that I most respectfully return to him."

Ivan follows this critique of the injustices of the world by telling a long parable. He asks Alyosha to imagine the reappearance of Christ during the Spanish Inquisition of the sixteenth century. Labeled a heretic, the Son of God is brought to judgment before the cynical

Grand Inquisitor, who launches a diatribe against Christ for having committed the unthinkable and unforgivable sin of giving humanity freedom of choice. This, the Inquisitor declares, is an intolerable burden, which humanity simply cannot carry. The church, out of a deeper concern for humanity, wishes to *deny* them freedom, and replaces the curse of freedom with the intellectual and spiritual opiates of miracle, mystery, and authority. By revering the mystery, believing and accepting the miracles, and following the dictates and directives of the church, people can live their lives without the heavy load of accepting responsibility for their own actions. The majority of people, according to the Grand Inquisitor, are weak and are to be likened to sheep. Happiness can only be achieved by the surrender of human freedom. People may cry out for it, but in fact they prefer slavery. Only the strong, those few at the top of the power structure, should have to bear the weight and responsibility of freedom.

The Brothers Karamazov explores some of the antireligious arguments that were circulating widely in Russian liberal circles at this time—most notably, the idea that atheism would liberate them from the stifling social customs and morals of the day, and allow society to break free from its servile past. Dostoyevsky clearly believes that this assumption is as superficially attractive as it is unexamined. Although the issue is explored to some extent in *The Brothers Karamazov*, a more explicit and engaging assessment of the idea is found in an earlier novel: *The Possessed*.

The Possessed, also known as *Devils*, is the third of Dostoyevsky's five great novels. The work, published over the years 1871–72, is loosely based on the Nechayev case of 1869. It describes the fortunes of a revolutionary group seeking to overthrow the Russian government and weaken the influence of the church. This demands absolute secrecy and the ability to commit a series of horrific crimes in pursuit of their political goal. In Dostoyevsky's hands, this becomes a major political tract in its own right, marked by a penetrating engagement with the appeal and implications of atheism.

For our purposes, the most important character in the novel is Kirillov, who argues that the nonexistence of God legitimates all forms of actions. The importance of this theme for the novelist is best appreciated from an 1878 letter to N. L. Ozmidov, in which he sets out the implications of atheism for morality: "Now assume that there is no God, or immortality of the soul. Now tell me, why should I live righteously and do good deeds, if I am to die entirely on earth? . . . And if that is so, why shouldn't (as long as I can rely on my cleverness and agility to avoid being caught by the law) cut another man's throat, rob and steal?"

In *The Possessed*, Kirillov adopts a related line of argument: if there is no God, it follows that he, Kirillov, is God. This puzzles Stephanovich, who asks him to explain what he means. Kirillov responds as follows: "If God exists, then everything is His will, and I can do nothing of my own apart from His will. If there's no God, then everything is my will, and I'm bound to express my self-will." Since the idea of God is a pure human invention, Kirillov reasons that he is free to do as he pleases—in this case, take his own life. Suicide is the ultimate expression of human autonomy. "There's no idea greater than the fact that God doesn't exist," Kirillov continues. "Human history supports me. The only thing man has done is to keep inventing God to go on living and not kill himself; this alone constitutes global history up to now. During the entire course of global history I alone am the first person who doesn't want to invent God."

What Kirillov regards as a rather hopeful possibility—that God does not exist and thus everything is permitted—was seen by Dostoyevsky himself as a threat. To remove limits to human action was to open the gates to less welcome developments, leading to unrestricted tyranny and violence. While Dostoyevsky's writings give little hint of the horrendous evils to come in the Stalinist era, there can be little doubt that he was trying to draw the attention of his readers to the darker side of atheism. Atheism, it has often been argued, was the necessary precondition for the Stalinist era. Yet many Russian bourgeois liberals of the 1870s saw atheism as a liberator that would free their culture from the oppressive political absolutism and moral conservatism of their age. Dostoyevsky, with the true vision of a prophet, foresaw something much more disturbing. To remove God is to eliminate the final restraint on human brutality.

NIETZSCHE AND THE DEATH OF GOD

If any philosopher is associated with the "death of God," it is Friedrich Nietzsche (1844–1900). We find no crisis of faith, no road away from Damascus, marking Nietzsche's commitment to atheism. As he himself remarked, it was more a matter of instinct than a response to any event. Yet Nietzsche's personal atheism must not be confused with his understanding of the essentially cultural development by which belief in the Christian God has become virtually untenable in modern Western society. Nietzsche's discussion of the grounds of (un)belief is actually rather disappointing, and is in any case not where his real interests lie. As Albert Camus pointed out, Nietzsche "did not form a project to kill God" but instead "found him dead in the soul of his contemporaries." The primary emphasis of Nietzsche's mature writings is that "belief in the Christian God has become unbelievable"—a statement that represents a cultural observation rather than a philosophical argument. "What is now decisive against Christianity is our taste, no longer our reasons." Western culture has not ceased to believe in God on account of unassailable philosophical reasons, but because of its shifted mood. Although clearly aware of the growing arsenal of atheist arguments, Nietzsche does not make much use of them. His basic approach is pragmatic: it is a simple matter of fact that God is gradually being eliminated from modern culture. Whether this is right or wrong, good or bad, it is happening. As a matter of observable fact, Nietzsche suggests, Western culture has ceased to find belief in God plausible. And what, he rightly wonders, might the implications of this be?

Nietzsche imagines news of the death of God being proclaimed to a disbelieving crowd by a madman—a visionary, even somewhat apocalyptic figure whose message is resisted. Nietzsche sets out his "Parable of the Madman" as follows in *The Gay Science*:

> Have you not heard of that madman who lit a lantern in the bright morning hours, ran to the market place, and cried incessantly: "I seek God! I seek God!" —As many of those who did not believe in God were standing around just then, he provoked much laughter. "Has he got lost?" asked one. "Did he lose his way like a child?" asked another. "Or is he hiding? Is he afraid of us? Has he gone on a voyage? emigrated?" —Thus they yelled and laughed . . . The madman jumped into their midst and pierced them with his eyes. "Whither is God?" he cried; "I will tell you. *We have killed him*—you and I. All of us are his murderers. But how did we do this? How could we drink up the sea? Who gave us the sponge to wipe away the entire horizon? What were we doing when we unchained this earth from its sun? Whither is it moving now? Whither are we moving? Away from all suns? Are we not plunging continually? Backward, sideward, forward, in all directions? Is there still any up or down? Are we not straying, as through an infinite nothing? Do we not feel the breath of empty space? Has it not become colder? Is not night continually closing in on us? Do we not need to light lanterns in the morning? Do we hear nothing as yet of the noise of the gravediggers who are burying God? Do we smell nothing as yet of the divine decomposition? Gods, too, decompose. God is dead. God remains dead. And we have killed him."

Unable to take this in, the crowd assumes it is the babbling of a fool. For Nietzsche, however, the unspeakable—the *unthinkable*—has happened, even if the crowd cannot and will not believe it. God has ceased to be a presence in Western culture. He has been eliminated; squeezed out. In short: we have killed God. The madman *wants* to believe in God (unlike many in the crowd); the problem is that he cannot. Yet he realizes that his audience is not yet ready to acknowledge the truth of his message.

The madman fell silent and looked again at his listeners; and they, too, were silent and stared at him in astonishment. At last he threw his lantern on the ground, and it broke into pieces and went out. "I have come too early," he said then; "my time is not yet. This tremendous event is still on its way, still wandering; it has not yet reached the ears of men. Lightning and thunder require time; the light of the stars requires time; deeds, though done, still require time to be seen and heard. This deed is still more distant from them than most distant stars—*and yet they have done it themselves.*"

So what are the implications of this development? Nietzsche insists that news of the death of God will be slow to travel; those in the know may expect to encounter resistance. "God is dead; but given the way of men, there may still be caves for thousands of years in which his shadow will be shown. And we—we still have to vanquish his shadow, too." Yet the day will come, he insists, when God will be finally eliminated from the world. "When will all these shadows of God cease to darken our minds? When will we complete our de-deification of nature?" The consequences of this de-deification of the world are immense. Morality is no longer defined with reference to God, but solely with reference to human needs and aspirations. "Morality is the herd-instinct in the individual." Moral and philosophical truths are simply beliefs that we create to enable us to cope with the world. There are no facts; simply interpretations—and those interpretations are to be judged by their utility in coping with a meaningless world.

For many, this nihilism was a new gospel. This was certainly not the case for Nietzsche himself, who spent many anxious moments trying to find a way around the conclusions that he knew must follow from nihilism. If there is no God, or if God has become a culturally discredited notion, then there are no absolute values or truths. "How much must collapse now that this faith has been undermined, because it was once built upon this faith, propped up by it, and grown into it—for example, the totality of our European morality." Yet others saw this erosion of the foundations of morality and truth as liberating.

Although best remembered for his dystopian novel *Brave New World* (1932), Aldous Huxley—grandson of Darwin's colleague T. H. Huxley—gave considerable thought to the question of how true human freedom could be attained. In his *Ends and Means* (1937), he pointed out how nihilism had some admirable qualities.

> For myself, as, no doubt, for most of my contemporaries, the philosophy of meaninglessness was essentially an instrument of liberation. The liberation we desired was simultaneously liberation from a certain political and economic system and liberation from a certain system of morality. We objected to the morality because it interfered with our sexual freedom; we objected to the political and economic system because it was unjust. The supporters of these systems claimed that in some way they embodied the meaning (a Christian meaning, they insisted) of the world. There was one admirably simple method of confuting these people and at the same time justifying ourselves in our political and erotical revolt: we could deny that the world had any meaning whatsoever.

If there is no meaning within the world, we are free to impose whatever meaning we please upon it. It is something that we freely and actively create, not something we are obliged passively to accept. To relinquish belief in God is simultaneously to affirm that our identity is placed beyond challenge or judgment, opening the way to new, creative ways of conceiving ourselves and the world in which we live. And this is Nietzsche's legacy to the West, however much he may have had misgivings concerning it.

One of the most penetrating criticisms of this approach is found in the writings of the Polish poet Czeslaw Milosz (born 1911), who won the Nobel Prize for Literature in 1980. Having found himself stifled intellectually, first under Nazism and then under Stalinism, Milosz had no doubt as to the ultimate source of despair and tyranny in the twentieth century. In a remarkable essay entitled "The Discreet Charm of Nihilism," he pointed out that it was not religion, but its nihilist antithesis, which lay at the root of the century's oppressive totalitarianism: "Religion, opium for the people! To those suffering pain, humiliation, illness, and serfdom, it promised a reward in afterlife. And now we are witnessing a transformation. A true opium of the people is a belief in nothingness after death—the huge solace of thinking that for our betrayals, greed, cowardice, murders, we are not going to be judged." The Marxist creed has now been inverted. The true opium of modernity is the belief that there is no God, so that humans are free to do precisely as they please. Life can become our privately scripted and controlled story, without any impeding thought of "a scale to weigh sins and good deeds."

For nihilism, a religious worldview is oppressive because it insists that we will be held accountable for our actions—that there will come a future judgment for crimes over which human courts are powerless to rule. Nihilism, Milosz argues, abolishes any such threat. There is no judgment against sins; indeed, there are no sins, other than those actions that we ourselves determine to be sinful. Earlier, Ludwig Feuerbach had argued that humanity constructed its own religious ideals for its convenience and consolation; we can see in Milosz's argument the recognition that both belief in God and a refusal to believe in God are themselves the result of human longings—the former a longing for consolation and immortality, the latter a longing for autonomy and a lack of accountability. Both are "opiums of the people"—different groups of people, it is true, but both needing their respective opiums.

Where some were attracted by the moral flexibility of nihilism, others found themselves drawn by its creative aspects. In his final volume of prose, *The Necessary Angel* (1951), the American poet Wallace Stevens (1879–1955) reflected on the imaginative possibilities of atheism. If there is no God, the imagination is liberated to create whatever possibilities it finds pleasing. The precondition for imaginative creativity is that there is nothing to constrain it, nothing to hold it down or limit its capacity to soar heavenward and create its own heaven and its own divinities. "To see the gods dispelled in mid-air and dissolve like clouds is one of the great human experiences. It is not as if they had gone over the horizon to disappear for a time; nor as if they had been overcome by other gods of greater power and profounder knowledge. It is simply that they came to nothing." Stevens argues that if one no longer believes in God, it becomes impossible to *dis*believe. It becomes necessary to believe in something else—and what else is there to believe in, other than the free creation of the unrestrained and unfettered human imagination?

Others were more hesitant concerning the proposed virtues of nihilism. To explore how this legacy was evaluated more critically, we turn to the French existentialist tradition, focusing especially on the remarkable writings of Albert Camus.

CAMUS AND THE ABSURD
SILENCE OF GOD

Albert Camus (1913–60) argued that human life is rendered meaningless by death, preventing the individual from making sense of existence. Any philosophy that believes it is possible to make sense of things is deluded, whether this takes the form of a "vertical" religion such as Christianity or a "horizontal" religion such as Marxism. In his first major work, *The Stranger* (1942), Camus argues that the only option is to rebel against the "ultimate negation" of death by throwing ourselves into life and making deliberate choices that challenge this futility. There is no god, no meaning—but we can create our own meanings, and throw ourselves into the world that they mediate.

In *The Myth of Sisyphus* (1942), Camus sets out his reasons for insisting that any form of faith in God is tantamount to "philosophical suicide." He uses Sisyphus, the mythical king of Corinth, as a metaphor for the absurdity of human existence. Having scorned the gods, Sisyphus was condemned by them to spend eternity in the underworld repeatedly rolling a rock to the top of a mountain, at which point the stone would roll back down again because of its own weight. Sisyphus was then obliged to begin the endless and pointless cycle all over again.

For Camus, Sisyphus is an image of the absurd hero. Condemned by the contingencies of history to a futile and meaningless existence, he sets out to make the best of things. The situation cannot be changed; it can only be accepted. There is no end in sight for Sisyphus, no respite from the pain of existence, and no possibility of knowing that what he is doing has any meaning. This is the metaphor that Camus chooses to illuminate the human predicament. If we eliminate the notion of God, we are left with a titanic and lifelong struggle that we can only lose. We are condemned by history to a painful struggle from which we cannot escape and which we cannot ultimately rationalize. "I don't know whether this world has a meaning that transcends it. But I know that I cannot know that meaning and that it is impossible for me just now to know it. What can a meaning outside my condition mean to me? I can understand only in human terms . . . I do not want to found anything on the incomprehensible. I want to know whether I can live with what I know and with that alone." There is no God to give meaning to events. The only way to be happy is by acknowledging the absurdity of the situation. "You have already grasped that Sisyphus is the absurd hero. He is, as much through his passions as through his torture. His scorn of the gods, his hatred of death, and his passion for life won him that unspeakable penalty in which the whole being is exerted toward accomplishing nothing. This is the price that must be paid for the passions of this earth."

For Camus, death is not to be seen as representing a release from our struggles, but as a denial of all that we accomplish by our efforts. Death is what makes life meaningless. So, in the face of death and in the face of the discouraging knowledge that we are defeated before we begin, can we be happy? Camus certainly thinks so.

I leave Sisyphus at the foot of the mountain! One always finds one's burden again. But Sisyphus teaches the higher fidelity that negates the gods and raises rocks. He too concludes that all is well. This universe henceforth without a master seems to him neither sterile nor futile. Each atom of that stone, each mineral flake of that night-filled mountain, in itself forms a world. The struggle itself toward the heights is enough to fill a man's heart. One must imagine Sisyphus happy.

Like *The Stranger, The Myth of Sisyphus* was written against a backdrop of despair and meaninglessness, during the depths of the Second World War. How could life have any meaning?

Camus is equally critical of the nineteenth-century tendency to divinize humanity, which found new expression in the works of Jean-Paul Sartre. For Sartre, the desire to be God is constitutive of human nature. To be human is to aspire to divinity as a rightful and meaningful goal: "To be human is to long to be God; or, if you prefer it, humanity is fundamentally a desire to be God." Sartre argues that we invent God in order to account for meaning in the world. We are haunted by the specter of cosmic meaninglessness, which we find unbearable. In consequence, we invent God so as to explain the unexplainable. For Sartre, atheism is both the presupposition and consequence of human autonomy—a freedom that must be affirmed. If there is a God, it is one which we have freely invented, and freely chosen to adopt—in other words, a humanized divinity, made in our own image.

Camus poured scorn on this crude divinization of humanity and human desires. In *The Rebel* (1951), Camus writes scathingly of the "horizontal religions of our times," which elevate humanity to the position of a deity—a role which, he argues, we are simply incapable of discharging responsibly and competently. The "metaphysical revolt" against God has caused humanity to grossly overestimate its capacities and overreach itself, leading to the messianic utopianism of Marxism. Camus argues that humanity is characterized by a double rebellion: the metaphysical revolt against the absurd and the historical revolt against injustice. In both cases, a link with atheism is established. The denial of God can be said to lie at the heart of Camus's understanding of politics and morality. Yet Camus rebels against both the idea that there is a God and one of its polemical inversions—namely, that humanity is God. In rejecting God, we must not succumb to the temptation of believing that we are divine.

The confident, optimistic atheistic faith that we find in the writings of Claude-Adrien Helvétius and Ludwig Feuerbach gave way to the darker, more uncertain questioning of Camus and many other writers, such as Franz Kakfa. The early atheist belief that a brave new world would result from the elimination of God and the deification of humanity gave way to a more somber estimation. Humanity may have revolted against God and declared itself to be autonomous; yet the outcome is a world ridden with anxiety, despair, and alienation—a far cry from the secular paradise envisioned by the dreamers of the eighteenth and early nineteenth centuries. Somehow, that paradise seemed to get postponed yet again. One of the most significant aspects of Camus's existentialism is his careful evasion of any suggestion that atheism leads to a brilliant new world, in which human alienation is overcome.

Convinced that the world is "unreasonable," Camus nevertheless yearns for it to possess some meaning. We find here nothing of the serene optimism of the Enlightenment concerning the idea of an entirely rational universe, and nothing of the agnostic's insistence that it does not matter that the universe is meaningless. These things matter profoundly to Camus. Yet he finds himself caught up in the anxiety of the contradiction between what he calls "the human need [for meaning] and the unreasonable silence of the world," which ultimately propels him toward the position that he calls the absurd—namely, the view that human life is rendered meaningless by death and that the individual cannot make any sense of human existence.

Camus does not know that God does not exist; he chooses to believe it. How could there be a God? If there is a God, he is silent, offering no justification of himself. For Camus, the idea of the death of God is best expressed in terms of his silence rather than his absence. Yet paradoxically, having rejected Christianity, Camus seems to embrace a faith of his own—a rather negative faith, it is true, but a *faith* nevertheless. We simply cannot know our situation; we are unable to make sense of it. The universe is silent when the question of "why" arises (*le "pourquoi" s'élève*), when we cry out for an explanation of our situation. We cannot make sense of things, and we obtain no answers from any other source. God and his antimetaphysical alternatives remain tantalizing hypotheses, not certainties. We simply cannot know, and must live our lives against the backdrop of a silent universe that declines to clarify its purposes—or ours.

THE DEATH OF GOD THEOLOGY

The 1960s marked a period of transition, in which the settled assumptions of the Western past were called into question with unprecedented vigor. It was as if there was an unrelenting impatience with the ways of the past, a sense of sheer boredom with existing ideas and values, and a strong belief that a new beginning lay just around the corner. The cultural mood of the period is caught well by Tom Wolfe in his essay "The Great Relearning." It was all about sweeping everything aside and starting all over again, "following a Promethean and unprecedented start from zero." To its critics, it seemed madness, a surefire recipe for chaos and superficiality. But to those who caught the vision, it was nothing less than entrancing, promising a rosy future unfettered by the outdated constraints of their parents' generation.

How could such a massive cultural upheaval leave Christianity unaffected? For the trendy young things of the 1960s, God was an outmoded idea that belonged to the past—or, even worse, to their parents' generation. Reaction against God was the hallmark of a right-thinking and intelligent young person. In Europe there was a surge of interest in Marxism in the 1960s. The May 1968 student riots in Paris were hailed as the harbinger of a shake-up at least as great as that which had swept away the *ancien régime* in 1789. "The existing moral order is the enemy," commented the editor of *Libération*, the left-leaning newspaper. The students were joined by nearly ten million workers—half the French workforce. For several weeks it looked as if France was facing a shutdown. Similar student protests at Columbia University in New York, together with widespread discontent with the Vietnam War, hinted at a global shift in values. In Northern Ireland, where I grew up, the vision of revolution also shimmered just over the horizon. The civil rights movement seemed poised to topple the old ways of living. A new dawn was just around the corner. Who could fail to be moved by such a powerful vision, especially when this one, unlike the pipe dreams of the past, seemed about to happen?

The 1960s marked a crisis point for Western Christianity. It suffered a severe crisis of confidence over these years, from which it has still not recovered. In the United Kingdom, the Church of England had been busy dealing with something that it regarded as being of ultimate importance: the revision of canon law, the internal legal codes of the church. While the bishops fiddled around with the arcane world of church legislation, their nation came close to losing its faith in God. John Robinson's book *Honest to God* (1963) suggested that Christians ought to dispense with the idea of a God "out there," and bring its ideas into line with some of the leading ideas of modern culture. This resonated with the cultural mood of the time. It made no small difference that Robinson was a bishop of the Church of England. Shortly before the publication of the book, Robinson had contributed an article to a leading British Sunday newspaper with the provocative title "Our Image of God Must Go." The book became a best-seller in England, and earned the nickname Honest John for its author. A new world had dawned, it was argued; Christians would just have to bring their ideas into line with it. The message was clear: Christianity had to update itself—or die. There was no shortage of those expecting the latter. If

God was dead, it was only a matter of time before the increasingly faint candle of faith in the West flickered, finally to die. Religion would be eroded, to be replaced with a secular, materialist world.

Still more radical developments took place in the United States, prompting the famous *Time* magazine cover story of October 22, 1965. The magazine highlighted a small group of theologians whose watchword was "God is dead." The most interesting of these theologians was Thomas J. J. Altizer, whose brief book *The Gospel of Christian Atheism* had recently been published. The story was picked up by the media and became a sensation. In its February 1966 issue, the leading theological journal *Christian Century* provided a satirical application form for its readers to join the "God-Is-Dead Club." The state of God's health was debated on TV talk shows, in the columns of the *New York Times*, and on car bumper stickers. Rarely, if ever, has a theological debate so captured the imagination of a nation. Yet the nation's attention span was brief. After discovering that the death of God did not, after all, mean that Americans had ceased to believe in God, the media lost interest in the movement. Altizer and the death of God ceased to be a hot item.

In the end, the debate probably generated more heat than light, due largely to Altizer's astonishing inability to express his ideas clearly in plain English, and his penchant for numbing overstatement. Like John Robinson in Great Britain, Altizer was convinced that the traditional notion of a transcendent God was problematic for modern culture. He was unpersuaded that his ideas would be misunderstood if he persisted with the slogan "the death of God." "My greatest failure," he once remarked, "was that I imagined I could write in such a way that it could affect the common reader. I couldn't even make myself clear to intelligent, educated readers with a background in theology."

Yet there were many who wanted to believe that God had indeed been eliminated from the public forum, who found the "death of God" movement a convenient, if temporary, ally. The elimination of religion as a serious public intellectual option has always been close to the heart of American intellectual life. God is to be respected, just as long as people don't get too serious about him. Talking about God was seen as something that consenting adults do in private. The 1960s seemed to represent the dawn of a long-awaited religionless era. It was no accident that many theological works speaking of a "religionless Christianity"—including Dietrich Bonhoeffer's letters and papers from prison—soared in popularity at this time. God had been squeezed out of the Western consciousness, and replaced with . . . well, what? Altizer's God substitute was mystifying and beyond comprehension, its obscurity only partly due to Altizer's prose. The growing interest in atheism in America around this time, however transient it may have been, was spurred by the incomprehensible concepts of God proposed by rattled liberals in the mainline denominations.

THE SUICIDE OF LIBERAL CHRISTIANITY

Atheism, like Marxism, never really caught on in America. Why not? The analogy with Marxism is illuminating, and we may pursue it briefly. Many Marxist writers in the early part of the twentieth century were deeply perplexed by the failure of their philosophy to gain a significant following in the United States. On the basis of its European experience, it ought to have built up a mass following. The same economic deprivation and social alienation that had led to the rise of Marxism in Europe ought to have precipitated a workers' revolt by this stage. Jim Connell's populist socialist song "The Red Flag" (1889) certainly anticipated some serious action in downtown Chicago:

> Look 'round, the Frenchman loves its blaze,
> The sturdy German chants its praise,
> In Moscow's vaults its hymns are sung
> Chicago swells the surging throng.

Large parts of France, Germany, and Moscow all saluted the red flag in due course. But *Chicago*? Hardly.

A ferocious and not a little impenetrable debate on the American failure of Marxism broke out between two leading Marxist theoreticians, Karl Kautsky and Eduard Bernstein. Bernstein's explanation has won wide acceptance: Marxism failed to win a following in the United States because its outlook was too deeply embedded in the social situation of 1840s Germany. It did not relate to the social realities of twentieth-century America, and Marxist theoreticians were making no effort to alter this situation by interpreting Marxism in a North American context. In short: it had become so conditioned by its original context that it failed to relate to dissimilar contexts.

The same was true of atheism in the United States. Its appeal was *standortsgebunden*, to use an inelegant but deadly accurate German term—specifically linked to one specific time and place. The appeal of atheism in Europe rested partly on its social role as a liberator from the bondage of the past and partly on the challenge it posed to the state. In Europe, the phenomenon of state churches (a relic of medieval Christendom) made Christianity an integral part of the establishment. To revolt against the status quo was to seek to overthrow Christianity. But the social situation in North America was quite different. The constitutional separation of church and state prevented any Christian body from exercising influence save through its function as an interest group. There was no link between church and state to revolt against, no established church to oppose. For much of its existence, American atheism had to actively seek out a meaningful enemy to oppose. Its moment finally came in June 1963, when *Murray* v. *Curlett* removed the reading of the Bible and prayers from America's public schools.

Buoyed by its new success, American atheism discovered it had an unlikely and largely unwitting ally—the intellectual leadership of the mainline Protestant denominations. The "death of God" controversy persuaded many more advanced thinkers that the glory days of God in heaven were over. God would have to be located somewhere else, and visualized in quite new and different ways. Convinced that nobody (well, nobody who really mattered, that is) could believe in a transcendent God anymore, revisionist theologians launched a makeover of their faith. Ideas such as eternal life, Resurrection, a "God out there," and any sense of the mysterious were unceremoniously junked as decrepit embarrassments.

If this was meant to pack them into the churches, it completely failed. The statistics reveal a grim picture. From 1955 to 1995—a generation in biblical terms—the mainline denominations suffered a massive loss of members, while churches that retained traditional teachings grew, not least from refugees aiming to escape from the rampant modernism of their denominations. The view of mainline church leaders has tended to be that modern America will take seriously only those churches that are progressive and liberal on core beliefs—such as the transcendence of God, the Resurrection of Jesus, and so on. This was certainly the perception of the 1960s, when many of the church leaders of the 1990s were in college. The decisive ethos of those years has remained firmly stamped in their minds. It's just too bad that things have moved on since then, leaving them beached. To their critics—and there are plenty of them—the mainline denominations have got stuck in a rut, and are being overtaken by new understandings of what it means to be a church—like the megachurches, with average Sunday attendances numbered in the thousands.

Wade Roof Clark, a sociologist at the University of California at Santa Barbara, published a pioneering study of the spirituality of the baby boomers demonstrating that a market-driven and culturally sensitive version of Christianity can be strong on the basics of its faith. A very different line is taken by James Spong, formerly Episcopal bishop of Newark, New Jersey. Spong argued that Christianity needs to ditch its outmoded ideas if it is to survive. If Bishop Spong applied his ideas in his own diocese of New Jersey before his recent retirement, they do not seem to have had much impact. The Episcopal church there seems locked into decline, when others are growing. What it thought was a confident manifesto has turned into a suicide note. Change is certainly needed, but the basics of faith are not the problem. Spong's remedy for the ills of the mainline denominations will probably just hasten their ending. The real issue is how well churches are able to adapt to their host populations and communicate their faith in ways that connect up with people's needs.

Even worse: these new ideas were so adapted to the ideas of modernity that they were fatally compromised by the death of modernity and the rise of postmodernity. Postmodernity reacted against just about every single aspect of modernity. The rather insipid ideas propounded by modernizers were not merely difficult to recognize as Christianity; they also turned out to be diametrically opposed to the new values and preferences of postmodernity, which often polemically inverted the certainties of its predecessor. The liberal church leaders of the 1960s and 1970s often seemed to advocate ideas that were temporarily popular at the time, but went out of fashion within a decade. They were unwise enough to believe that the cultural mood of the 1960s represented a permanent shift in Western culture, valid for at least another century. As it happened, that mood was on the skids within a decade. A movement that had tried to make God relevant to one social grouping ended up making that same God irrelevant to just about everyone else.

The settled view in the West throughout the 1960s was that God would die of old age and exhaustion, probably within the next decade. It was just a matter of time. The conventional wisdom of the sociologists of religion was that a secular age lay ahead. Admittedly, most of these were based in Western Europe and made the unwise assumption that the pattern of decline in religious belief and fervor typical of that region applied globally. Yet this seemed entirely reasonable at the time; it became the accepted wisdom of the age.

Yet many were impatient, and were not prepared to wait around for God to die. Their social and political experiments required the permanent elimination of God. Sterner—and rather more permanent—measures would be required.

THE EXECUTION OF GOD: THE ATHEIST STATE

The Russian Revolution of 1917 is, by any standard, one of the most important events in the history of the world. Although one of Europe's most backward nations, Russia possessed the potential to dominate a substantial geopolitical arena. Its traditional sphere of influence was immense. With the overthrow of the czar and the formal adoption of Marxism-Leninism, Russia was poised to export a radical new ideology throughout Eurasia, whether by argument or by force. Although the French Revolution had experimented with atheism, not entirely successfully, Marxism-Leninism held that a true socialist state was necessarily atheistic. The road to socialism demanded the death of God. Yet in Russia, faith obstinately persisted—to a far greater extent than anyone realized, as recently published material makes clear. So what was to be done?

The persistence of faith following the Russian Revolution was something of an embarrassment to Marxist theory. It had been assumed that religion would disappear once social alienation had been abolished through revolutionary action. As Lenin wrote in his essay on religion: "Religion is opium for the people. Religion is a kind of spiritual intoxicant in which the slaves of capital drown their humanity and blunt their desire for a decent human existence . . . The class-conscious worker of today . . . leaves heaven to the priests and bourgeois hypocrites. He fights for a better life for himself, here on earth." Yet religion refused to die, causing a serious problem for Marxist-Leninist theory. The accommodation of observation to theory became an increasingly difficult issue. There were limits to which Marxist theory could be adjusted to cope with the anomalous persistence of religion.

In the end, the theory triumphed: reality would have to be brought into line with what the theory predicted. Religion would have to be forcibly suppressed.

A desire to eliminate belief in God at the intellectual or cultural level has the most unfortunate tendency to encourage others to do this at the physical level. We simply cannot separate means and ends here. Lenin, frustrated by the Russian people's obstinate refusal to espouse atheism voluntarily and naturally after the Russian Revolution, enforced it, arguing—in a letter of March 1922—that the "protracted use of brutality" was the necessary means of achieving this goal. A further judicious application of this foolproof approach during the Stalinist era ensured that the official atheism of the Soviet Union would not be blemished by any unfortunate lapses into religious belief. The December 1927 edition of *Pravda*, the ideological publication of the Communist Party of the Soviet Union, pilloried religion as the class enemy of the proletariat and socialism. It was to be eliminated.

Yet it must not be assumed that the state-sponsored campaign against religious belief and practice was entirely effective. Stalin is known to have been angered by the failure of the League of Militant Godless to suppress religious belief, especially in rural areas, which remained obstinately committed to the old faith. In 1937 the league was obliged to admit that possibly as much as one-third of the urban, and two-thirds of the rural, population of the Soviet Union were still practicing religious believers. Twenty years after the Revolution, God was still a living reality in the life of most of its population.

There were many who defied the silencing of God within the Soviet Union. The writer and Orthodox priest Gregory Petrov, who died in a Soviet labor camp in 1940, found the beauty of the natural world beyond his prison camp to be an indelible reminder of the presence of God. God might have been silenced within the Soviet Union. But who could prevent nature from singing God's praise? Did not Psalm 19 declare that the heavens proclaimed the glory of the Lord?

O Lord, how lovely it is to be your guest.
Breezes full of scents; mountains reaching to the skies;
Waters like boundless mirrors, reflecting the sun's golden rays and
the scudding clouds.
All nature murmurs mysteriously, breathing the depth of
tenderness.
Birds and beasts of the forest bear the imprint of your love.
Blessed is mother earth, in your passing loveliness, which awakens
our yearning for the happiness that will last for ever,
In the eternal native land where, amid beauty that will never grow
old, the cry rings out: Alleluia!

Petrov found immense consolation in such thoughts, allowing the natural world that surrounded the inhuman and degrading life of the labor camp to remind him of his future homeland free of oppression and pain. The forests, mountains, and lakes around the camp signaled a future hope, which illuminated and transfigured his present situation. It was his opium, in Marx's terms; yet in the terms of Petrov's Orthodox faith, it was simply a confidence that God possessed a richness that could embrace and transfigure his present appalling situation and promise him security and peace in a place that lay beyond the reach of Marxist-Leninist ideology.

It is now clear that the various antireligious campaigns of the Stalinist era failed to eliminate personal faith. Yet perhaps this was not Stalin's intention. If it is assumed that Stalin's concern was to comprehensively break the power of organized religion, a much greater degree of success was achieved, especially during the 1930s. Apart from some awkward and clumsy concessions to believers during the darker days of the Second World War, when national unity was of critical importance in the face of the Nazi invasion, Stalin's program of suppressing religion achieved considerable success.

Stalin's death in 1953 did not lead, as some had hoped, to a relaxation of antireligious propaganda. In July 1954, the Communist Party of the Soviet Union ordered an increased atheist commitment within the nation's schools. Schoolbooks repeatedly asserted the malevolence of religion. Some examples: "Religion is a fanatic and perverse reflection of the world"; "Religion has become the medium for the spiritual enslavement of the masses." Alarmed at the persistence of religion, the party decreed that "the teaching of school subjects (history, literature, natural sciences, physics, chemistry, etc.) should be saturated with atheism."

Atheism was now the state religion of the Soviet Union, in much the same way as Christianity had become the state religion of the Roman Empire following the conversion of the emperor Constantine. If that precedent was anything to go by, atheism could expect to be around and influential for a *very* long time. The accuracy of that perception seemed confirmed by the expansion of Soviet influence following the Second World War, as nation after nation in Eastern Europe and the Baltic region came within the Soviet sphere, economically, politically, and atheistically. East Germany, Poland, Czechoslovakia, Lithuania, Estonia, Latvia, Romania, Bulgaria, and Hungary gradually fell into place within the Soviet bloc. Farther eastward, additional expansion seemed imminent, as Mao Zedong's revolutionary armies triumphed over their opponents in China.

Although its heartland was Eastern Europe, atheism was also gaining momentum in the West following the Second World War. Although there were some within Western Europe who hoped to eliminate religion through Communist revolutions similar to those that shook Eastern Europe, the dominant mood was that of the historical inevitability of atheism. Religious faith was eroding, partly through the breaking of the intergenerational transmission of faith in the 1960s and partly through the growing public perception of the fragility of faith. The final elimination of God from Western culture was felt to be at most a generation away.

These perceptions were reinforced by the sociologists. A secular society—in the sense of a society that had no place for religion, and saw no need for it either—was the inevitable outcome of the process of modernization, begun by the Enlightenment back in the eighteenth century. A minority argued that religion would be extinct by the year 2000; the majority regarded it as in terminal decline throughout the world, and supremely in the West. A landmark publication by a leading Christian theologian confirmed this inexorable trend. In 1965, Harvard theologian Harvey Cox wrote a book entitled *The Secular City*. It became a best-seller. The book took its stands on a series of what it regarded as incontrovertible core beliefs. Secularism was here to stay; God was dead; Christianity would have to accommodate itself to modern thought and values; religion was about humanity, not God. And that, in the view of most writers, was the end of the matter.

But it wasn't.

PART 2

TWILIGHT

THE UNEXPECTED
RESURGENCE OF RELIGION

B Y 1970 MANY HAD COME TO THE VIEW THAT RELIGION was on its way out. Some saw this as the glorious culmination of the process of secularization within Western culture; others as a sad and traumatic end to the history of faith in the West. What would a post-theist world look like? Many imagined one, and liked what they saw. Elimination of belief in God would lead to a more peaceful and stable world. That, at least, was the judgment of John Lennon (1940–80), whose song "Imagine" invited its audiences to envisage an ideal world, devoid of conflict precisely because it was devoid of religion: "Imagine there's no heaven; it's easy if you try / No hell below us, above us only sky."

By eliminating religious, political, social, and economic differences, humanity would finally be able to achieve unity. The song was released on September 9, 1971, in the United States, and achieved an instant resonance with the zeitgeist, then dominated by the Vietnam conflict and the rise of the peace movement. Beliefs were firmly identified as the enemy of peace. Once religion had been eradicated, there would be only a "brotherhood of man" with nothing left "to kill or die for." Sadly, Lennon was shot dead in New York on December 8, 1980, a victim of his own fame rather than of religious belief. But the vision remained persuasive.

But what if Nietzsche is right? What if the great revolt against God of the nineteenth and early twentieth century is not a matter of reason, but of taste? What if the appeal of atheism is culturally conditioned and historically located—in other words, its attractiveness is the outcome of a specific set of historical circumstances that have now ended, giving way to a quite different situation?

Everywhere there are signs that atheism is losing its appeal. To speak of the "twilight of atheism" is to evoke an association with Richard Wagner's "twilight of the gods" or Nietzsche's "twilight of the idols," suggesting that its day of influence is passing, and its sun setting. The term "postatheist" is now widely used to designate the collapse of atheism as a worldview in Eastern Europe and the resurgence of religious belief throughout many of those areas that had once been considered officially atheist. Yet it is now clear postatheism is not limited to the East; it is becoming a recognizable presence within Western culture. Atheism, once seen as Western culture's hot date with the future, is now seen as an embarrassing link with a largely discredited past.

One of the surest signs of this loss of confidence is a not particularly subtle attempt at redefinition within the atheist movement. Faced with numerical decline and a growing revolt against their dogmatism, some within the movement are suggesting that "atheism" should not designate those who positively reject belief in God; instead, they argue, it should refer to those who do not, at this moment, actually believe in any supernatural beings. So "the new atheism" now embraces those who are still thinking about God and those who regard the question of God as being beyond adjudication this side of heaven—in other words, those who prefer to call themselves agnostics.

It's a smart public relations move. But it means that "atheism" has lost its cutting edge, dulled and grayed from overextension. The college graduate who has suspended judgment on God while she reflects on the issues cannot be designated an atheist for that reason; she might in-

deed be a potential atheist—but she might equally end up as an agnostic or a Christian. It's a neat way of redefining atheism, extending its
numerical embrace at a time of decline and demoralization. Yet it is
clearly unacceptable to call a person an atheist because he doesn't
presently believe in God. This impoverishment of a once-proud concept will simply persuade atheism's growing army of critics that it is on
the retreat, and anxious to swell its ranks by any means possible.

But this is not atheism in the grand and dignified sense of the
word—a bold and courageous word that I myself was once proud to
own. Atheism is not about the suspension of judgment on the God
question; it is a firm and principled commitment to the nonexistence of
God, and the liberating impact of this belief. The very idea of God is
declared to be outdated, enslaving, and a downright self-contradiction.
The history of atheism is a mirror image of faith. For at its best and
most authentic, atheism is a protest—a protest against the social and
personal injustices often linked with religion and certain of its ideas in
the past, which are held to be reactionary, oppressive, or even demonic.
It is impossible not to respect atheism at these points. To abuse the
term by applying it to those who are still thinking about things, or who
believe that the matter cannot in fact be settled, represents a dilution
of the concept born of demographic desperation.

A LOSS OF FAITH:
A PERSONAL NARRATIVE

I used to be an atheist. Let me be clear what I mean by that. I am not
using the watered-down definition of someone who does not (yet)
believe in God, or is not particularly religious. By "atheist," I mean
precisely what the word has always been understood to mean—a
principled and informed decision to *reject* belief in God. I write this
book as a wounded yet still respectful lover of the great revolt against
God. In the late 1960s, as a high school student in Belfast, Northern
Ireland, I came to the view that religion was the source of all of hu-

manity's ills. It was the wisdom of the age, which I reflected faithfully, though perhaps a little too passively. Religion was, to my youthful eyes, an inherently violent presence within Western culture, whose elimination was only a matter of time. I had read A. J. Ayer's *Language, Truth and Logic*, and believed firmly, if a little prematurely, that it was utterly meaningless to talk about God. I came to regard Christianity and the natural sciences as mutually incompatible, on the basis of the incorrigible certainties about life widely entertained by teenagers. I tried, without much success, to found an Atheist Society at my school, the Methodist College in Belfast.

The principal cause of my atheism was Marxism, a movement that I believed held the key to the future. The late 1960s were a time of immense optimism concerning the future. It was widely believed that a new world was waiting to be born, and that we would not have long to wait before a new era of justice, peace, and freedom would emerge, sweeping away the discredited old order. Religion was part of that order, and I confidently believed that it would not be around for much longer. Attending a very religious school did little to increase my enthusiasm for faith. The progressive books that I read—such as Bertrand Russell's *Why I Am Not a Christian*—encouraged me to believe that mine would be the last generation to have to put up with this nonsense.

I had specialized in the natural sciences, hoping to go up to Oxford University to study chemistry after finishing high school. I was firmly of the view that the natural sciences offered perfectly adequate explanations for every aspect of reality. My views at this stage were very similar to those later expressed by Richard Dawkins. Religion was irrational superstition, which depended on blind faith on the part of very stupid people; science proved its theories for certain. It was an extremely simple worldview—probably deriving much of its appeal from precisely that simplicity—that I was able to maintain without undue difficulty. Until, that is, I began to study the history and philosophy of science in my final year at school, in preparation for going up to Oxford. Suddenly, things seemed rather more complicated and rather less straightforward than I realized.

Why did I then find atheism so attractive? I have no doubt that I, along with countless others, saw atheism as attractive for three interlocking reasons. First, it offered a break from the religious past. Northern Ireland had a long history of religious strife and violence; the elimination of religion would therefore lead to peace and prosperity within my troubled homeland. Like many, I longed for peace, and saw atheism as the solution to the world's problems. If religion was to be abolished throughout the world, how many fewer wars there would be!

Let me stress this point: the appeal of atheism for me lay in its proposal to eradicate religion. If atheism had represented itself simply as commending the merits of a godless worldview, I would not have been attracted to it—and neither would many others. Its lure lay in its proposal to change the world rather than to create a little club of the godless in the midst of a religious world. As Karl Marx had pointed out many years earlier, philosophers had merely offered interpretations of the world; what was really needed was a transformation. The atheist vision was totalizing—a panoramic view of a society that had been liberated from its chief enemy and oppressor, whether that was defined as God or religion (I knew just enough at this stage to appreciate that not all religions believed in God).

Second, atheism seemed to make a certain degree of sense of things. If there was no God, then life was what we chose to make of it. It was, in some ways, a rather bleak philosophy of life—but if it was right, who cared? Having read Camus and Sartre, I had come to the view that there was a real integrity, not to mention a certain degree of bravery, in embracing such an austere philosophy, which contrasted rather pleasingly with what I regarded as the superstitious delusions of Christianity. To my slightly confused way of thinking, the bleaker an outlook, the greater the chance of its being right in the first place.

But third, atheism offered hope—the hope of a better future and the possibility of being involved in bringing this future about. It has often been suggested that Marxism offers a secular messianic outlook, and I certainly found it to be so. There had to be a better future for humanity—and to enter and embrace that future demanded breaking with the oppression and superstitions of long ago. Atheism offered humanity the possibility of transforming itself, starting all over again without the encumbrance of outmoded ideas inherited from a distant past.

It was only when I went up to Oxford in 1971 to study chemistry in detail that I began to realize how little I knew about the history and philosophy of the natural sciences, or the nature of Christian belief. Like my fellow countryman C. S. Lewis, I found myself experiencing "the steady unrelenting approach of Him whom I so earnestly desired not to meet." To cut a long story short, I discovered that I had rejected what I did not really understand, and accepted what I increasingly came to realize was an imaginatively impoverished and emotionally deficient substitute. The trite antireligious slogans of writers such as Robert Ingersoll came increasingly to seem empty and uncomprehending as I began to discover a dimension to life that I had hitherto suppressed.

I do not for one moment imagine that I am typical of those who once embraced atheism and then lost their faith. With the passing of time since then, I have increasingly come to think that it is impossible to read the great works of the golden age of atheism without feeling a sense of distance, even dislocation. The conventional validations of atheism seemed to presuppose a social order that had long since vanished. Works of atheist propaganda seemed to relive long-forgotten battles; they paid disturbingly little attention to the more worrying aspects of the twentieth century, not least the highly ambivalent legacy of institutionalized atheism itself.

Writing this book has thus been an unsettling experience. It is like the Irishman who leaves his native land to settle in America, retaining fond memories of Ireland—memories made even fonder by a sense of dislocation, physical and cultural, from his homeland. As the years pass, those memories become increasingly romanticized, softened by the passage of time, tinged with nostalgia. On revisiting the homeland, some of its fondly remembered bright colors turn out to be rather drab, its idealized vast landscapes more cramped, and its cities more derelict than the memory allowed. The ideas that once excited and enthralled me seem, on being revisited, rather humdrum and mundane. The distorting effects of memory soon became clear to me; the rooms of the intellectual house I had once inhabited now appeared uncomfortably cramped, dingy, and stale. I had moved on, and, to my surprise, found less than I had expected in the revisiting to make me wish to move back.

In revisiting atheism, I found some of those familiar and much-loved places I recalled from my youth: a passion for liberation, a principled demand for an end to oppression, for intellectual rigor in our thinking, and for courage in the face of the world's evils and ambiguities. Yet I also became aware of the sheer humanity of the movement— its failures, both moral and intellectual, which jostled uneasily alongside its more publicized successes; its pathological sense of entitlement to sit at the head of the high table of religious discussion; and a disturbing ambivalence, even vulnerability, within the ideas and systems that I had once thought to be impregnable.

THE STALLED INTELLECTUAL CASE AGAINST GOD

It is increasingly recognized that philosophical argument about the existence of God has ground to a halt. The matter lies beyond rational proof, and is ultimately a matter of faith, in the sense of judgments made in the absence of sufficient evidence. As Thomas Huxley rightly pointed out, no such decision may be reached on the basis of the evidence available, forcing us to reach one of two conclusions: either no decision can be reached (a position that Huxley designated "agnosticism"), or a decision is reached on other grounds. As Blaise Pascal (1623–62) pointed out, "reasons of the heart" play a far greater role in shaping our attitudes to God than we realize.

The belief that there is no God is just as much a matter of faith as the belief that there is a God. If "faith" is defined as "belief lying beyond proof," both Christianity and atheism are faiths. While this suggestion might seem astonishing to some atheists, it is not only philosophically correct but also illuminating in shedding light on the changed fortunes of atheism in recent years. The strength of atheistic feeling has been directly proportional to that of its religious antithesis: with the weakening of religious faith in many parts of the West, especially Western Europe, there has been a concomitant erosion in the attractiveness of its atheistic alternatives. In the Western European context at least, a swelling public indifference toward religion has led to the loss of the potency of both poles of religious culture, Christianity and atheism.

In recent years there has been a growing recognition of the ultimate circularity of the great atheist philosophies of recent centuries. The explanations of the origin of the idea of God put forward by Feuerbach, Marx, and Freud have one all-important feature in common: they presuppose atheism. It is the fundamental assumption that there is not—indeed, that there cannot be—a God that prompts them to offer explanations of why perfectly intelligent human beings should think that there is a God to believe in. As there is no God, the origins of this idea must lie in the malfunctioning of the mind, the subtle influence of the human unconscious, or the complex social forces that shape our beliefs and values, often without our being aware of them. Yet when all is said and done, these explanations of religious belief start out from atheist premises and duly arrive at atheist conclusions. They are, in their own way, coherent: they are not, however, compelling. They simply offer an atheist explanation of religious belief, in much the same way as Christianity offers a theistic explanation of the same phenomenon. They explain observation on the basis of a preconceived standpoint;

they most emphatically do not establish that standpoint in the first place.

How can they? God is simply not an empirical hypothesis that can be checked out by the scientific method. As Stephen Jay Gould and others have insisted, the natural sciences are not capable of adjudicating, negatively or positively, on the God question. It lies beyond their legitimate scope. There is simply no logically watertight means of arguing from observation of the world to the existence or nonexistence of God. This has not stopped people from doing so, as a casual survey of writings on both sides of the question indicates. But it does mean that these "arguments" are suggestive and nothing more. The grand idea that atheism is the only option for a thinking person has long since passed away, being displaced by a growing awareness of the limitations placed on human knowledge and the need for humility in religious and antireligious advocacy.

There is an interesting and seldom noticed parallel between the arguments against the existence of God and the classic arguments for the existence of God set out by Thomas Aquinas in the thirteenth century. On close examination, Aquinas's arguments have Christian assumptions—for example, that there is a God, and that this God has created the world. The arguments then proceed to demonstrate that these beliefs are consistent with the way the world actually is. For example, Aquinas asks where human values such as truth, goodness, and nobility come from. What causes them? He argues that there must be something which is in itself true, good, and noble, and that this brings into being our ideas of truth, goodness, and nobility. The origin of these ideas, Aquinas suggests, is God, who is their ultimate cause.

A similar line of argument is found in Augustine of Hippo (354–430), who reasons that, on the basis of a Christian understanding of creation, it is to be expected that humanity will long for the presence of God. If we have been created to relate to God, there is something intrinsic in human nature that will cause us to yearn for God. As Augustine himself put it in a prayer to God: "You have made us for yourself, and our heart is restless until it finds its rest in you." The longing for God that Feuerbach regarded, on the basis of atheist premises, as a dysfunctional delusion, is seen by Augustine as the natural outcome of a humanity that mirrors the contours of the mind of God.

As has often been pointed out, such arguments as we find in Augustine and Aquinas are really addressed to Christian believers, intended to reassure them that their take on the world makes sense and is self-consistent. The existence of God is actually assumed; what is offered is a post hoc rationalization of that faith. In precisely the same way, the arguments of Feuerbach, Marx, and Freud really offer little more than a post hoc rationalization of atheism, showing that this position, once presupposed, can make sense of things. None of the three approaches, despite what their proponents claim, is any longer seen as a rigorously evidence-based, empirical approach that commands support on scientific grounds. Each sets out from, and duly returns to, atheist presuppositions. The journey may have been interesting, but it leads back to its starting point.

In terms of their impact and intrinsic interest, the arguments of these three atheist giants merit being placed alongside those of Aquinas. But none of these considerations—whether atheist or theist—are compelling, save for those prepared to accept their hidden presuppositions in advance of their more public conclusions. At a purely intellectual level, the arguments for both atheism and theism—whether based on reason or science—lead to a stalemate.

Perhaps the best way of appreciating this is to read the excellent recent dialogue between J.J.C. Smart and J. J. Haldane, published as *Atheism and Theism*, which demonstrates the possibility of a gracious and generous exploration of the issues while at the same time showing how purely rational arguments are incapable of resolving the issues. Knockdown and foolproof arguments simply are not available to us. It is for this reason that polemicists on both sides of the argument are so often reduced to rhetorical devices, bludgeoning their audiences into submission by crude verbal bullying rather than by careful evidence-based reasoning. The jury is out on this one: final adjudication on the God question lies beyond reason and experiment. Maybe T. H. Huxley was right: agnosticism is the only credible option here.

THE SUFFERING OF THE WORLD
AND ATHEISM

Atheist writers often appeal to the presence of suffering in the world as a decisive refutation of the existence of God. How can there be a God, when there is so much suffering and pain in the world? Annie Besant's influential book *Why I Do Not Believe in God* (1887) is typical of many atheist comments on this issue: "I do not believe in God. My mind finds no grounds on which to build up a reasonable faith. My heart revolts against the spectre of an Almighty Indifference to the pain of sentient beings. My conscience rebels against the injustice, the cruelty, the inequality, which surround me on every side. But I believe in Man. In man's redeeming power; in man's remoulding energy; in man's approaching triumph, through knowledge, love, and work." We find here a contrast between a God who is indifferent to human pain and sorrow, and a caring, loving humanity, passionately committed to the well-being of all.

Besant is typical of the many who echo Ivan Karamazov's inclination to hand God back his ticket. Who wants to believe in a God who is detached from the pain and sorrow of the world—who somehow evades the suffering of the world he is supposed to have created? For many, the trauma of Auschwitz can only mean the supreme triumph of atheism: who could believe in God in the face of such horrifying acts of violence and brutality?

It is only fair to point out that those who planned the Holocaust, and those who slammed shut the doors of the Auschwitz gas chambers, were human beings—precisely those whom Ludwig Feuerbach declared to be the new "gods" of the modern era, free from any divine prohibitions or sanctions, or any fear of future divine judgment. Annie

Besant does not seem to have dreamed that the humanity she so venerated could do such shocking, immoral, and inhumane things. If any worldview is rendered incredible by the suffering and pain of the twentieth century, it is the petty dogma of the nineteenth century, which declared that humanity was divine. It requires an act of blind faith that ignores the moral wasteland of the twentieth century to agree with the shallow judgment of Algernon Charles Swinburne (1837–1909): "Glory to man in the highest! / For man is the master of things." This "master of things" has much to answer for—more violence, bloodshed, and oppression than any naive Victorian optimist could ever have imagined.

Nearly two hundred years' experience of the moral failings of this humanity-turned-divinity have been enough to convince most that it has been a failed experiment. While some continue to argue that Auschwitz disproves the existence of God, many more would argue that it demonstrates the depths to which humanity, unrestrained by any thought or fear of God, will sink. There are many today who affirm a belief in humanity in preference to a belief in God. Yet this humanity has been responsible for a series of moral, social, and political catastrophes, some inspired by a belief in God, others by a belief that God must be eliminated, by all means and at all costs. The common denominator here is humanity, not divinity.

For some, the existence of God is called into question by suffering; for others, however, the presence of God is a consolation and support in suffering. For these, the existence of a God who suffers alongside humanity is a lifeline, without which they would sink into despair. The idea of a God who suffers alongside his people is already present in the Christian Bible. It was, however, developed in particularly significant directions by writers such as Dietrich Bonhoeffer (1906–45). For Bonhoeffer, "our God is a suffering God," one who bears our sin, pain, and anguish. The deepest meaning of the cross of Christ is that there is no suffering on earth that is not also borne by God. The church, for Bonhoeffer, is the continuing presence of the suffering Christ in history, a body of persons called to share in the messianic suffering of God by being there for others, carrying their burdens and thus fulfilling the duty laid on them by Christ himself. It is through suffering that Christians learn to turn the final outcome of their actions over to God, who alone can perfect them in glory. And it is in dying that they find true freedom as they meet God face to face. A suffering God, according to Bonhoeffer, has not abandoned his people. Far from it; he stands by them as a fellow sufferer, and will bring them home to a place from which suffering and pain have been removed.

The twentieth century witnessed much ink being spilled over the question of what the existence of suffering has to say about the existence of God. The results have been inconclusive, not least because there has been a growing realization that the debate is going precisely nowhere. As philosopher William Alston has pointed out, any logical argument which attempts to show that evil is logically incompatible with the existence of God "is now acknowledged on (almost) all sides" to be completely bankrupt. So if human reason cannot finally settle the matter, then it will have to be sorted out in other ways. And so attention has shifted away from reason to the human imagination. Might this be the battleground on which atheism finally triumphs, given the signal failures of religion to captivate the imagination of Western culture in the recent past?

THE IMAGINATIVE FAILURE
OF ATHEISM

The failure of the religious imagination in the late eighteenth and early nineteenth century was, as we have noted, a significant contributing factor to the erosion of faith. The human reason might persuade that something was *true*; it was, however, the human imagination that persuaded that it was *real*. As the nineteenth century proceeded, many concluded that Christianity—at any rate, in those Protestant forms that dominated Great Britain and North America—offered a rendering of reality that was less than compelling, a somewhat bleak and imaginatively impoverished account of things. In his remarkable work *Christ and Apollo* (1975), the Jesuit writer William Lynch pointed out that an appeal to the imagination was essential if Christian theology was to remain a viable option.

> The Christian faith should never think of itself as a conceptual bundle of ideas which must beg imaginative support from literature and art. This faith is also a life of the imagination—historical, concrete, and ironic. There will, hopefully, never be an end to collaboration between theology and literature, but it must be a collaboration of (theological) imagination with (literary) imagination. Otherwise theology loses its nerve and does not have the strength to collaborate with anything.

In the twentieth century, following the Great War, something of a rebirth of the "baptized imagination" took place, with a growing number of Christian writers rediscovering the potency of an appeal to the imagination. G. K. Chesterton, C. S. Lewis, J.R.R. Tolkien, Dorothy Sayers, and Flannery O'Connor might be mentioned by way of illustration. A rebirth of the Christian imagination was under way.

Yet curiously, atheism seems to have lost its appeal to the imagination around the time Western Christianity was rediscovering it, however tentatively. Why? What went wrong? Why did a worldview that proved the imaginative victor over a weary Christianity in the nineteenth century come to lose its crucial superiority in this area? The simplest answer lies in the history of the twentieth century.

Atheism invited humanity to imagine a world without God. For many in the eighteenth and nineteenth century, this was a morally compelling vision—a world in which humanity could think and do as it pleased, without having to look over its shoulder at some disapproving deity. In what seemed an intellectually and socially stifled situation, it was entirely understandable that many should dream of a world from which the tedium of social respectability had been eliminated, a world in which humanity was declared to be God and was hence free to do as it pleased. It was a pleasing vision, appealing to the imagination precisely because it was so obviously imaginary. In real life, Western culture continued to be dominated by belief in God, to the immense irritation of many, until the end of the Victorian era.

Yet the twentieth century brought about a radical transformation of things. It was no longer necessary to imagine a world without God. The Soviet Union represented precisely such an atheocracy. What humanity had previously been asked to imagine as presently unfulfilled had now come to pass. And the more people learned about the Soviet Union and its European dependencies, the less they liked what they saw. It was a world evacuated of God, to be sure—but the process of extraction appeared to have sucked that world dry of many of the vital stimuli for creativity and exhilaration. There were limits to the human imaginative capacity to laud the joys of Stalinism.

Yet there is a deeper failure here—a failure noted by Rowan Williams, archbishop of Canterbury, in his 2002 Raymond Williams memorial lecture, delivered at the Hay-on-Wye book festival. The archbishop points out that secularism, in common with modernity in general, "leaves us linguistically bereaved." For Williams, the secular tendency to set limits to what may be known, spoken, and depicted truncates the human potential by failing to "allow room for the inaccessible in what we perceive." The prohibition of even an attempt to engage with "agencies or presences beyond the tangible" seriously impoverishes humanity, which leads people to seek (illicitly, in the view of the atheist) a "spiritual" dimension to existence in the face of secularist protests that this cannot, or should not, be done. "Secularism fails to sustain the imaginative life and so can be said to fail; its failure may (does) produce a fascination with the 'spiritual.'"

The fundamental question implied throughout Williams's analysis will not go away. It is this: is there something about human nature that impels it to seek the spiritual? To press beyond the boundaries of the tangible? On an atheistic understanding of things, this is certainly not

the case: there are no "spiritual" realities save those of our own making, arising from the exigencies of our social location and the secret
dreams of our hearts. It may be a pleasing fiction to imagine that such
longings actually correspond to something; nevertheless, such initially
pleasant lines of thought might lead to a belief in the transcendent, and
hence a reversion to the intellectual servility of a bygone age. But the
thought will not go away.

On a Christian reading of things, such longings for God are only to
be expected. They are part of the way things are. Even the most modest
statement of a Christian doctrine of creation holds that God has created
human beings in order to love, cherish, and fulfill them. We have been
created to relate to God; if that relationship is absent, we experience a
sense of longing. This sense of yearning for something of real significance is, for writers as diverse as Augustine of Hippo and C. S. Lewis, a
disguised longing for none other than God. As Augustine put it, in a
prayer to God: "You have made us for yourself, and our heart is restless
until it finds its rest in you." Another prayer to make the same point is
attributed to Anselm of Canterbury (1033–1109), one of the greatest
thinkers of the Middle Ages: "Lord, give me what you have made me
want; I praise and thank you for the desire that you have inspired; perfect what you have begun, and grant me what you have made me long
for." For these writers, the deep human longing has its origins in God,
and can only find its true fulfillment in God. God is the name of the one
we have been looking for all our lives, without knowing it.

The experience of longing, of yearning for the transcendent, will be
interpreted by atheists along the lines suggested by Feuerbach, Marx,
or Freud. It is the outcome of psychological or sociological forces, and
cannot be assumed to correspond to anything real or transcendent beyond us. Yet the credibility of these great atheist systems themselves
has been seriously eroded, to the point where some see them simply as
arbitrary doctrines designed specifically to undermine religious belief.
The same experience that some put down to purely social, economic,
or psychological factors can easily be interpreted in a theistic manner—

as a God-given means of prompting humanity to find and achieve its true destiny by finding its rest in God.

THE REBIRTH OF INTEREST IN THE SPIRITUAL

Faith in God will die out by natural means, or it should be eliminated through forcible suppression. That, in a nutshell, was the expectation of the golden age of atheism. It was the certainty of an age, a secure belief for which Feuerbach, Marx, and Freud had offered robust and compelling philosophical, sociological, and psychological defenses. Religion was expected to disappear from all but the more primitive sections of Western culture. Yet by 1980 it was clear that these great prophecies had failed. As William S. Bainbridge and Rodney Stark pointed out in their magisterial study of Western religion, *The Future of Religion: Secularization, Revival, and Cult Formation*, "The most illustrious figures in sociology, anthropology and psychology have unanimously expressed confidence that their children—or surely their grandchildren—would live to see the dawn of a new era in which, to paraphrase Freud, the infantile illusions of religion would be outgrown."

But they have not been outgrown. If anything, the reverse is true. Perhaps Carl Jung was right when he argued that, in mythological archetypes, God's death is always followed by his resurrection. The cultural perception of the death of God has given way to a renewed interest in spirituality, to the astonishment and intense irritation of those who hold such things to be superstitious nonsense. In postatheist Russia, there has been a remarkable rebirth of interest in religion, found both in the resurgence of traditional religions, especially Russian Orthodox Christianity, and in popular flirtation with various new religions—including a growing interest in angels as means of mediating between earth and heaven. As Robert Fulford remarked in a 2001 column in the *National Post*:

It is a melancholy truth that most of us are wrong most of the time about the way the world is going. We watch it, we hear about it, we experience it, and usually we don't know what it means. Of all the smug and foolish delusions that were part of conventional wisdom when I was young in the middle of the 20th century, two stand out in memory. One was the idea that nationalism was a 19th-century concept, on its last legs. The other was that religion, as a force in worldly affairs, was slowly but inevitably fading away. At times I was stupid enough to believe both of these preposterous fallacies; but then, so was nearly everyone else.

The simple fact is that interest in religion has grown globally since the high-water mark of secularism in the 1970s, even in the heartlands of the West. A telling indicator of the resurgent popular interest in religion is the change in direction of the long-running television series *Star Trek*. Classic *Trek* episodes from the period 1966–69 were strongly influenced by the humanist philosophy of their creator, Gene Roddenberry. In a 1991 interview with *Humanist* magazine, Roddenberry dismissed religion as "nonsense—largely magical, superstitious things." Early *Star Trek* episodes were saturated with an ideology of the excellence of science, the triumph of logic, and the inevitability of progress. Religion was one of the evils of the past—along with poverty, prejudice, and war—that progress would leave behind. Religious beliefs were to be expected among the primitive alien societies favored by a visit from the starship *Enterprise*. But the crew of the *Enterprise*, enlightened modern progressives thoroughly familiar with Freud's advanced theories, themselves held no such beliefs. Religion was best left to the savages of the more backward parts of the galaxy, who had yet to discover the great eternal truths of psychoanalysis.

Roddenberry's death in 1991 led to the breaking of this outdated rationalist stranglehold on the program. Suddenly, the series aligned itself with the new interest in spirituality in American culture of the 1990s, rather than the time warp of the 1960s. Science and progress were toppled from their throne. Where Dr. Spock relied upon logic, Commander Chakotay preferred to trust in spirit guides. While *Star Trek* deliberately avoided the question of what religious beliefs were true, the message was clear: spirituality was a good thing. As a legitimate part of a cultured person's world, it was to be respected, not despised.

This new interest in things spiritual has swept through Western culture in the last decade. The burgeoning bookstore sections dealing with "Body, Mind, and Spirit" are a telling indicator of a shift in Western thought away from the world of the Enlightenment. This has not been welcomed by old-fashioned rationalists, who have seen their cherished deities of reason and logic dethroned, to be replaced with angels, spirits, forces—not to mention Jesus. Marxism—which was even declared to be a religion by several doubtless well-meaning theologians in the rather uncritical euphoria of the 1960s—has lost the appeal it once had for an alienated youth of yesteryear. Postmodern culture seems fed up with the rather boring platitudes of scientific progress and longs for something more interesting and exciting. Even those who try to get rid of religious beliefs often seem to end up by offering alternatives. The earlier episodes of *Star Trek* were obsessed with such fundamentally religious motifs as suffering, resurrection, and sacrifice, even if these were subtly restated in the cool and logical terms of modern science.

Early *Trek* episodes reflected the sociological wisdom of the late 1960s and early 1970s, which predicted with a confidence that now looks rather pathetic the demise of religion and emergence of a secular society. The problem was that most sociologists of the period were European, based in Germany or France, and made the fallacious (but to them, entirely natural) assumption that their local situations were determinative for the entire world. Religion was in decline in Western Europe; it was only a matter of time before the same thing happened everywhere. The fact that many of these sociologists were hostile to religious belief was conveniently overlooked by their supporters and inadequately understood by their foes. By the 1990s, confident predictions of the elimination of religion were a thing of the past. A new realism developed: religion is here to stay. One of the most important elements in this new evaluation of the situation is the growing attention paid by sociologists to Pentecostalism, a rapidly growing worldwide form of Christianity. In what follows, we shall explore why this development is of such importance to the observed waning appeal of atheism.

THE REMARKABLE CASE OF PENTECOSTALISM

As Christian writers such as John Henry Newman (1801–90) have consistently stressed, Christianity is a living organism, still in the process of evolving and developing. It has learned from its past failings and evolved away from those forms and structures that once attracted justifiable criticism. Without in any way ceasing to be Christian, it has learned to exist in more accountable and responsible forms. Thus the atheist criticism of the too cosy relationship between church and state in medieval and early modern Europe is regarded as having merit; yet this potentially compromising relationship is not of the essence of Christianity, but is a historical contingency arising from the evolution of medieval Europe. Christianity is not a historically fixed monochrome entity, but a diverse and dynamic faith that evolves in different manners at different points in history. That process of evolution is guided and stimulated by successes and failures, including—as Newman pointed out—valid criticism of the church from those outside its walls. The atheists who want to take potshots at Christianity end up shooting at a moving target. The rise of Pentecostalism illustrates this point particularly well, pointing to both the historically situated nature of atheist criticism of the church and the ability of Christianity to develop in new forms as it learns from the past.

In 1965 Harvard theologian Harvey Cox published *The Secular City*, a work arguing that Christianity would have to face up to a secularized culture that had no time for religion. Cox's work is a useful weathervane, slavishly following the dominant cultural trends of the time, faithfully echoing what leading sociologists were predicting rather than critiquing them. Yet everyone now knows that they were completely wrong, including, it seems, Cox himself. In his most recent book, *Fire from Heaven* (1996), Cox turns his attention to the spirituality of Pentecostalism, which he argues holds the key to the religious life of the twenty-first century. It is no longer secularism that holds the future for Christianity, but Pentecostalism—"a spiritual hurricane that has already touched half a billion people, and an alternative vision of the human future whose impact may only be at its earliest stages today." The book represents an about-face, a pointed and deliberate rejection of what seemed obviously true to its author—and to American academia—only thirty years earlier.

So what is this Pentecostalism, which has made such massive inroads globally since the Second World War, and has largely been ignored by sociologists until very recently? The origins of the movement are complex, but are usually traced back to the first day of the twentieth century—January 1, 1901. Charles Parham (1873–1929) had launched the Bethel Bible College in Topeka, Kansas, a few months earlier. One of his particular interests was the phenomenon of speaking in tongues, which is described in Acts 2:1–4. Most Christians had taken this to be something that happened in the early church, but was no longer part of the Christian experience. On New Year's Day, 1901, one of Parham's students experienced this phenomenon. A few days later, Parham experienced it for himself.

Parham began to teach about this apparent recovery of the gift of tongues. One of those who heard him speak was the African-American preacher William J. Seymour (1870–1922), who opened the Apostolic Faith Mission in Los Angeles in April 1906. Over the next two years, a major revival broke out, characterized by the phenomenon of speaking in tongues. The term "Pentecostal" began to be applied to the movement, taking its name from the Day of Pentecost—the occasion, according to the New Testament, when the phenomenon was first experienced by the early Christian disciples.

The movement spread rapidly in America, appealing especially to the marginalized. Unusually, it seemed to appeal to and be embraced by both white and African-American Christian groupings. Although Pentecostalism can be thought of as traditionalist in its Christian theology, it differs radically from other Christian groupings in placing emphasis on speaking in tongues and in its highly experiential forms of worship, which involve prophesying, healings, and exorcisms. A direct, transforming, personal encounter with God is seen as a normal feature of the Christian life. The worshiping style and lack of intellectual sophistication of the movement led to its being ignored by mainline denominations and the academy—including theologians, church historians, and, above all, sociologists. Yet after the Second World War, a new phase of its expansion paved the way for massive growth in the second half of the twentieth century.

The incident that brought Pentecostalism to wider public attention in the United States took place in Van Nuys, California, in 1960. The rector of the local Episcopalian church, Dennis Bennett, told his astonished congregation that he had been filled with the Holy Spirit and had spoken in tongues. Reaction varied from bewilderment to outrage; the local Episcopalian bishop promptly banned speaking in tongues from his churches. However, it soon became clear that others in the mainline denominations had shared Bennett's experience. They came out of their closet and made it clear that they believed that they had experienced an authentic New Testament phenomenon, which would lead to the renewal of the churches.

By the late 1960s it was evident that some form of renewal based on charismatic gifts (such as speaking in tongues) was gaining a hold within Anglican, Lutheran, Methodist, and Presbyterian circles. Perhaps most important of all, a growing charismatic movement began to develop within the Roman Catholic church. Using "Pentecostal" to describe this became problematic, as this term was used to refer to a family of churches—such as the Assemblies of God—which placed particular emphasis on speaking in tongues. Accordingly, the term "charismatic" was used to refer to movements within the mainline churches based upon the ideas and experiences of the Pentecostalist movement.

The Pentecostalist movement—which we shall here take to include charismatic groups within mainline churches—has changed considerably since the Second World War. The most obvious change is a massive surge in growth. It is now estimated that there are 500 million Pentecostalists in the world, with a very wide geographical distribution. Although the movement may be argued to have its origins primarily within African-American culture, it has taken root in South America, Asia, Africa, and Europe.

Why has this form of Christianity become so popular? Two factors are generally agreed to explain the growing global appeal of Pentecostalism. First, Pentecostalism stresses a direct, immediate experience of God and avoids the rather dry and cerebral forms of Christianity, which many find unattractive and unintelligible. It is thus significant that Pentecostalism has made significant inroads in working-class areas of the developing world that have been resistant to traditional forms of Protestantism, especially in traditionally Roman Catholic Latin America.

Second, the movement uses a language and form of communication that enables it to bridge cultural gaps effectively. Sociologist David Martin argues that the most important feature of Latin American Pentecostalism is its "indigenous character," pointing to the movement's remarkable ability to adjust itself and become "incarnate" in any culture, particularly in Africa and Asia.

In terms of the number of its adherents, Pentecostalism is already the most significant Christian alternative to Roman Catholicism. It has sidelined those Protestant groupings that once saw themselves as mainline. Nobody likes to be shunted off to the sidings like this, and there has been lots of grumpy sniping at Pentecostals from anxious Protestant intellectuals as a result. Yet the more perceptive of their number have realized that a massive transformation in global Christianity is taking place, and have urged their fellows to take the movement seriously. Harvey Cox's *Fire from Heaven* blazes a trail that many will need to explore. One of the reasons that Pentecostalism has succeeded is that mainline Protestantism has failed to meet the needs and aspirations of the marginalized and disadvantaged. The development of the charismatic movement within the Roman Catholic church in Brazil and other Latin American nations has radically changed the appeal of Christianity to the region. And the movement is spreading.

The wider relevance of Pentecostalism to the fortunes of atheism is not difficult to discern. Christianity is perfectly capable of reinventing itself (although Christians are careful to speak of this process in terms of renewing or reclaiming lost or neglected themes of apostolic Christianity). This new variant of Christianity is experientially grounded and socially activist, having no complex ecclesiastical hierarchy worth speaking of, thus bypassing many of the traditional grounds of criticism of Christianity. Atheist critiques originally aimed at the Christianity of French Roman Catholicism of the early eighteenth century prove ineffective against this new variant of faith. As Denys Turner pointed out in his witty inaugural lecture as Norris-Hulse Professor of Divinity at Cambridge University (October 2001), atheism has rather come to rely upon Christian traditionalism as a means of preserving its own identity:

> It is indeed extraordinary how theologically conservative some atheists are, and one might even speculate that atheists of this species have an interest in resisting such renewals of Christian faith and practice as might require the renewal of their rejection of it. I suppose it must be upsetting for atheists when the target of their rejection moves; for insofar as a moving Christian target does upset the atheist, it reveals, depressingly, the parasitical character of the rejection. So a static atheism can have no wish for a moving theism.

In part, atheism gained its appeal in the past through the failures of the churches, rather than on account of its own intrinsic merits. The appeal of atheism to many socially alienated individuals lay in their sense of disconnection and alienation from the churches, which often seemed to be located at a sociological address a million miles away from them. The churches spoke a language they could not understand, addressing realities they did not experience. Pentecostalism changed all that, engaging directly with the cultural, social, and experiential world of the masses. In many ways, Pentecostalism has become the new Marxism of the third world, displacing its secular rival for the affections and loyalty of the dispossessed. This is supremely the case in Latin America, which has seen Marxism, either as a philosophy in itself or as a significant secularizing influence within the Roman Catholic church, slip into headlong retreat in the face of massive Pentecostal expansion. But where, in some deplorable cases, Marxism made use of firing squads and force in securing its power base, Pentecostalism seems to put its trust in the power of God to change people's lives.

Pentecostalism is of importance to our story in another respect. For its sense of the immediacy of God's presence through the Holy Spirit is of potentially immense importance in repairing the felt loss of the presence of the divine in everyday life in the West. The rise of atheism mirrored the parallel erosion of any expectation of an encounter with divine reality in personal experience or group worship. Controversially, many historians suggest that the cause of this wearing away of the sacred within the secular was the Protestant Reformation—the movement that brought about massive change and reform within the Western European church in the sixteenth century. So can the Protestant Reformation be seen as somehow—however indirectly and unintentionally—having contributed to the rise of atheism? In what follows, we shall give thought to this provocative possibility.

8

DISCONNECTION
FROM THE SACRED:
PROTESTANTISM AND ATHEISM

T HE PROTESTANT REFORMATION OF THE SIXTEENTH CEN-
tury is a landmark in the history of Western thought, religious
and secular. The rise of Protestantism changed the shape of Western
European culture and had a decisive effect on the subsequent transformation of global culture. Protestant émigrés from Europe settling in
North America, especially during the first half of the seventeenth century, established their faith in that region, seeing themselves as a chosen people entering a new promised land. During the nineteenth
century, Protestant missionaries from North America and the United
Kingdom undertook an unprecedented level of evangelistic work in
Asia, Australasia, and Africa, with the result that Protestant forms of
Christianity became established far beyond their original homeland of
Western Europe.

To suggest a link between Protestantism and atheism might, at first
sight, seem improbable, perhaps even bizarre. How could a movement
so dedicated to the propagation of the Christian faith conceivably be
said to have encouraged the rise of atheism? In making this suggestion,
I am drawing together a number of scholarly studies of the origins and
development of Protestantism, which indicate that there is a significant

link between the movement and the emergence of atheism. Given the importance of this suggestion, however uncomfortable it may be for Protestants (among whom I unabashedly number myself), it is essential to explore its foundations, and, if it is found to be cogent, ask what its consequences might be.

Sociologists have often drawn attention to the radical changes in Western culture that are implicated in the rise of Protestantism. Protestantism was the preferred religion of the new middle classes, often enterprising tradesmen and artisans who felt that they were hindered in their economic and social advancement by the old social order of the Middle Ages. The traditionalist ethos of that period gave precedence to patrician families. There was little possibility of self-made people bettering their position through talent or achievements. By the end of the Middle Ages, a social revolution was under way in the cities of Western Europe. Power was shifting, sometimes slowly but always irreversibly, from the old patrician families to the mercantile middle classes.

It has often been noted that Protestantism had a special appeal to city populations, and especially the new urban middle classes. The new religion was seen as strongly supportive of the emerging individualism of the period. Martin Luther's doctrine of justification by faith alone is an example of this tendency to move away from a corporate understanding of society. Salvation was no longer determined by membership in the church, but by one's individual relationship with God. No longer was salvation dependent upon social position; it was a matter of the individual's relating correctly to God. The institution of the church, including its sacramental system and its priesthood, was no longer to be seen as essential to the individual's securing admission to heaven (although Protestant reformers such as Calvin stressed the importance of the church as a means of supporting believers in their spiritual development).

Protestantism may thus be seen as a religion with a particular concern for the middle classes. The history of the Reformation certainly supports this suggestion, indicating that those most hostile to Protestantism were generally drawn from the traditional upper classes and those most supportive from the middle classes. Even some apparent exceptions to this pattern fall smoothly into place on closer examination. For example, Calvinism had a strong appeal to the middle classes in France in the 1560s, but was also regarded favorably by some aristocrats. On closer examination, the aristocrats in question were generally middle-class entrepreneurs elevated to the aristocracy by virtue of their newly acquired wealth.

Interesting though this observation may be, it is still a long way from establishing any connection between Protestantism and atheism. In his famous work *The Protestant Ethic and the Spirit of Capitalism* (1904), Max Weber argued that there was an intrinsic connection between Protestantism and capitalism. Although this thesis has been widely challenged and is perhaps not adequately grounded in the historical evidence, it has drawn attention and study. Protestantism is seen to be allied to the cultural trajectories that have determined the shape of the modern Western world. This is not to adjudicate the question of whether modernity caused the rise of Protestantism, or vice versa; it is simply to note that some connection seems to exist. The connection with atheism lies in another feature of the modern era that is widely associated with the rise of Protestantism—the divorce of the realms of the sacred and secular.

THE DIVORCE OF THE SACRED AND THE SECULAR

A distinctive feature of the Reformation, particularly associated with the leading reformers Huldrych Zwingli and John Calvin, is the "desacralization" of nature. The distinction between the sacred and the secular is widely thought to have contributed to the rise of the natural sciences, which is particularly (but by no means exclusively) associated with Protestantism. The declaration that the natural world was not in any way sacred opened the way to its scientific investigation. There could be no religious obstacles to the analysis of the world. The world increasingly became seen as a machine or instrument—of divine origins, of course, but increasingly distant from God. The material world might have been created by God; it could not, however, convey the divine presence. God's presence was no longer channeled directly into the world through natural means; God had to be known *indirectly*.

Medieval Catholicism had a strong and pervasive sense of the presence of the sacred in the world, seeing an intimate, direct link between God and the world. The spiritual, social, and political worlds were interwoven and seen as inseparable. Every level of society was understood to be interlocked with another, in one vast organic entity that was ultimately grounded in God as its origin and source. Popular religion often centered on the affairs of rural communities, reflecting its rhythms and seasons. The agrarian needs of such a rural community—such as haymaking and harvesting—were firmly enmeshed in popular religious cults. Thus in the French diocese of Meaux in the early sixteenth century, religious cults were well established in which the saints were invoked to ward off animal and infant diseases, the plague, and eye trouble, or to ensure that young women found appropriate husbands. The direct connection of religion and everyday life was taken for granted. The spiritual and the material interconnected at every level.

As Eamon Duffy points out in *The Stripping of the Altars* (1992), a massive and well-researched study of traditional English religion on the eve of the Reformation, in popular Catholicism sacred and secular times, events, and places were so closely associated that they were often indistinguishable. The rhythms of the year were primarily determined by the feast days of the church and the necessities of agriculture. The individual had a strong sense of place within a cosmos that radiated the glory of God and displayed a divine structure. The sacred was present within the world's events, rhythms, and patterns. One expected to encounter and experience the divine in everyday life.

The Protestant reformers were strongly critical of any such suggestions. Not entirely without reason, they suspected that medieval Catholicism occasionally degenerated into a folk religion of nature. An immediate encounter with God through nature was excluded, almost as a matter of principle. God had chosen to reveal himself through the Bible, and the authorized mode of knowing God was therefore through reading that Bible, and hearing sermons based upon its contents. The architecture of Protestant churches was developed in accordance with this emphasis. Whereas medieval Catholicism saw the focus of worship as the altar of the church, the pulpit now became the focal point of Protestant worship. Attention was thus shifted away from the idea of a direct presence of God in the sacramental bread and wine to an indirect manner of knowing God through preaching.

Throughout the Middle Ages, God was held to be encountered in the natural world and through the sacramental mysteries of baptism and the mass. Whatever risks such an understanding entailed, it nevertheless affirmed that it was possible to experience God in the patterns of day-to-day living. This point was developed further by medieval mystics—such as Meister Eckhart (1260–1327)—who argued for a direct encounter between the believer and God. In the seventeenth century, the church made some halfhearted attempts to control the influence of mystics, generally by stressing the importance of revelation channeled through the centralized authority of the church. Yet the fundamental principle that the sacred could be known through and be present in the secular, the spiritual in and through the material, was not challenged.

Protestantism, on the other hand, insisted that the ways and will of God were to be known through the Bible, and preaching based on that sacred text. For the great Swiss reformer Huldrych Zwingli, this knowledge tended to take the form of *information*—for example, the great foundational truths of the Christian faith, or the moral duties of believers. For medieval Catholicism, the Mass made Christ physically present for believers, as an object of adoration and devotion. For Zwingli, the Lord's Supper reminded believers of Christ's death, and its implications for humanity in Christ's absence. Where Catholicism allowed a direct encounter between the believer and spiritual realities, Zwingli resolutely refused to acknowledge that spiritual realities could ever be known through the material world. Christ was in heaven; Christian worship was about recalling what Christ had done in the past and looking forward to his future return. But in the present—in the here and now—Christ was known only as an absence.

The rise of Protestantism thus gave rise to an absent God who was known only indirectly—and then through the mind rather than the imagination. For Protestants, especially those tracing their lineage back to Calvin or Zwingli, there can be no sense of sacred space or place— no possibility of a direct encounter with the sacred or an experience of the divine other than that which is mediated indirectly through reading the Bible and the public exposition of its message. The Bible sets out God's will and God's ways, providing information about what was to be believed and what was to be done. Preaching and the study of the Bible were seen as being of supreme importance in bringing about a sound knowledge of God. But this knowledge all too often took the form of direct familiarity with the Bible, and a highly indirect and circumspect knowledge of God.

The outcome was inevitable and predictable. God became an absence in the world. Where Catholic writers might speak of the world's being "charged with the grandeur of God" (a phrase attributed to the Jesuit poet Gerard Manley Hopkins), Protestant writers tended to think of God in terms of a divine architect or mechanic. It was very clear what God required people to believe and do; a direct knowledge of the living presence of God was, however, regarded as theologically unsound. Any sense of immediate contact with the divine was thus excluded from nature, which was "disenchanted" (Max Weber).

By the end of the seventeenth century, Protestant theology was seen as spiritually dry and dusty, of interest only to those with a troubling obsession with pure ideas. The idea that God could be encountered directly was considered dangerous. One of the most significant reactions against this bookish conception of an absentee God is found in Pietism, which argued that God could be known through the personal experience of believers. It was possible to feel the living presence of Christ in the soul, and thus be reassured of God's love and care. Consider, for example, a verse from Charles Wesley's hymn "And Can It Be?" (1738), which speaks of a subjective conviction of the truth and relevance of faith:

> Still the small inward Voice I hear,
> That whispers all my Sins forgiv'n;
> Still the atoning Blood is near,
> That quench'd the Wrath of hostile Heav'n:
> I feel the Life his Wounds impart;
> I feel my Saviour in my Heart.

This remarkable hymn speaks of Christ as a living experienced reality—something that Wesley clearly expected his audiences to share and appreciate.

Pietism was an important correcting influence in Protestantism, restoring an awareness of the possibility of experiencing God directly in everyday life. Yet the dominant voices of mainline Protestant orthodoxy presupposed a disembedded God—a God who was now dislocated from the world of nature, culture, and human experience. It is a relatively small step conceptually from an absentee God, who is uninvolved in the workings of an autonomous natural world and who cannot be known directly, to a God who does not exist. The God of Protestant orthodoxy, as Thomas Hobbes pointed out, might as well not exist, in that his supposed existence seemed to make very little difference to anything. A permanently absent God can quickly become a dead God. If the existence of God makes little or no impact upon the experiences of everyday life, the business of living might as well be conducted without reference to Him. As Hugo Grotius (1583–1645), the great Dutch Protestant lawyer, pointed out, the end result of all this was a world in which people lived *etsi Deus non daretur*, "as if God did not exist." Many were happy to make the increasingly easy jump from a pragmatic atheism (we will live as if there is no God) to an ontological atheism (there really is no God).

This point has been stressed by a series of sociologists—including Max Weber, Charles Taylor, and Stephen Toulmin—who have, in their different ways, shown how Protestantism was the means by which a society that originally possessed a strong sense of the sacred became "desacralized" or "disenchanted," eventually leading to a culture which, to all intents and purposes, had no sense of God's presence in its midst. The inevitable result of this was secularization—the final elimination of God from the world. As Francis Fukuyama points out in his *End of History and the Last Man* (1992), "the generally accepted agent for this secularization in the West was Protestantism."

Why is this point so important? At a recent conference in Oxford, which brought together leading Christian writers and statesmen from across the world, I had the opportunity of exploring some of the themes of this book with some senior Christians from Nigeria, Kenya, Uganda, and Tanzania. They found themselves having some difficulty appreciating the plausibility or attraction of atheism. From their African perspective, everything about the natural world and human existence proclaimed the existence of a spiritual reality. The sense of a divine presence within nature and human experience was self-evident. Many villagers throughout this region are highly aware of spiritual forces, which they often seek to consult or control through a complex system of divinations, charms, and spells. With the arrival of Christianity, these spiritual forces are understood to have been tamed or conquered—though not eliminated—through the death and resurrection of Christ. The Christian gospel is interpreted in terms of deliverance from spiritual oppression, release from the power of curses, and liberation from the baleful influence of ancestors. Significantly, my colleagues commented that the only part of Africa in which atheism had secured any meaningful presence was the highly Westernized (and largely Protestant) nation of South Africa; even then, the movement seems to be limited to the white population.

A major determinant for atheism is whether a sense of the divine has been eliminated from a culture. The absence of any expectation of encountering the divine directly through nature or in personal experience inevitably encourages belief in a godless world—a world that lives *etsi Deus non daretur,* "as if God did not exist." The charge against Protestantism is that it has brought about precisely such an erosion of any sense of direct encounter with the divine. Protestantism can respond, with excellent grounds for doing so, that the expectation of an encounter with the divine can lead to paganism, idolatry, or the vagueness of a nature religion. Far better to limit such knowledge of God to what can be known reliably about God through reading or studying the Bible. Yet by limiting knowledge of God to what can be known about God's words and God's will, some highly influential forms of Protestantism have ended by placing an embargo on any direct knowledge or experience of God. It is a high price to pay.

Protestantism is open to another related criticism—namely, that it has impoverished the Christian imagination, and by doing so, made atheism appear imaginatively attractive. For Protestantism has been severely critical of any appeal to imagery in the Christian life, holding that words are to be preferred to images in representing God. As we shall see, this understandable concern has once more had unintended consequences.

THE IMAGINATIVE FAILURE OF PROTESTANTISM

Medieval Christianity valued the importance of imagery, seeing this as a vitally important means of keeping the people of Europe in direct contact with the realities of faith. The distinctive architecture of Gothic cathedrals was intended to accentuate a sense of spaciousness and light, anticipating the Christian hope of heaven. As Bonaventure (1221–74), the great Franciscan theologian of the Middle Ages, pointed out, imagery played a vitally important role in Christian piety and spirituality. Religious images enabled the less educated members of the church to learn about their faith, offering anchor points for theological education. The wisdom of this insight is evident from the church architecture of the era: the altarpieces of the great churches of the Renaissance helped to stress the importance of the crucified Christ, and imprint the scene in the "baptized imagination." Furthermore, Bonaventure noted that since human "emotions are excited more by what is seen than what is heard," images offered a far greater capacity to stimulate personal devotion among the faithful.

This use of images seemed entirely natural to medieval Catholicism. If the Bible spoke of heaven, why not try and depict heaven visually, to help the faithful focus on it? After all, the Bible used images—such as the "New Jerusalem"—to depict heaven; why not allow the believing imagination to linger on these images? If the Gospels placed great weight on the devotional and theological importance of the Crucifixion, why not depict this artistically in altarpieces, or represent it in wooden carvings?

While the great theologians of the era—such as Thomas Aquinas and Bonaventure—were careful to insist that it was not the physical image itself, but the transcendent reality to which it pointed, that was the proper object of Christian adoration and reflection, there is no doubt that religious paintings, stained-glass windows, sculptures, and woodcuts came to play a very significant role in popular Catholic devotion. It was widely assumed that physical images—such as altarpieces, crucifixes, statues of saints, and manuscript illuminations—were invaluable aids in maintaining the public presence of divine realities in the culture of the day.

Worship was seen as a means of connecting up with the divine—of anticipating entry into heaven and imagining what is encountered. It is impossible to understate the place of worship in sustaining the Christian life in the Greek and Russian Orthodox churches. Especially within the Greek Orthodox tradition, in public worship the faithful seek to draw close to the threshold of heaven itself and peer through its portals to catch a glimpse of the worship of heavenly places. The Orthodox liturgy celebrates the notion of being caught up in the worship of heaven, and the awesome sense of mystery that is evoked by gazing beyond the bounds of human vision.

In the Orthodox view of things, whenever the divine liturgy is celebrated on earth, the boundaries between heaven and earth are removed, and earthly worshipers join in the eternal heavenly liturgy chanted by the angels. During these moments of earthly adoration, worshipers have the opportunity of being mystically transported to the threshold of heaven. Being in a holy place and about to participate in holy things, they on the one hand become aware of their finitude and sinfulness, and on the other gain a refreshing glimpse of the glory of God.

The idea of liminality—that is, being on the threshold of the sacred, peering into the forbidden heavenly realms—is represented visually in the structure of Orthodox churches, especially the way in which the sanctuary and the altar are set apart from the people, thereby enhancing the awesomeness of the mystery of God. In their treatises on worship, John Chrysostom and other early Greek-speaking Christian writers repeatedly draw attention to the liturgical importance of this sense of the sacred. The altar is the "terrifying table"; the bread and the wine are "the terrifying sacrifice of the body and blood of Christ which worshippers must approach with fear and trembling." For the Orthodox, there is an especially close link between the Eucharist— the sacrament celebrated with and through bread and wine—and the experience of the worship of heaven. Although physically located in the empirical world, the worshiper is transported over the mystical threshold of heaven, and enabled to anticipate its future delights. Religious imagery (especially icons) and architecture serve to focus the worshiper's attention on the transcendent.

The Protestant Reformation saw any such use of imagery in worship subjected to devastating criticism. Although Martin Luther opposed the abuse of religious images, he had no doubt of their positive role in stimulating and informing the Christian imagination. Christian pedagogy and devotion were aided by images as much as by words. Yet Luther would be a minority voice in this debate. Religious unrest often led to the violent destruction of religious images at the hands of angry crowds. Had not the Second Commandment (Exodus 20:4–5) forbidden making images, or worshiping them? Throughout Western Europe, the Reformation was generally accompanied by the smashing of religious statues in churches and the whitewashing of their walls to destroy imagery. Nothing would be allowed to remain that could become the object of false worship for believers.

This concern is particularly well expressed by Huldrych Zwingli, whose reforming ministry was based in the city of Zurich. While conceding that religious images had considerable imaginative potential, Zwingli believed that this was more likely to lead people away from the true religion rather than confirm them in its truths. Images of God or Christ were held to be potentially idolatrous, and were not to be tolerated within churches. Protestant churches should be devoid of anything that would distract from the preaching of the word. In Zwingli's view, churches should have plain, whitewashed walls, to prevent worshipers from thinking about anything other than the sermon and the reading of the Bible.

John Calvin shared this critical attitude toward religious imagery. It has often been pointed out that Calvin's views on the manner in which buildings designed for public worship should be decorated resonate with those of Islam. No portrayals of God in human form were to be permitted within churches. It was, Calvin suggested, all too easy for something created to be confused with the creator. It was to open the way to idolatry, "to imagine or possess something in which to put one's trust in place of or in addition to the one true God who has revealed himself in his word." For Calvin, the point is not simply that God should not be pictured; it is that God is intrinsically incapable of being pictured.

While many Roman Catholic churches around this time adopted elaborate styles of ornamentation, with extensive use of visual aids to piety in the form of religious images and portraits, these were rigorously excluded from Calvinist places of worship. While it would be inaccurate to say that Protestantism was intrinsically iconophobic, there is no doubt that a profound mistrust of any form of imagery is characteristic of the movement. There is perhaps more than a hint of intellectual superiority in the Calvinist *Heidelberg Catechism* (1563). Calvinists do not need visual images of God, being perfectly capable of understanding and making full use of the wide range of verbal images conveyed in Scripture:

QUESTION 96. What does God require in the [second] commandment?

ANSWER: That we should not portray God in any way, nor worship him in any other manner than he has commanded in his Word.

QUESTION 97. So should we not make any use of images?

ANSWER: God cannot and should not be depicted in any way. As for creatures, although they may indeed be depicted, God forbids making use of or having any likeness of them, in order to worship them or to use them to serve him.

QUESTION 98. But should we allow pictures instead of books in
churches, for the benefit of the unlearned?

ANSWER: No. For we should not presume to be wiser than God,
who does not want Christendom to be taught by means of dumb
idols, but through the living preaching of his Word.

The religious concerns that lay behind the Reformation ought to
be respected. There is no doubt that religious imagery was abused
during the Middle Ages, often being seen as objects of adoration in
their own right, rather than as means of focusing the mind on the
transcendent reality they were intended to point to. For writers such
as Calvin, the use of images in personal worship or personal devotion
could distract from the "word of God," or compromise the critical distinction between the realm of the created and its ultimate ground in
God himself. Yet this concern for theological correctness was achieved
at a price. God ceased to be a living reality in the popular Protestant
imagination.

The contrast with Roman Catholicism and Eastern Orthodoxy on
this point could not be greater, in that both were convinced of the need
to engage with the human capacity to imagine. Convinced of the importance of the imagination in nourishing personal faith, the Roman
Catholic church sought to challenge the Protestant Reformation at the
level of church decoration as well as in the more abstruse arena of theology. The period of the high baroque in the seventeenth century made
extensive use of all the visual arts—architecture, painting, and sculp-
ture—to create ensembles intended to exert an overwhelming emotional impact on worshipers and visitors. Classic examples of this style
include the crossing of St. Peter's Basilica and the Cornaro Chapel in
the Church of Santa Maria della Vittoria, both in Rome. The intention
was to imprint the realities of the Catholic faith on the minds of the
faithful through a deliberate appeal to the senses. Originating in Italy,
the new style was soon taken up in Spain, Southern Germany, and Austria. Churchgoers could listen to the proclamation of spiritual realities

and have them reinforced by the visual art and architecture around them.

Protestantism offered a God who was known through the preaching of the word of God; Roman Catholicism, while not being inattentive to the importance of preaching, reinforced that message visually. Slowly but surely, any sense of God as a living, engrossing reality began to slip from Protestantism. The dull, joyless, and unattractive churches of Protestantism conveyed the subliminal message that the God who was to be found in them shared these disagreeable characteristics. Protestantism has been chided by many cultural analysts for its failure to stimulate the arts. The great Welsh poet R. S. Thomas castigated the movement for this failure, dubbing it "the adroit castrator of art" and "the bitter negation of song and dance and the heart's innocent joy." Our concern is, however, rather more profound. Protestantism encouraged the notion that God was absent from human culture and experience.

A substantial part of my activity as a scholar focuses on the history and thought of the Protestant Reformation. As a result, I am a frequent visitor to some of the great centers of the movement, including Zurich. I have often sat within the Great Minster of that city, looking around its vast interior, unadulterated by imagery or decoration, and noting the values it affirms—most notably, the absolute priority accorded to preaching, made clear by the size and location of the pulpit. Its simplicity is admirable, and totally in conformity with the spirit of Zwingli's reform program of the 1520s. But the building speaks subtly of a silent, absent, and distant God. The Protestant reluctance to picture God has all too often led to an envisioning of the world that is bleak and barren, where it ought to be saturated with the radiance of the glory of God. Once more, it is a small step from declaring that God cannot be pictured to suggesting that he cannot be conceived as a living reality in the rich imaginative life of humanity.

THE ATHEIST CHALLENGE AND THE
FUTURE OF PROTESTANTISM

A book on atheism cannot be anything other than controversial. Indeed, it might be argued that anyone dealing with the topic who neglects to be contentious has failed to do justice to it. Given the complexity of the issues and the clear absence of agreement within society, such a work can hope to encourage debate, but hardly settle the matter. If the arguments presented in this chapter are correct—which I believe them to be—there are clear implications for the futures of both Protestant Christianity and atheism, not least that certain traditional forms of Protestantism will decline further, while those which affirm and celebrate a direct engagement with the divine will grow at the expense of the former. I can only present this as something for debate, not something that has in any way been settled. Yet given the importance (and intrinsic interest!) of this point, I propose to explore it further, asking what its implications might be for the future of Protestantism.

It might reasonably be argued that Protestantism is perfectly capable of responding to such criticisms by rediscovering some of its foundational themes, as they are found, for example, in the works of Martin Luther. Only a form of Protestantism that is obsessed by theological correctness, and fails to articulate the experiential aspects of faith, is vulnerable at this point. It is true that within both the mainline Protestant denominations and the evangelical constituency there are some who commend a purely "text-centered" understanding of the Christian faith, seeing preaching as nothing more than teaching the contents of the Bible and spirituality as a deepened understanding and internalization of its message. Yet, as the rise of Puritanism, Pietism, and "experiential religion" in England and elsewhere in the seventeenth and eighteenth centuries makes clear, it is entirely possible to develop an approach to Christianity that is rigorously grounded in theological principles, yet sees these as laying the foundation for an encounter with the living God.

Nevertheless, some sects of Western Protestantism, often deeply influenced by the rationalism of the Enlightenment, continue to this day to place an emphasis upon "theological correctness," stressing the overarching importance of having right ideas about God. These prescribed notions of God are to be determined by a reading of the Bible, which is understood primarily as a doctrinal handbook. Faith thus becomes an indirect knowledge of God, stated in terms of beliefs about God which, however correct they may be as far as they go, convey the impression that Christianity is little more than abstract theorizing about a God whose will is revealed in the Bible. The mind is engaged; the emotions and imagination remain untouched. Historically, it is precisely such a spiritually and imaginatively impoverished reading of Christianity that resulted in Hugo Grotius's argument that people of his day had come to live and think *etsi Deus non daretur*.

The contrast with Pentecostalism on this point could not be greater. Pentecostalism's emphasis on a direct, immediate experience of God avoids the rather dry and cerebral forms of Christianity that many find unattractive and unintelligible. It is thus significant that Pentecostalism has made huge inroads in working-class areas of Latin America, Africa, and Asia, in that it is able to communicate a sense of the divine and its implications without the need for prayer books and the other traditional paraphernalia of Protestant culture.

As we noted earlier, Pentecostalism is the fastest-growing form of Protestant Christianity, having established itself firmly throughout Asia, Africa, and Latin America in the second half of the twentieth century, and shed any characteristics associated with its original North American context. This dramatic and rapid expansion has taken many by surprise. At the time of writing (2003), there are estimated to be more than half a billion Pentecostals throughout the world. Although unquestionably a global movement, it has shown itself able to adapt itself to a wide variety of cultural contexts, developing distinctive local characteristics in response.

Pentecostalism declares that it is possible to encounter God directly and personally through the power of the Holy Spirit. God is to be known immediately and directly, not indirectly through study of a text. Whereas traditional Protestantism is wary of allowing any such direct experience of God, Pentecostalism celebrates it and makes it a hallmark of Christian living. God impacts upon the totality of existence, and is not confined—as in some traditional Protestant traditions—to the world of the mind. Walter Hollenweger, the most distinguished historian of the movement to date, points to the importance of this aspect: "When you become a Pentecostal, you talk about how you've been healed, or how your very life has been changed. That's something that Pentecostals talk about over and over, partly because people are interested in hearing that sort of thing. Pentecostalism today addresses the whole of life, including the thinking part. More mainline forms of Christianity address the thinking part first, and that often affects the rest of life—but not always." This may be contrasted with what Harvey Cox describes as "text-orientated believers"—that is, those Protestants who believe that God can only be accessed (and then to a limited extent, in the form of abstract religious ideas) through reading the Bible or hearing an expository sermon. For Cox, Pentecostalism celebrates the resurgence of "primal spirituality" and absolutely refuses to allow its experience of God to be limited to ideas. God is experienced and known as a personal, transformative, living reality.

If the analysis that we have sketched in this chapter has any validity, it is this form of Protestantism that may be expected to resist erosion by atheism. Pentecostalism is strongly predisposed toward the dispossessed and oppressed, undermining one of the most effective atheist critiques of religion—that it oppresses. Just as significantly, Pentecostalism offers a direct, personal, transformative encounter with God in the worship of the church and in personal experience. On discussing the issues raised in this book with leading Pentecostals, especially in the great urban sprawls of Asia, I found them responding with an appeal to their experience. How can God's existence be doubted, when God is such a powerful reality in our lives? And how can God's relevance be doubted, when God inspires us to care for the poor, heal the sick, and work for the dispossessed?

On the basis of recent statistics, Pentecostalism is by far the largest strand of Protestantism, and shows continuing growth patterns globally. This has not really impacted as yet on Western observers, as this explosive growth has taken place outside Western Europe and North America. Yet the globalization of the movement is well under way. The immigration of Asian and African Christians to the cities of the West has made Pentecostalism a growing presence. Will it eventually come to have the influence in the West that it now has in the developing world? And if so, what are the implications for the slowly setting sun of atheism?

Alongside these developments, however, another must be noted. It has often been pointed out that atheism is the ideal religion of the modern period, reflecting its ideas, values, and agendas. Modernism has decisively shaped Western culture. Yet as Tennyson pointed out many years ago in his poem *In Memoriam*, things change: "Our little systems have their day, / They have their day, and cease to be." If there is a symbiotic relationship between atheism and modernity, what happens if that synergy is ruptured through radical cultural change? Or if modernity were to die, to give way to a quite different cultural system in the West? Or if a new worldview arose out of a revolt against precisely what modernity cherished? The reason for asking these questions is simple: in the view of many analysts, this is precisely what has happened through the rise of postmodernity, with important—and largely negative—implications for atheism.

9

POSTMODERNITY:
ATHEISM AND RADICAL
CULTURAL CHANGE

I N 1972, STEPHEN JAY GOULD AND NILES ELDREDGE proposed a theory of biological evolution that has since come to be known as punctuated equilibrium. This holds that most evolution occurs in short bursts, interspersed with long periods of stability. Gould and Eldredge attacked the idea that organisms continually change, adapting by small degrees to fit their environment. Where Charles Darwin had viewed evolution as a slow, continuous process, without sudden jumps, Gould and Eldredge noted that the fossils of organisms found in successive geological strata indicated long intervals in which nothing changed (hence "equilibrium"), "punctuated" by short, revolutionary transitions, in which species became extinct and were replaced by wholly new forms. New species appear in large numbers over short periods, perhaps because of dramatic events such as asteroid impacts. Gould—perhaps the most influential and best-known evolutionary biologist since Charles Darwin—was widely criticized by more conventional Darwinists, who dubbed his theory "evolution by jerks."

The relevance of this to our discussion? A culture also undergoes change—sometimes slowly over many years, sometimes with such speed that the settled assumptions of generations are overthrown, even inverted, within a single generation. After periods of relative stability, massive change can take place, often without much warning that this is about to happen. What was entirely plausible in one cultural context now becomes seen as eccentric, possibly even irrational. The same belief may appear as the accepted wisdom of the age at one point, and fifty years later be regarded as hopelessly old-fashioned and outdated. Our story in this chapter concerns two massive cultural upheavals, one at the dawn of the golden age of atheism, the other at its closing.

The first such upheaval is the rise of modernity—a confident, ebullient movement, convinced of the supreme ability of human reason to understand the world and hence to master and control it. There was no longer any need for a God to confirm or underwrite a settled and stable order of moral values, social relations, or rules of thought. All could be established with certainty and universality through human reason. Atheism was the religious belief of choice for this movement, in that it resonated profoundly with its presuppositions and goals. It is no accident that the rise of atheism in the West is so closely tied to that of modernity; they are as two sides of the same coin.

Yet the excesses, failures, and ultimately the uninhabitability of modernity led to a loss of enthusiasm for its goals, and eventually a complete inversion of many of its leading ideas. Far from providing eternal and universal truths of reason, by which humanity might live in peace and stability, modernity found itself implicated as the perhaps unwitting accomplice of Nazism and Stalinism. Certainty, once prized as the goal of true knowledge, now came to be seen as the grounds for coercing belief. Reacting against the simplistic overstatements of the Enlightenment, postmodernity has stressed the limits to human knowledge, and encouraged a toleration of those who diverge from the "one size fits all" philosophy of modernity. The world in which we live is now seen as a place in which nothing is certain, nothing is guaranteed, and nothing is unquestionably given.

In this new outlook, the best we can hope for is to know partially rather than totally. The Enlightenment stereotype of the all-knowing mind has been replaced by the image of the searcher, questing for truth as she journeys through an ambivalent and complex world, where simple answers are likely to be wrong answers. Atheism, as a totalizing system, is ill at ease in such a world, whose growing openness to the spiritual aspects of life has led to a resurgence of interest in religion and the realm of the transcendent. The symbiosis between atheism and modernity has proved to be the Achilles' heel of the movement. The decline, then death, of modernity has robbed its partner of its self-evident plausibility and appeal. While all religions have been affected in some way by the rise of postmodernity, its most significant casualty has been atheism itself. The established religion of modernity suddenly found itself relegated to the sidelines, increasingly to be viewed more as a curiosity than as a serious cultural option.

Why is this point of relevance? One of the most striking features of Nietzsche's account of the "death of God" is that this rests on a cultural perception. God has not been argued out of existence; a cultural mood developed, which tended to see God as something of an irrelevance, and relegated him to the sidelines. Yet culture is not static; it continues to change. What if a new cultural shift took place, rekindling interest in the spiritual and reacting against the very ideas that once made atheism such an attractive option? For that, in a nutshell, is what many observers consider to have happened in the last few decades, as modernity faltered, uncertain of its own values, and unwillingly gave way to postmodernity.

The importance of this major cultural transition naturally leads us to consider the matter in more detail. We begin with the dawn of the modern era in the West.

THE BIRTH OF MODERNITY

At some point around 1750, a massive cultural shift began in the West, as the movement that we know know as modernity came into being. The new movement dawned slowly, its illuminating rays taking longer to penetrate some of the darker corners of the West than others. Yet there was no doubt as to what was happening. An older way of looking at the world, of understanding the place of humanity in the universe, was dying. In its place, a new outlook was coming to birth. It is easy to point to landmarks defining this transition to modernity, such as the American and French Revolutions, following in quick succession. Its fundamental themes were clear: humanity was already fully in possession of the resource it needed to master the world—reason.

It is no historical accident that the reemergence of atheism as a serious intellectual option dates from the dawn of modernity. Atheism is the religion of the autonomous and rational human being, who believes that reason is able to uncover and express the deepest truths of the universe, from the mechanics of the rising of the sun to the nature and final destiny of humanity. There is a single, universal rationality, which human beings are able to identify and uncover through the appropriate use of rational reflection and scientific experimentation. A unified, coherent worldview could be created from the fragmentation that defines existence. It was a powerful, self-confident, and aggressive worldview. Possessed of a boundless confidence, it proclaimed that the world could be fully understood and subsequently mastered. Barriers to this understanding and conquest could be swept aside as irrational, reactionary, and pointless.

The modernist emphasis on the explicability of the world led to an impatience with what was seen as intellectual pussyfooting. There was only one correct, rational way of viewing the world; the important thing was to identify that privileged position, from which everything could be seen in its proper perspective—and kept there. The right use of reason permitted the intelligent human being to rise above the world and see everything from this unique and omnicompetent vantage point.

Atheism was perfectly suited to this rational and logical worldview. It was the established religion of modernity. There was no God. But from the privileged vantage point of modernity, it was possible to see why some very sad and misguided people should believe that there was—and how others, more worryingly, could use religion as a means of exploiting and oppressing such naive fools. The theories of Feuerbach, Marx, and Freud both explained the origins of the human illusion of God and allowed the idea to be controlled. Atheism did not give permission or create free space to believe in God—a belief that it regarded as irrational, reactionary, or just plain mad. The believer was thus relegated to the category of the subnormal or the subversive—both of which were threats to modernity, and hence demanded to be controlled. Soviet-style communism, having thus explained the origins of religion on ideological grounds, was able to control this irrationality—for example, through the education process and the use of psychiatric hospitals, both of which allowed those who stepped out of line with modernist orthodoxy to be controlled and neutralized.

A leading theme of modernity was its emphasis on uniformity. The Other was relentlessly reduced to the Same. There was only one right way of seeing things; once this had been determined, it was to be enforced. To observe everything from the privileged vantage point of modernity is to master everything and subjugate anything that is regarded as a menace. The threat to human existence caused by the unpredictability and chaos of the natural order and the irrationality of human affairs would thus be eliminated, giving way to paradise—an ordered and structured world in which humanity could dwell without anxieties. Yet this emphasis upon uniformity and control demanded the suppression of differences and diversity. The place of religions could be firmly controlled, assigning each a strictly limited space within which it could exist—but exist only as a prisoner. The space allocated was not the vast open plains of public accessibility, but the confines of a prison cell.

In 1791 the English philosopher Jeremy Bentham proposed an architectural innovation designed to make prisons safe and humane. He envisioned a prison space constructed as a circular array of inward-pointing cells. Solid walls between the cells would prevent any communication between prisoners, and a small window in the back of the cell would let in light. At the center of this ring of cells, Bentham proposed to place an observation tower with special shutters to prevent the prisoners from seeing the guards. This *panopticon* was designed as an "all-seeing place" to permit complete observation of every prisoner. Its ultimate goal was to control the prisoners through both isolation and the possibility of constant surveillance.

The postmodern philosopher Michel Foucault seized upon this idea of a controlling space and applied it as a metaphor for the oppressive control of modernity and its complete failure to respect difference and diversity.

> Each individual, in his place, is securely confined to a cell from which he is seen from the front by the supervisor; but the side walls prevent him from coming into contact with his companions. He is seen, but he does not see; he is the object of information, never a subject in communication. The arrangement of his room, opposite the central tower, imposes on him an axial visibility; but the divisions of the ring, those separated cells, imply a lateral invisibility. And this invisibility is a guarantee of order. If the inmates are convicts, there is no danger of a plot, an attempt at collective escape, the planning of new crimes for the future, bad reciprocal influences; if they are patients, there is no danger of contagion; if they are madmen there is no risk of their committing violence upon one another.

Applied to matters of religion, Foucault's critique of modernity leads to the recognition that atheism saw itself as the panopticon, the vantage point from which religion could be viewed and mastered. Marx argued that religion arose from social conditions; the control of religion could then be brought about by appropriate social engineering. Freud argued that it came about through the dark recesses of the human unconscious; control of religion could then be achieved through manipulating mental processes. Religion could be isolated, restricted to a safe space, and then allowed to die—or, in the case of some more aggressive modernist proposals, eliminated through violence. As Foucault points out, infections were best controlled by a series of limits on individual freedom and movement, followed by more radical measures to eliminate them from the community once they had been brought under control. Modernity treated religion as an outbreak of madness—occasionally socially acceptable, but invariably a cause for concern.

By 1950, modernism found itself in such serious tension with the human experience of life that its credibility was stretched to the breaking point. Paradise was postponed to the point where it became increasingly clear that it was little more than a visionary utopia. Instead of admitting its own failure to deliver what it promised, modernity kept deferring and delaying the arrival of its utopia. Paradise was always around the next corner. The vision may remain living for some; nevertheless, it stands in the midst of a landscape scarred by the debris of its failures. Perhaps the most visionary critique of modernism is credited to the German Marxist writer Walter Benjamin (1892–1940), who saw the rise of Nazism in the 1930s as a telling sign of the futility of modernism. Benjamin viewed the Nazi-Soviet Pact of 1939 as a devastating indicator of the failure of Marxism, and, unable to live with the despair of this realization, or perhaps fearing imprisonment by the Vichy authorities in France, committed suicide shortly afterward. For Benjamin, it was as if modernity had created a world within which he could not bear to live.

Modernism's great break with the past and declaration of its intention to begin all over again once seemed novel and exciting. Yet as the rise of Nazism and Stalinism in the 1930s made clear, breaking with tradition just meant breaking with civilization and all its inbuilt safeguards against totalitarianism. The modernist tendency toward the enforcement of universalization and uniformity can be seen particularly well in the field of architecture. The ideology of design associated with modernism is based, at least in part, on the International Style, founded in the 1920s and 1930s by Walter Gropius and others. The movement was committed to simple, functionally efficient design without ornament, the use of concrete, steel, and glass, and a particular use of the rectangle and straight line. To those who conceived it in the 1920s, this style would be liberating; in reality it proved to be deeply oppressive. The utter tedium of Stalinist city planning demoralized those who lived in such modern cities. To its growing body of critics, modernism had fathered a meaningless uniformity and uniform meaninglessness. The design of Nazi concentration camps, such as Auschwitz and Birkenau, showed the modernist concern for functional efficiency and its prioritization of rectangles and straight lines at its worst. The neatly arranged rows of rectangular huts came to symbolize the oppression of both Nazism and the architectural style it favored.

By the end of the Second World War, the social, moral, and intellectual failings of modernity were all too obvious. Western culture was shaken by a new series of convulsions, as the settled assumptions of modernity were cast aside, to be replaced by a new way of thinking and seeing the world—postmodernity.

THE POSTMODERN RESPECT
FOR DIVERSITY

Postmodernity is a complex, perhaps ultimately undefinable notion (in that "definition" implies limitation, something to which most postmodern writers take exception). Nevertheless, a number of common themes can be identified within the movement. Pehaps the most important of these is the rejection of modernism's quest for objective, essentially knowable truth and beauty; its belief that a totality and unity can still be found within the fragmented world we inhabit, so that the world can be known, understood, and mastered through rational and scientific means. Postmodernity has reacted against such notions, for two major reasons: first, that it was untenable philosophically, and second, that it encouraged the rise of intolerance and lack of respect for the Other.

Neither modernity nor postmodernity is to be regarded as "right"; each represents a cultural mood, the latter heavily determined by the perceived failings of the former. Where Enlightenment writers believed that it was possible to lay down some fundamental axioms and proceed to erect a major philosophical system upon them, postmodern writers point to the failure of this entire project. The notion of a self-grounding philosophy has become seriously unfashionable, and every attempt to propagate one today is greeted with suspicion on account of its pretensions to totalization. Where modernism spoke of rationality in the singular—for there is only one legitimate way of thinking—postmodern writers recognized a variety of rationalities, insisting that philosophical adjudication between them was not possible. As Os Guinness points out in a penetrating account of recent trends:

> Where modernism was a manifesto of human self-confidence and self-congratulation, postmodernism is a confession of modesty, if not despair. There is no truth; only truths. There is no grand reason; only reasons. There is no privileged civilization (or culture, belief, norm and style); only a multiplicity of cultures, beliefs, norms and styles. There is no universal justice; only interests and the competition of interest groups. There is no grand narrative of human progress; only countless stories of where people and their cultures are now. There

is no simple reality or any grand objectivity of universal, detached knowledge; only a ceaseless representation of everything in terms of everything else.

There is no privileged standpoint from which everything else can be seen. There is no "metanarrative"—a grand, overaching scheme of things that offers a totalizing view of reality. As Terry Eagleton points out, this underlies postmodernity's vigorous rejection of "one size fits all" philosophies, which refuse to tolerate dissent, difference, or divergence from their preconceived norms.

> Post-modernism signals the end of such "metanarratives" whose secretly terroristic function was to ground and legitimate the illusion of a "universal" human history. We are now in the process of awakening from the nightmare of modernity, with its manipulative reason and fetish of the totality, into the laid-back pluralism of the post-modern, that heterogeneous range of life-styles and language games which has renounced the nostalgic urge to totalize and legitimate itself . . . Science and philosophy must jettison their grandiose metaphysical claims and view themselves more modestly as just another set of narratives.

This leads to a growing respect and tolerance for differences and a principled rejection of the modernist reduction of the Other to the Same. As Jean-François Lyotard declared, postmodernism "refines our sensitivity to differences and reinforces our ability to tolerate the incommensurable." Local and partial insights are to be welcomed and respected, in contrast to the suspicion with which totalizing claims are to be treated.

Although many postmodern writers identify themselves as atheists, two important points must be made immediately. First, the postmodern rejection of the possibility of a "God's-eye" standpoint does not for one moment entail the rejection of God. While postmodernity is quite clear that humanity does not occupy the position of God—assuming that such a position would allow a total account of reality—this does not for one moment imply or entail that there is no God. Postmodernity affirms a philosophical modesty, noting limits to our knowledge; it does not—and, indeed, cannot—make declarations concerning what exists and what does not exist. But second, and perhaps more importantly, postmodernity seriously undermines the plausibility of atheism—for reasons that we shall explore in what follows.

ATHEISM AND THE CHALLENGE OF POSTMODERNITY

Postmodernism is a cultural mood that celebrates diversity and seeks to undermine those who offer rigid, restrictive, and oppressive views of the world. Modernism—which tried to reduce everything to a uniform set of ideas—is excoriated by postmodern writers as a form of intellectual Stalinism, a refusal to permit diversity in our readings of the world. Postmodernity celebrates diversity of belief, seeing any attempt to coerce individuals to accept the viewpoints of another as being oppressive.

At first sight, the postmodern enterprise might seem to work in atheism's favor. Many postmodern writers are, after all, atheists (at least in the sense of not actively believing in God). The very idea of deconstruction seems to suggest that the idea of God ought to be eliminated from Western culture as a power play on the part of the churches and others with vested interests in its survival. Yet this is not how the leading postmodern writer Jacques Derrida would wish the concept to be interpreted. The issue is about openness and a willingness to respect the Other: "Deconstruction is not an enclosure in nothingness, but an openness to the other."

Derrida describes the liberating consequences of postmodernity in terms of the image of "decentering." According to Derrida, modern Western thought is based on the idea of a center—an origin, a truth, an ideal form, a fixed point, an "immovable mover," God, which is the ultimate guarantor of meaning. This excessive use of the image of the center, according to Derrida, leads to a systematic attempt to exclude by ignoring, repressing, or marginalizing others. Derrida notes the importance of the notion of a center in the fostering of oppression by the West, arguing that on its basis, the great Western powers have attempted to fashion the world to resemble the theoretical structure of their ethnocentrism, often using violence. Unwilling to tolerate difference or divergence, they have sought to eliminate it, forcing the periphery to conform to the center—for example, during the periods of European colonial rule, German control over Europe during the Second World War, and American hegemony during the Vietnam War. In each instance, the representatives of Western culture, on the basis of a misplaced confidence concerning the ethically imperative nature of their beliefs and practices, attempted to deny and ultimately destroy beliefs and practices that deviated from their own, either by suppressing them completely or assimilating them to culturally acceptable alternatives. This attempt to totalize the center through a universal definition of what it means to be a human must be subjected to a radical deconstructive critique as a necessary precondition to the elimination of oppression.

The implications of this for any religious worldview can hardly be overlooked. Oppression arises through a refusal to tolerate alternatives, leading to their suppression. Atheism may have begun as a liberating attempt to "decenter" Western culture from the oppression of the state churches of Europe. Yet instead of following that process of decentering through to its legitimate conclusion, atheism merely proposed an alternative center. By positing a view of humanity that necessarily denied the existence of God as a precondition of authentic human existence, atheism once more sought to totalize the center by proposing a single, universal definition of what it means to be a human that deliberately excluded and marginalized those who did not accept this severely limiting definition.

Atheism is obliged to define the Other either as the idea of God itself or as those who believe in God—a category that embraces the vast majority of the inhabitants of planet earth. The Other is therefore reduced to the Same—a process we can see in the critiques of religion mounted by Feuerbach, Marx, and Freud. Each argues that the Other (God) is simply another instance of the Same (such as social and economic forces). While these three writers have different understandings of what the Same might be, they share a common reductionist methodology that insists that God can be completely and conveniently reduced to their categories. While these approaches are completely consistent with the outlook of modernity, postmodernity's emphasis on the necessity of respect for the Other radically calls their propriety into question. A lack of respect for the Other, it is argued, ultimately leads to an unacceptable repression of the Other.

While there are indeed some atheists who are respectful of religious belief, the dominant tone within the movement is rather more strident. Belief in God is evil, and must be eliminated. In his Lowell Lecture, given at Harvard University on April 20, 1992, Gore Vidal argued that monotheism was the source of America's many evils.

> The great unmentionable evil at the center of our culture is monotheism. From a barbaric Bronze Age text known as the Old Testament, three anti-human religions have evolved—Judaism, Christianity, and Islam. These are sky-god religions. They are, literally, patriarchal—God is the Omnipotent Father—hence the loathing of women for 2,000 years in those countries afflicted by the sky-god and his earthly male delegates. The sky-god is a jealous god, of course. He requires total obedience from everyone on earth, as he is not just in place for one tribe, but for all creation. Those who would reject him must be converted or killed for their own good.

Setting to one side the slightly hysterical overstatements that make this lecture such entertaining reading (well, when did accurately reported facts make good reading?), its darker side cannot be overlooked. Vidal argues for "all-out war on the monotheists." Parallels with such demands can be found elsewhere, especially in the writings of Richard Dawkins, who calls for the eradication of faith as the world's greatest evil. Yet the twentieth century gave rise to one of the greatest and most distressing paradoxes of human history: that the greatest intolerance and violence of that century were practiced by those who believed that religion caused intolerance and violence.

This mention of coercive means of eliciting support for atheism brings us to what is now recognized as one of the most disturbing aspects of the history of atheism in the twentieth century—its violence.

THE EMBARRASSING INTOLERANCE OF ATHEISM

The confident secularist predictions of the demise of religion are things of the past. So if religion will not lie down and die of its own accord, can it be eliminated by other means? Yes, it can—provided the norms of civilization are totally disregarded. For the only alternative is the eradication of religion by force. The forcible suppression of religion is one of the most troubling aspects of atheism—especially to those of a postmodern inclination, for whom tolerance is the supreme social and personal virtue. Modern Western society prizes tolerance and has limited patience with those who demand the elimination of beliefs—or, even worse, believers.

Those who speak of the elimination of religion—for example, by comparing it to a malignant infection that must be eradicated—often fail to ask, let alone explain, how this elimination is to take place. What happens if people rather like religion, and refuse to abandon it? Atheists often speak about the eradication of religion as if this would be a painless, even pleasant process. Perhaps they are not un-like naive carnivores, who believe that animals conveniently lie down at an appropriate moment and die painlessly so that they may be eaten by appreciative humans. The naive atheist seems to believe that a so-phisticated seminar in godlessness is all that is required to eliminate religion, showing a grateful people that they can be liberated from an oppressive and debilitating illusion. The reality of the situation is bloody, messy, and brutal: the eradication of faith tends to involve fir-ing squads and gas chambers.

The myth of the painless eradication of religion is still found in Philip Pullman's recent *Dark Materials* trilogy (1998–2000), which posits a universe oppressed by a malevolent and apparently senile de-ity. The only way in which the sadistic brutality of the "kingdom of God" can be ended is by overthrowing this divinity and establishing a "republic of heaven." The death of God demands that we cease to speak of a kingdom of God; in its place we must substitute the "re-public of heaven"—a phrase that ends the final volume of Pullman's trilogy. The God who dies, according to Pullman, is the God who burns heretics and hangs witches. He will not be mourned.

It is a fascinating and intriguing story. Yet the reader is left with an awkward, enduring, and perturbing question. Is that *really* where everything ends? It's like reading *Animal Farm* no further than the bit where the animals have evicted the nasty humans and established their own republic with its catchy slogan "four legs good; two legs bad." But the story simply doesn't stop there. What about poor old Boxer, the nice old horse who was sent off to the glue factory? In Or-well's narrative, Boxer represents the oppressed peasants, in whose name the revolution took place, who were initially manipulated by their new masters and subsequently ended up being just as oppressed as under the old system.

The Russian Revolution did not end with the oppressed peasants expelling the czar, taking over the land, and living happily ever after. A new elite took over, who then proceeded to oppress the peasants, although in a creatively different manner. Stalin's liquidation squads took care of those more obstinate peasants who were unwise enough to resist forcible collectivization. And then there were the purges of those who got in the way of the new world order. As Martin Amis points out in his brilliant recent study of Stalin, *Koba the Dread*, Westerners just didn't want to know about the violent excesses of this psychopath. Pullman has secured closure at the literary level—but is this *really* where the story can be said to end? In one sense, it has only begun.

If atheism saw itself simply as one (ir)religious option among many, there would not be a problem. Atheism, however, has a disturbing tendency to see itself as the only true faith, and demands that everyone conform to its beliefs. Yet Soviet atheism is the true religious philosophy of modernity—a totalizing worldview which demanded that all else give way to its claims. As the history of the atheist state makes clear, this inevitably sets an agenda for repression and oppression. A worldview that was once acclaimed as a liberator thus became an oppressor, requiring in turn to be overthrown.

It was relatively easy to overlook the dark side of atheism in the heyday of Western liberalism. Reports of terror, torture, famine, mass deportations, and massacres in the Soviet Union were once easily dismissed as the propaganda of reactionaries and political conservatives. Truth, however, has a habit of emerging. The fall of the Berlin Wall in 1989 did more than allow inhabitants of the Soviet bloc access to the West; it also paved the way for Western scholars to inspect the archives of the Soviet Union and its allies. What was found was shocking. The opening of the Soviet archives led to revelations that ended any notion that atheism was a gracious, gentle, and generous worldview. *The Black Book of Communism*, based on those archives, created a sensation when first published in France in 1997, not least because it implied that French communism—still a potent force in national life—was tainted with the crimes and excesses of Lenin and Stalin. Where, many of its irate readers asked, were the Nuremberg trials of communism? Communism was a "tragedy of planetary dimensions" with a grand total of victims variously estimated by contributors to the volume at between 85 million and 100 million—far in excess of those murdured under Nazism.

With the publication of this volume, any meaningful talk in the West about atheism as a liberator came to an abrupt end. The authors adopted Ignazio Silone's maxim that "revolutions, like trees, should be judged by their fruit." Communism promised liberation from the illusion of religion; it ended up with a body count exceeding anything previously known in history. In a powerful and compelling analysis, *The Black Book* demonstrated how exclusion leads inexorably to extermination. When religion is declared to be an enemy, the outcome is as inevitable as it is criminal.

> Terror involves a double mutation. The adversary is first labeled an enemy, and then declared a criminal, which leads to his exclusion from society. Exclusion very quickly turns into extermination. [The] idea [of a purified humanity] is used to prop up a forcible unification—of the Party, of society, of the entire empire—and to weed out anyone who fails to fit into the new world. After a relatively short period, society passes from the logic of political struggle to the process of exclusion, then to the ideology of elimination, and finally to the extermination of impure elements. At the end of the line there are crimes against humanity.

A demand to eliminate deficient beliefs leads to an obsession with power as the means by which that elimination can proceed. Again, as *The Black Book* pointed out, the imposition of a theory became an end in itself, leading to a mind-set that could not tolerate, nor even conceive of, alternative belief systems.

Why should maintaining power have been so important that it justified all means and led to the abandonment of the most elementary moral principles? The answer must be that it was the only way for Lenin to put his ideas into practice and "build socialism." The real motivation for the terror thus becomes apparent: it stemmed from Leninist ideology and the utopian will to apply to society a doctrine totally out of step with reality . . . In a desperate attempt to hold onto power, the Bolsheviks made terror an everyday part of their policies, seeking to remodel society in the image of their theory, and to silence those who, either through their actions or by their very social, economic, or intellectual existence, pointed to the gaping holes in the theory. Once in power, the Bolsheviks made Utopia an extremely bloody business.

The appeal of atheism to generations lay in its offer of liberation. It promised to liberate the enslaved and exploited masses from their cruel oppression by the state and church. Yet wherever atheism became the establishment, it demonstrated a ruthlessness and lack of toleration that destroyed its credentials as a liberator. The Promethean liberator had turned nasty.

Prometheus, according to Greek mythology, stole fire from the gods so that humanity might benefit from its warmth. Humanity had been trapped, and was powerless to change its situation or improve itself. Without fire, it could not create tools that would allow it to assert its control over the world. By stealing the fire of the gods, Prometheus had empowered humanity, enabling it to achieve a destiny that the gods feared and sought to prevent. It was little wonder that modernity saw Prometheus as a figure of liberation, pointing to the need and ability of humankind to break free from the repressive stranglehold of the gods and achieve its own destiny.

Yet there is a second part to the Greek myth, studiously overlooked by the apologists of the Enlightenment. The gods retaliated when Prometheus stole their fire and gave it to humanity. Zeus sent Pandora to Prometheus's brother, Epimethius, bearing a jar (not a box, incidentally) that she was instructed not to open. Pandora could not resist the temptation and removed the lid, allowing various calamities to escape and invade the world. Enlightenment writers are generally a little coy about this aspect of the Prometheus myth, which seems to imply that the human attempt to possess the powers of the gods will end with the unleashing of forces that could not have been foreseen, with disastrous results. But its implications for atheism are obvious.

Atheism presented itself as a liberator, destroying the myth of the gods and thus enabling humanity to step outside the arbitrary limits placed upon it by religious bigots. Religion stopped people from doing things that were fun, useful, and productive. Abolishing the idea of God eradicated these arbitrary limits. Yet, as Dostoyevsky foresaw, the elimination of God led to new heights of moral brutality and political violence in Stalinism and Nazism. The opening of Pandora's jar turned out to bring just as much woe as joy.

The particular appeal of atheism to generations of religiously alienated people was that it was different. Where religions oppressed, atheism liberated. The first step to authentic human existence was to throw out the outdated and destructive idea of God. By 1997, with the publication of *The Black Book*, this view had become untenable. Atheism was just as bad as any other religion. Its distinctive claim had been irreversibly discredited. No longer could anyone take the suggestion that atheism was the liberator of humanity with any seriousness. The archives of the Soviet Union told a very different story, which made harrowing reading.

Of the many criticisms that can be directed against the world's religions, the most serious is their history of violence and oppression. Yet this is not a criticism that can be made with integrity by atheists, precisely because their own recent history contains too much cruelty, oppression, and violence at the hands of those determined to rid the world of religions. To those who stand outside the religious debate altogether, atheists and their opponents seem equally tainted.

One of the more disturbing patterns of history is that movements that began as liberators end up becoming oppressors in their own right. It is as if the abused seems historically predetermined to become an abuser. A movement that promised intellectual liberation ended up being seen as an institutionalized oppressor. Had atheism itself, many wonder, now fallen victim to this baleful pattern of inversion? And does this account for its gradual eclipse? After the violence and intolerance of institutionalized atheism had become public knowledge, it became a matter of public necessity to confine these untamed passions in a private space. Atheism was a legitimate view for consenting individuals; it could not, however, be allowed to be the ideology of the public arena.

Postmodernity "reinforces our ability to tolerate the incommensurable" (Jean-François Lyotard). It encourages toleration and excoriates those who, by actions or beliefs, seek to marginalize, oppress, or dominate. Michel Foucault's sustained assault on the notion of "objective truth" rests on his belief that those who claim possession of such truth use it to dominate others, forcing them to fall in line with their views or be excluded. As is well known, this critique of such a notion has major implications for religions such as Christianity and Islam. Yet atheism is also affected—perhaps even more so. For postmodernity is intolerant of any totalizing worldview, precisely because of its propensity to oppress those who resist it.

As the history of the twentieth century makes clear, atheists can be just as nasty, prejudiced, stupid, and backward as their religious counterparts. In retrospect, this was only to be expected. After all, atheists are human beings, like everyone else, and their refusal to believe in God or any other spiritual force makes them no better and no worse than anyone else. Yet many expected that atheism would morally elevate its followers. It was much easier to believe this in the nineteenth century, when atheism held the moral high ground, never having been exposed to the corrupting influences of power and government. When atheists kept a discreetly low profile, nobody could be bothered to look into their beliefs and lifestyles. But when they launched high-profile social and political campaigns advocating an atheist agenda, people started asking awkward questions. And they began getting disturbing answers.

In what follows, we shall tell the fascinating story of one of the most bizarre figures in recent American religious history, and ask whether it has anything to tell us about the future of atheism.

10

THE ATHEIST'S REVOLT:
MADALYN MURRAY O'HAIR
AND OTHERS

ONE OF THE GREAT THEMES IN THE HISTORY OF ATHE-ism is the rebellion of son against father. This powerful personal quest for identity is often linked with the rejection of the father's beliefs. In the high noon of atheism, this story often took the form of the rebellion of an atheist son against the stale and barren worldview of a Christian father. The wisdom of the age was that atheism was exciting and liberating, promising an end both to the interminable boredom occasioned by religious indoctrination and to its baleful and despotic impact on personal development. This pattern of the accumulated intergenerational rejection of faith must, it was widely believed, lead to the end of faith and the triumph of some form of atheism. Yet the situation is far from being as simple as this pattern might suggest, as we shall see.

FATHER AND SON:
EDMUND GOSSE

One of the most fascinating works to deal with a son's revolt against his father's faith is Edmund Gosse's *Father and Son*, published in 1907, some forty to fifty years after the events it relates. Gosse's book describes, movingly yet relentlessly, the movement of a son away from the religious beliefs of his father. Admittedly, those religious beliefs were quite extreme, particularly by British standards. Philip Henry Gosse, a noted naturalist, was a member of the Plymouth Brethren, a pugnaciously introverted group of Christians who held that just about every aspect of late Victorian culture was inspired by Satan and designed to lead believers away from the true faith. The celebration of Christmas was deemed to be "popish." Gosse would have no formal celebration of the birth of Christ. A moving passage describes how the two housemaids decided to mark Christmas Day 1857 by cooking a plum pudding. Young Edmund, then aged eight, was offered a small piece. On learning of this, his father flew into an uncontrollable rage—angered more by the sheer sacrilege of the event than by the challenge it posed to his authority.

At times the book seems to verge on the comic; at others on the tragic. Gosse's narrative recounts the vivid and disturbing memories of a lonely boy reading aloud works of theology to his dying mother, of his pressing his pale cheek against the windowpane for interminable hours, and of the silence between father and son "in which you could hear a sea anemone sigh." Although, following the researches of Ann Thwaite, the work is now widely regarded as factually inaccurate, perhaps written more to make a point than to tell the truth, it remains a fascinating portrayal of what the religious alienation of son from father in the Victorian period might have been like.

As the work unfolds, its readers begin to sense that there is more to the elder Gosse than might at first seem the case. He is a moderate by the standards of his colleagues. When a preacher remarks, perhaps with a little too much enthusiasm, that William Shakespeare is a "lost soul now suffering for his sins in hell," Gosse objects. How do we know? Might not God's mercy extend to such a soul? Edmund himself begins to appear as something of a bore, inclined to a rather tedious form of rationalism at one moment and a love of poetry and art at another.

Edmund Gosse's rebellion against his father and his mental world parallels that of the age. The Victorian father was widely depicted as an authoritarian despot, making demands of his children that they could not possibly meet. To reject the faith of the father almost becomes a routine element of the process of growing up. A popular stereotype began to emerge and then to crystallize into the rigidity of a fossil: Christianity is the unthinking, unreflective faith of the previous generation; atheism the dynamic and informed worldview of its successor.

DAUGHTERS AND SONS: IVY COMPTON-BURNETT

This view is set out with particular stridency, fortunately tempered by an engaging wit, in the novels of Ivy Compton-Burnett (1884–1969)—such as *Brothers and Sisters* (1929) and *Daughters and Sons* (1937). One of the themes explored in her writings is the manner in which the present is damaged but not defeated by the past. Part of the legacy of the past, with which the present must struggle, is religious belief. Compton-Burnett's view on this matter was simple: religion was credible and powerful in the past; now, it had no relevance for anyone. A mere fifty years was sufficient to erase its power. She makes this point, for example, in *Daughters and Sons* by stressing the historically situated character of religious belief. The novel is set in 1894, and we are asked to imagine Sabine, now over eighty years of age, absolutely settled in her beliefs and morals. She knew what God was like and what he expected of her. The narrator comments: "Her feeling for [God] was of such a nature that she only needed to have been born fifty years later than her date of eighteen hundred and ten, to fail to recognize him at all."

There is no doubt that this pattern can be seen repeated throughout the nineteenth and early twentieth centuries. The religious beliefs of an older generation were an embarrassment to their children. In Compton-Burnett's *A Family and a Fortune* (1939), a funeral prompts

Oliver, an elderly grandfather, to own up to a slightly tenuous belief in life after death. "His grandsons," the narrator observes, "looked at him with incredulous eyes, startled by the faith of a man who was in other respects a normal being." The children of Anglican clergy were often the most aggressive atheists, and the most critical of the institution their parents served.

If this worldview had prevailed, the Christian faith in England would have died out years ago. Each generation seems to have believed that Christianity would disappear within its lifetime. Let us assume that a new generation arises every thirty years; that the rate of decline of religion is such that one in three will rebel against the faith of their parents; and that the entire British population in 1880 would have defined itself as Christian. (This hypothetical rate of erosion is actually rather modest in comparison with the cataclysmic decline presupposed by some atheist propagandists in the early 1990s.) The figures would then be:

DATE	CHRISTIAN PERCENTAGE OF POPULATION
1880	100
1910	67
1940	45
1970	30
2000	20

This crude analysis does not take into account the substantial postwar immigration into Britain from the Indian subcontinent, which resulted in large Hindu and Muslim communities' becoming established in the nation. Although not reducing the number of Christians in Britain, this phenomenon would significantly reduce the proportion of Christians within the population as a whole.

Yet the 2001 census of Great Britain, which allowed people the opportunity to self-define religiously, came up with a figure that must give cause for thought to those who have bought into this model. About 42 million people—72 percent of the population—defined themselves as

Christian. Relatively few of these attend church—a pastoral problem that the Christian churches must clearly explore and address. But there has simply not been the erosion of faith that earlier generations predicted with such confidence. The glib and simplistic predictions of a secular or atheist society simply have not come about. Christianity turned out not to be a marginalized anachronism doomed to terminal decline, but instead a remarkably resilient and enduring part of the social and intellectual order.

My concern in this chapter is not to document the failure of the confident predictions of well-meaning atheist pundits of the past, interesting and illuminating though they may be. This failure is widely conceded, and I have already given some thought to the critical weaknesses that it exposes in atheism. Instead, I want to tell another story. It is not the story of the son who comes to reject Christianity by rebelling against his father—the cultural stereotype of the late nineteenth century—but of a son who comes to Christian faith by rebelling against the atheism of his mother. The story casts light on why atheism is highly unlikely to achieve cultural or intellectual dominance in the United States, and why its appeal is declining elsewhere. The story we shall tell is of William J. Murray's relationship with his mother, Madalyn Murray O'Hair.

MOTHER AND SON:
MADALYN MURRAY O'HAIR

Madalyn Elizabeth Mays was born in Pittsburgh on April 13, 1919.[1] As it happened, that day was Palm Sunday, the day traditionally observed

---

[1] *This account is based on information freely available in the public domain, especially William J. Murray,* My Life Without God *(Eugene, Oreg.: Harvest House Publishers, 1992); Madalyn Murray O'Hair,* The Atheist World *(Austin, Tex.: American Atheist Press, 1991); and Jon Rappoport,* Madalyn Murray O'Hair *(San Diego: Truth Seeker Press, 1998); supplemented by reporting from ABC News, Associated Press, the* Atheist News, *the* Austin Chronicle, *the* Dallas Morning News, *the* Los Angeles Times, *the* National Review, *the* San Antonio Express-News, *and* Time *magazine.*

by Christians as marking Christ's entry into the city of Jerusalem, where he would die a week later. She married John Henry Roths in October 1941. The Japanese attack on Pearl Harbor in December of that year plunged the United States into war against Japan. Madalyn and her husband signed up and went to war—separately, as it happened. John was shipped out to the Pacific theater of war, while Madalyn ended up in Italy, working as a cryptographer. Her work brought her into contact with many senior American officers, including William J. Murray, serving in the Eighth Army Corps. She became pregnant with her first child in September 1945.

Murray declined to acknowledge the child as his own. On his return to the United States in late 1945, Roths offered to remain as Madalyn's husband, despite her infidelity, and act as father to her child. Madalyn declined and sued for divorce. Her first child was born in May 1946. By this time, Madalyn had begun to refer to herself as Madalyn Murray, even though no relationship now existed between herself and William J. Murray. In a further sign that she regarded herself as married to Murray, she named her son William Joseph Murray III. In February 1954, Madalyn became pregnant once more as the result of an affair with Michael Fierello, a local man. Although Murray was not the father, she named her second son Jon Garth Murray. Interestingly, both children were baptized.

Madalyn now began to become involved with radical political groups. Although the nature of those groups remains unclear, they can probably be described as Communist. Although it is uncertain when Madalyn became an atheist, or for what reason, there seems little doubt that she regarded this as an integral aspect of her new radical identity. She attempted to find employment in the Soviet Union, believing that this was where the future of the world would be shaped. In the event, nothing came of these advances.

To modern readers, this naïveté seems incredible. Yet it must be recalled that many idealists in the United States at this time genuinely believed that the Soviet Union was a bastion of freedom and enlightenment, offering a model that avoided the multiple failings of American capitalism—above all, unemployment. Lee Harvey Oswald, for example, was one such idealist. Having linked up with much the same radical groups as Madalyn, Oswald defected to the Soviet Union in October 1959. He returned to the United States in June 1962, only a little disillusioned. The rest, as they say, is history.

The episode that propelled Madalyn to nationwide fame took place in the fall of 1960. William was just about to begin attending school in Baltimore as a fourteen-year-old ninth grader. He had enrolled late because of the family's delayed return to the United States from Europe, where Madalyn had tried to defect to the Soviet Union through the Soviet Embassy in Paris. Much to her irritation, she had been refused. She was not in a particularly positive frame of mind after this humiliation. While visiting her son's school, she noticed that the children were praying and reading the Bible. She took immediate exception to both, and ordered her son to begin keeping a log of any religious activity that took place at school. William himself had no objection to these activities. But Madalyn saw him as a pawn in a larger game. He would be her passport to celebrity. William later recalled his mother's words: "The United States of America is nothing more than a fascist slave labor camp run by a handful of Jew bankers in New York. They trick you into believing you're free with those phony rigged elections . . . If they'll keep us from going to Russia where there is some freedom, we'll just have to change America. I'll make sure you never say another prayer in that school." Madalyn would not be the first attention-seeking mother to exploit her child in this way; it was, however, a classic example of the phenomenon.

William's log gradually filled up, until Madalyn judged the time was right to make a protest. She wrote to the school board, demanding that her son be exempted from Bible reading and prayer. When the school board turned down her request, she wrote to the *Baltimore Sun*, setting out her grievances. Eventually, the *Sun* decided to run a story. On October 27, the front page of the *Sun* was dominated by its headline:

"Boy, 14, Balks at Bible Reading." The story was taken up in the media and rapidly became a national issue. The American Civil Liberties Union expressed interest, then backed off. They had another virtually identical case under way nearby. The school agreed to a compromise. In the first week in November, they announced that they regarded the reading of the Bible as perfectly constitutional. They were, however, prepared to allow any student who took exception to Bible reading or prayer to remain silent or be excused from the class at that point. It seemed that the matter was closed.

But it wasn't. Madalyn's protest led to a tenfold increase in her mail, and a substantial number of checks began to arrive. She could afford to hire a lawyer. In December, she filed a petition, in the name of her son, demanding that illegal Bible readings and prayers should cease. The event attracted her more publicity. She became a lightning rod for alienated Americans of all kinds, who saw in her protest the potential beginnings of something much greater. The Baltimore courts threw out the petition, forcing Madalyn to appeal all the way to the U.S. Supreme Court. By this stage, funds were rolling in, and there was no problem about coping with legal costs. Madalyn's genius for self-promotion was paying off in a big way. Suddenly a new opportunity for advancing her agenda and heightening her profile opened up.

Early in 1962, the founder of the *Free Humanist* magazine (circulation 600), finding he no longer had the time to manage his pet project, handed the entire enterprise, including the mailing list, over to Madalyn. It was promptly renamed the *American Atheist*, and became a key means for promoting Madalyn and atheism in about equal measure. It became a nonprofit corporation in May of that year. It would prove the ideal vehicle for the advocacy of Madalyn and her ideas.

Arguments before the Supreme Court began on February 26, 1963, and generated immense debate nationwide. Madalyn was given free rein to express her atheist views in the columns of newspapers. The tone of her approach can be judged from these comments in the April 12, 1963, issue of *Life* magazine: "We find the Bible to be nauseating, historically inaccurate, replete with the ravings of madmen. We find God to be sadistic, brutal, and a representation of hatred, vengeance. We find the Lord's Prayer to be that uttered by worms groveling for meager existence in a traumatic, paranoid world."

On June 17, the Supreme Court announced its decision. By a majority of eight to one, the Court ruled that the Bible and prayer were to be kept out of the public schools. It was a landmark decision, one of the most important milestones in the long history of clarification of the constitutional relation of church and state. It propelled Madalyn into the forefront of public debate. *Life* called her "the most hated woman in America," a label she accepted with pride. It was her badge of honor.

Some local difficulties (such as charges that she assaulted five Baltimore police officers) now forced Madalyn to relocate to Hawaii, from which she gave an interview to *Playboy* in October 1965. She made it clear that she had no time for traditional morality. As a "radical feminist," she was convinced that celibacy was absurd, even pathological— especially for nuns who believed in some kind of spiritual marriage to Christ. "You think I've got wild ideas about sex? Think of those poor old dried-up women lying there on their solitary pallets yearning for Christ to come to them in a vision some night and take their maidenheads. By the time they realize he's not coming, it's no longer a maidenhead; it's a poor, sorry tent that *nobody* would be able to pierce—even Jesus with his wooden staff. It's such a waste. I don't think *anybody* should be celibate—and that goes for priests as well as nuns."

After flirting with the idea of moving to Cuba, then still viewed by the American radical left as a socialist paradise, Madalyn transferred to Texas in 1965, where she would remain for the rest of her days. She married Richard O'Hair, a former FBI informant. A spate of activism followed. Her organization, American Atheists, began to grow, reaching a claimed membership of fifty thousand with chapters in thirty states and a high-profile national convention. She ran a weekly talk show on 150 radio stations. She busied herself with a flurry of lawsuits—including a 1978 lawsuit against the state of Texas to abolish the requirement that public officials swear their belief in a supreme be-ing—with an enthusiasm that even some of her supporters worried about. She seemed almost pathological in her hatred of religion. In 1979 she even filed a lawsuit against the pope, who was due to visit the United States and celebrate a "stupid, archaic" Mass on public land.

Her high public profile was confirmed in November 1967, when she was invited to appear in the first episode of Phil Donahue's pioneering TV talk show. Although the Vietnam War dominated the news and tem-porarily eclipsed her, she was never far from the center of public de-bate about religion. Public donations reached a new high, allowing her to fund the building of a new headquarters and various other organiza-tions—including the Society of Separationists, United World Atheists, and United Secularists of America. Bumper stickers began to appear with uniquely sophisticated messages like "Honk if you love Madalyn!" and "Apes evolved from Creationists." If Billy Graham was the spokesman of evangelical Christianity across the nation, there was no longer any doubt as to whom the public identified as the public face of atheism.

Madalyn's reputation as an atheist propagandist certainly did not rest on the quality of her arguments, which were generally superficial and banal. Rather, that reputation was based on her pugnacious atti-tude to religion, linked with her unwillingness to give up even the slightest ground to her opponents. Her case for atheism, set out in her radio shows and published in books such as *The Atheist World*, was conventional, even dull, and intellectually vapid to the point of being self-defeating. Here, for example, is a rather predictable attack on the history of religion, which Madalyn broadcast on November 11, 1972: "The horrible record that has been compiled over the centuries by re-ligious fanatics and zealots of whatever creed would be incredible if it were not so well documented and if it did not indeed persist to our own time." Quite so. But one looks in vain for any recognition that the twen-tieth century witnessed some of the most appalling massacres and re-pressions perpetrated by those *opposed* to religion. The great paradox of our time, which apparently eluded O'Hair, is that the worst slaughters in the twentieth century were carried out against people on account of their religion. If a creed is judged by its human rights record, atheism cannot be said to have a record of distinction.

Then a double whammy hit home. The blows were fifteen years apart, but no less lethal on that account. First, in 1980, William Murray—Madalyn's son, in whose name the famous lawsuit of 1960–63 was brought—became a Christian believer. Second, in 1995, Madalyn went missing, precipitating massive public interest in her financial affairs and personal life. What came out was far from flattering.

William's long and complex journey to faith is described in his book *My Life without God* (1992), which provides intimate and generally unattractive details of his mother's personal life and convictions, as well as his own private reflections on what led him to the Christian faith. In 1995 he authored *Let Us Pray*, a manifesto for the reintroduction of prayer into public schools—precisely the issue on which his mother had campaigned on his behalf thirty years earlier. *My Life without God* tells the story of a life without God—but with Madalyn. It makes for excruciatingly embarrassing reading for American atheists. Some little snippets will give an idea of what life with Madalyn was like, and the total contradiction between her public posturing and private behavior.

One of Madalyn's standing arguments for atheism was that by liberating people from the ludicrous demand to love God, they could love other people more effectively. Atheism was *pro bono publico*, a surefire recipe and catalyst for philanthropy and social justice. But not in Madalyn's home, it seems. Madalyn lived together with her parents and two children. It was not an easy situation, partly because of their limited income (which only ceased to be a problem once Madalyn was launched on the lucrative lecture circuit), and partly because of the social dynamics of the family. Madalyn regularly ended up having dogfights with her parents, forbidding her children to speak to them.

By 1960 Madalyn had reached the conclusion that the problems her family faced were entirely due to her father, John Mays. Get rid of him and the family would be at peace. Unfortunately, John showed not the slightest interest in leaving home or conveniently dropping dead. Madalyn decided to help nature take its inevitable course, and instructed William to add a judicious dose of rat poison to his grandfather's coffee. "He's just a rat anyway," she remarked. "You put sick animals to sleep, and this is no different." William declined.

In the end, nature helped out. On January 9, 1963, Madalyn and her father had a ferocious argument before breakfast, which ended with Madalyn leaving the house in a rage, firing off some pastorally sensitive words as she did. "I hope you drop dead! I'll dump your shriveled body in the trash!" John Mays had a heart attack that same afternoon and died almost immediately. On returning home from work, Madalyn was informed of the news. William recalls the conversation as proceeding along the following lines:

> "Well, I'll be. Where's the stiff?"
> "At the Memorial Hospital Morgue."
> "Have you made any arrangements?"
> "Not yet."
> Then she turned to [William], and said, "Bill, call up some undertakers and find the cheapest one. Then have them pick up the stiff from Memorial."

Of course, this proves nothing. America has more than its fair share of dysfunctional families and insensitive individuals. Yet somehow, people expected better than this. If atheism really is about changing lives and society, might it not be reasonable to expect it to have changed Madalyn into something a little more civilized?

It is a fair question, and one that will not go away. Initially, concerns about Madalyn were limited to her behavior toward her employees at American Atheists and toward minority groups. She had a special dislike for homosexuals, as an incident with gay activist John Lauritsen made clear. In 1976 Lauritsen attended a convention of the Society of

Separationists, one of Madalyn's organizations, at which Madalyn attacked homosexuals. Lauritsen wrote to protest, evoking a robust response from Madalyn, dated May 20, 1976, in which she expressed her stridently homophobic views. Madalyn, it seems, was not really into the atheist equivalent of ecumenism.

Nor was she into networking or the cultivation of personal relationship, normally regarded as an integral aspect of American corporate life. She was vulgar, rude, and contemptuous, especially to those who donated to her causes. But the real problems began in 1993, when rumors of fraud within Madalyn's empire began to circulate. It would not be long before she would be likened to Jimmy Swaggart, the fallen TV evangelist, rather than to the unblemished Billy Graham.

Initially, the rumors focused on the inflated membership claims of American Atheists. Estimates that its membership was in the region of fifty to seventy thousand were increasingly ridiculed. A leaked *Handbook for Chapter Directors* advised American Atheist chapters to give "optimal" figures and speak of a "national mailing list of about 70,000 families." At a time when the actual membership was rumored to be about two thousand and dropping, the document noted that "if the media knew our actual number of members or subscribers they will know that we do not have enough clout numerically to kept [*sic*] them from saying anything they like about us."

Through a combination of abuse and mismanagement, American Atheists began to fall apart at the seams in the early 1990s. The state chapters started to break away, alienated by Madalyn's aggressive personality and her dysfunctional approach to management. Her decision to impose her son, Jon Garth Murray, on her fellow board members as her successor proved unwise in the extreme. His lack of social skills was aggravated by a most unfortunate speech impediment. Yet the corporate charter of American Atheists, Inc. (1987), gave three of the five seats on the board to members of Madalyn's family: Madalyn herself, her son Jon, and her granddaughter Robin.

Also during the early 1990s, a dispute arose over the ownership of

an atheist publication entitled the *Truth Seeker*. Madalyn had been trying to take over the Truth Seeker Company of San Diego since January
1989. The story broke on April 30 of that year, when the *Los Angeles
Times* ran a front-page story alleging that Madalyn was trying to seize
the *Truth Seeker* and its multimillion-dollar estate, bequeathed by
James Hervey Johnson. Madalyn argued that Johnson had left his millions to promote atheism. So why hadn't Johnson left his fortune to
her? Reporter Armando Acuna had no doubts: "Because he despised
her. And she loathed him. She continues to refer to the man she says
she knew for 40 years as James Scurvy Johnson." Madalyn was not a
stockholder in the Truth Seeker Company; her declared interest in the
estate rested solely on her public profile as the most prominent American atheist. In reporting later developments in this case on July 19,
1990, *San Diego Union-Tribune* staff reporter Anne Krueger wrote
scathingly of Madalyn's imperious claims to sovereignty over lesser
atheists: "[O'Hair] cannot be considered an implied beneficiary of
atheist Johnson's estate merely because she considers herself the country's 'pre-eminent spokesperson for mainstream atheism' . . . O'Hair's
attorney, Georgine Brave, argued that . . . [Johnson's] entire estate
should go to her client as the world's leading atheist." It was a public
relations disaster for Madalyn and her organization. But worse was to
come.

In response to Madalyn's predatory attempts on his client, San
Diego attorney Roy Withers sued American Atheists for $6 million,
claiming that they had improperly conspired to gain control of the estate of James Hervey Johnson. Things began to look bad for the Atheists. Faced with the very real possibility of losing the lawsuit and hence
incurring massive payouts, Madalyn decided to resort to concealing
their assets. Jon was instructed to ship out the 50,000-volume Charles
E. Stevens American Atheists Library—their greatest single asset—in
such a way that it could not be traced. David Waters, who had been
hired by American Atheists in 1993, was given the job of organizing the
covert disposal of assets, including converting some bank accounts into

cash. (In 1998 he showed secret correspondence to the *Austin Chronicle*, which broke the story of the deception.) David R. Travis, a Vietnam "foxhole atheist" who was employed at the headquarters, came across statements from the New Zealand Guardian Trust Co., which showed that Madalyn and her two family board members had stashed $900,000 in offshore accounts. Shocked at the implications of this discovery, he took the story and the documents to the Internal Revenue Service and the local press. The publicity got worse for Madalyn, day by day.

In August 1995, Madalyn, Jon, and Robin left Austin for San Antonio. The following month, Jon ordered $600,000 worth of gold coins from San Antonio jeweler Cory Ticknor, using funds from the New Zealand bank account. He collected the bulk of them a week later. Then they disappeared. According to records from the U.S. bankruptcy court, Robin left town owing $30,075 on nine different credit cards (plus a couple of department store cards). Jon left owing $47,782 on eleven different cards. All the indications were that the trio were building up huge cash holdings. But why? And where did they intend to go? Phil Donahue certainly wanted to know. His final program was due to be broadcast in May 1996, and he wanted to end the series as he had begun—by interviewing Madalyn. But not even the private detective he hired was able to track her down.

Conspiracy theorists had a field day. Suspicion immediately fell upon the American Christian right. Perhaps some fundamentalist had kidnapped the O'Hair family and was holding them for ransom. Or even trying to convert them? On September 24, 1996, William Murray filed a missing persons report at the Austin Police Department, which began an investigation. The trail went cold, with the Austin police refusing to accept that any crime had actually been committed. Others, however, were not so sure. The investigation passed up to the federal level. Eventually, the true story emerged.

The trio had been kidnapped by David Waters, Gary Karr, and

Danny Fry in August 1995. The motivation for the crime was money, pure and simple. Neither Christians nor aliens were involved. The kidnapping, it turned out, had been organized by Waters, a former employee of American Atheists, who had been sacked in 1994 for financial misappropriation. Waters never faced trial for the kidnapping and murder of the Murray O'Hairs, but can expect to spend the rest of his life in jail. In March 2001 he was sentenced to twenty years (in addition to earlier sentences of sixty and twenty-five years). As a result of a plea bargain, he finally revealed the location of the three corpses. Their dismembered bodies were eventually found by the FBI on a five-thousand-acre ranch near Camp Wood, Texas. Madalyn's corpse was positively identified from the serial number of a 1993 replacement hip.

The story did not quite end at that point. William Murray claimed the remains of his mother, half brother, and daughter, and arranged for their burial in Austin—their last abode. He respected their last wishes, and arranged a quiet funeral service according to their requests. No prayers were said over her. Madalyn had often expressed anxiety over a Christian funeral—she did not want a "crucifix shoved up her ass," as she delicately put it. In a bizarre twist, American Atheists demanded possession of the three cadavers, apparently believing that they were somehow their property.

So what happened to American Atheists, the organization that Madalyn founded and from which she siphoned off millions of dollars for her own ends? (An investigation by ABC-TV's *Nightline* on June 1, 1998, suggested a figure of eight million dollars.) Well, it is still there. Ellen Johnson took over as president at a board meeting. In an article in *Atheist Nation*, Howard Thompson—editor of the the *Texas Atheist* newsletter—argued that there were grounds for challenging the legality of that decision. With the three O'Hair members removed from the board, how could the remaining two members appoint a new president? The small-minded squabbles that broke out over this matter reminded critics of the movement of the kind of petty political infighting that they thought was limited to church organizations. The organization, however, recovered from these difficulties, and remains America's best-known atheist organization.

What do American Atheists actually do? The *National Review* decided to find out. On Easter weekend 2002, their reporter Andrew Stuttaford attended the twenty-eighth national convention of the organization, held at Logan Airport, Boston. Attendance was pretty good. In the June 2002 issue of the *National Review*, he commented on his impressions:

> Around 250 souls (maybe that's not the word) had turned up for the fun, typically bright, somewhat eccentric sorts, often with the style sense of faculty members at a failing community college. Guys, shoulderlength hair does not work with bald on top. Oddballs? Well, the affable man sitting next to me did spend a surprising amount of time busily crossing out the word "God" from his dollar bills. Cranks? Judging by the pamphlets on display outside the main auditorium, quite possibly, although, to be fair, I did not witness anyone actually picking up a copy of *The Unpleasant Personality of Jesus Christ*.

They could have fitted these souls easily into a corner of one of the megachurches that are springing up all over the United States at the moment, with congregations in the thousands. In fact, American Atheists seemed just like a small denomination, with their own religious goals and gripes, and the same sense of entitlement to representation in the public arena. Theologically, atheists may be totally different from small Protestant denominations; sociologically, they seem indistinguishable, not least in their petty squabbles.

Where most atheists just ask to be left alone, getting on with their lives peacefully and Godlessly, Stuttaford found American Atheists to be decidedly more militant, awkward, and angrier. "There are no horns on their heads, but watch out for the chips on their shoulders." Stuttaford clearly regarded the whole event as a gathering of the forlorn and social misfits, busy fighting yesterday's battles and seeking to preserve the heritage of their great founder—Madalyn Murray O'Hair. "Oppressed by their sense of oppression, they also show signs of succumbing to the temptation of that most pernicious of contemporary cults, the cult of the victim." Stuttaford relates how he heard tales of social snubs and embarrassment that demonstrated unequivocally that atheists were a persecuted minority, reduced to defending their integrity and bravery in the face of relentless criticism by telling jokes about "foreskins, nuns, and a hermaphroditic divinity." The crude and abusive spirit of Madalyn clearly hovers over her successors. The best way of ridding America of religion, it seems, is to tell dirty jokes.

There were some high points to the convention, however. Most impressive of all, Stuttaford reported, was a lecture by Michael Cuneo, a professor from New York City, an expert on Satanism and those who exploit this for their own rather sordid ends. "In an amusing presentation, he spoke of ceremonies that combine the best of *The Exorcist* with the worst of *Elmer Gantry*. This was skepticism at its good-humored, informative best, an inspiration, one would think, to the Hyatt's godless horde. But there was one small irony. Prof. Cuneo teaches at Fordham, a Jesuit university, and, yes, he's a Catholic." Stuttaford left the convention with the new realization that you don't have to believe in God to be a fundamentalist.

So is atheism going to take over America? Or anywhere else for that matter? Not on this showing. The history of American Atheists, Inc., suggests that atheism can be just as arrogant, deceitful, and downright outrageous as anything that the churches have managed to put together over their much longer history. Far from ushering in a new age of antireligious virtue, atheism just seems to end up aping the vices of its religious rivals. If Americans are looking for something to rid them of the institutional corruption and personal arrogance that have tainted the religious life of their nation, then institutional atheism singularly and publicly fails to provide it.

It is, of course, entirely fair to object at this point. The legitimacy of

self-appointed representatives will always be a matter of debate. Madalyn Murray O'Hair, it might reasonably be argued, is simply not typical
of the movement at large. Yet this is a dangerous strategy, offering a
slightly evasive means of deflecting criticism for atheist and Christian
alike. "They're not typical!" begs awkward and difficult questions over
the boundaries of movements, and who is to be regarded as "representative" and who is not. The point being made here is simply that,
under Madalyn Murray O'Hair, America's most prominent atheist organization projected an immensely unattractive image of a Godless
world, which has helped to shape American perceptions of atheism. A
movement that began with a sense of outrage at the injustices of the
world seems to have ended up either by parodying itself or by appro-
priating the excesses—moral and intellectual—of its opponents.

Atheism in twenty-first-century America has become little more
than one among many self-serving religious interest groups, competing
for the attention of the media and public policy makers. In its more
fundamentalist forms, American atheism aspires to universality and a
sense of entitlement to sit at the top of the public table; these pretensions exude an arrogance and complacency that are increasingly out of
place in a postmodern culture. Perhaps it is not surprising that its star
is waning. A movement that was always on the periphery of American
public life seems doomed to remain there.

Yet that sense of decline and decay is by no means limited to atheism in America, where it was never a major player anyway. Throughout
those regions of the world in which atheism was once a significant intellectual force, there are signs of a loss of confidence in the movement, both in the wider public arena and within its own ranks. The sun
seems to be setting on yet another empire—this time, an "empire of
the mind."

11

END OF EMPIRE:
THE FADING APPEAL
OF ATHEISM

The celebration of Queen Victoria's Diamond Jubilee in June 1897 marked the high point of British imperial history. It was, without doubt, a supreme moment of national self-confidence and self-congratulation, exceeding in enthusiasm even the Golden Jubilee of a decade earlier. The British had created the greatest empire that the world had ever known, on which the sun never set—and much of its colorful diversity was on display in the streets of London that summer. Londoners watched amazed as processions of native soldiers of all races paraded past in dazzling uniforms. If ever the British needed reassurance of the grandeur of their empire, this was it.

But earth's proud empires fade away, as an old hymn had it. Rudyard Kipling (1865–1936) had his doubts. Writing at the height of the Jubilee celebrations on June 22, he expressed his deep unease with things in the poem "Recessional." The crowds were "drunk with sight of power"; but was there anything to sustain the empire other than force? Unless founded upon God's will, the empire must surely pass into history, to join others that were great in their day, and now lay forgotten.

Far-called, our navies melt away;
*   On dune and headland sinks the fire:*
Lo, all our pomp of yesterday
*   Is one with Nineveh and Tyre!*
Judge of the Nations, spare us yet,
Lest we forget—lest we forget!

Perhaps Kipling had realized that the foundations of that empire were already shifting beneath his feet. It could not go on. Something had to give. But for many on that momentous day, such thoughts would have been completely out of order. What could go wrong?

The same process of rise and fall, growth and decay, can be seen in the great empires of the human mind. There comes a point when their growth stalls, their attraction pales, and their credibility falters. And often it comes as a surprise, its predictability—like a decline in the stock market—only evident with the benefit of hindsight. Atheism is in trouble. Its glory days lie far behind it. Its future seems increasingly to lie in the private beliefs of individuals rather than in the great public domain it once regarded as its natural habitat. The attraction of atheism proved not to be universal, but was limited to certain situations—situations that were rapidly disappearing into the past, losing their impact on the popular imagination. Distant memories of atheism as a liberator competed with more recent memories of atheism as an oppressor. So how did this reversal of roles come about?

LIBERATORS AND OPPRESSORS: ON ATHEIST ROLE REVERSAL

One of the attractions of the form of atheism that I encountered as a high school student was that it saw the world in black-and-white terms. There were no confusing shades of gray to complicate things. Atheism was the great liberator of humanity, religion its oppressor. When religion was abolished, there would be peace and light, and everyone would live in harmony. At that stage, of course, I was too young and naive to realize that just about every worldview and religion that has ever existed has preached pretty much the same message: Come around to our way of thinking and everything will be just wonderful. Every dogma is wrong (except ours, of course).

But my young mind was not quite ready for such complicating ideas; I preferred to keep things simple, and the fundamentalist atheism I knew was ideal for my purposes. Religion was bad for you, at every level—socially, personally, and politically. The French and Russian Revolutions showed us what atheists could do when they put their mind to changing the world. It was time for another major revolution, to accomplish at the global level what these had achieved locally. I freely admit that with the benefit of hindsight, these ideas were simplistic in the extreme, making many religious ideas look sophisticated by comparison. But these were the ideas that were in circulation in the 1960s, and I and many others found them entrancing.

The bottom line of the argument is that liberation is an excellent thing and oppression a bad thing. As religion oppresses and atheism liberates, you can work out the politics for yourself. But what if these roles are historically conditioned? In other words, what would happen if the role of atheism as a liberator was determined by the specifics of a given historical situation, and was not universally true? Or if religion was only oppressive in certain contexts, and liberating in others? There is no doubt that many French intellectuals of the mid-eighteenth century despised the church for its social backwardness and its unsophisticated theology, and saw atheism as a much-needed and long-overdue breath of fresh air.

But it is not a universal pattern, as can be seen from a more detailed study of history. One case study—the development of Christianity in Korea during the twentieth century—illuminates the point at issue with special clarity and force. The origins of Christianity in Korea go back to the late eighteenth century, when a small Catholic community was established following initiatives from Beijing, China. The small

Christian community was vigorously persecuted during the nineteenth century. Of the total Christian population of about 18,000, it is thought that 8,000 were massacred. However, a degree of stability resulted when a friendship treaty was signed with the United States in 1882. Shortly afterward, American Protestant missionaries arrived in Korea and began to establish major medical and educational missions in the country. Nevertheless, at the dawn of the twentieth century only a tiny proportion of the country was Christian—just under 1 percent, according to the best estimates. Yet an authoritative survey of the religious commitments of the Korean people published in 2000, the closing year of the twentieth century, showed that 49 percent of the population was Christian. So how and why did this massive change come about? How did a country with virtually no Christian presence come to be very nearly a Christian nation?

There is no doubt that a decisive factor in this development was that Christianity was perceived as a liberator, not an oppressor, by Koreans in the twentieth century. Korea was annexed by Japan in 1910 and remained under Japanese rule until the end of the Second World War. Christianity was seen as allied with Korean nationalism, especially in the face of Japanese oppression. Elsewhere in Asia, Christianity was easily depicted by its critics as the lackey of Western imperialism. In Korea, however, the enemy was not the West, but Japan. Throughout this time, Christians played an active role in the Korean independence movement out of all proportion to their numbers. Of the 123 people tried for insurgence by the Japanese in the 1911 popular revolt against Japanese rule, 98 were Christians. At this time, Christians made up just over 1 percent of the Korean population. Though a tiny presence in the nation, Christianity was a liberator in the Korean context. History is about the specifics of any given situation, and religion is seen as liberating in some contexts, and restrictive and oppressive in others.

Today, South Korea sends out Christian missionaries to nations throughout Asia. The large Korean populations in major Western cities, from Sydney to Los Angeles, from Melbourne to New York, are closely linked in a network of churches, which often act cooperatively and provide mutual support and spiritual nourishment. And as North Korea shows signs of economic crisis and political instability, the question of the future religious development of this hardline Communist state remains completely open. The anecdotal evidence suggests that Christianity has already made deep inroads within the northern population, and is expected to grow further in the next decade.

The credentials of atheism as a political and intellectual liberator have also been called into question. Once more, its social role is found to be determined by the historical context. Without doubt, atheism was seen as a liberator in France in the 1790s, in Germany in the 1840s, and in Russia during the 1910s, to mention just a few especially important moments in recent Western history. But at other times and places, atheism has been seen as socially and intellectually repressive—for example, throughout Eastern Europe after the Second World War. The ruthless repression of academic freedom at that time (largely ignored, it must be said, by the Western liberal intelligentsia) is a powerful reminder that a worldview that demands freedom when in opposition can become astonishingly intolerant of its rivals when in power. It is not of the essence of atheism to be a liberator, nor of religion to be an oppressor. Those roles are determined by the contingencies of history. Perhaps the social conditions may return under which atheism is once more liberating, and religion oppressive. But that day now seems far away.

"New presbyter is but old priest writ large." With these words, written in 1646, John Milton expressed the depressing insight that radical religious change often led to tinkering with the vocabulary, rather than eliminating the vices, of the religious establishment. Rather than proving the exception to this rule, atheism has simply confirmed it. Atheism was once new, exciting, and liberating, and for those reasons held to be devoid of the vices of the faiths it displaced. On closer inspection, and with greater familiarity over time, it turned out to be just as bad, possessed of just as many frauds, psychopaths, and careerists as its religious alternatives. Many have now concluded that these personality types are endemic to all human groups, rather than being the peculiar preserve of religious folks. When young and innocent, and seen against the backdrop of a weary and stale religious establishment, atheism possessed the double appeal of novelty and integrity. With Stalin and Madalyn Murray O'Hair, atheism seems to have ended up by mimicking the vices of the Spanish Inquisition and the worst televangelists, respectively. Yet this is not to say anything especially negative about atheism—merely that it is just as prone as any other system of thought to the frailties and failings of human nature. Far from being a solution to the human dilemma, it has become part of the problem.

A further question may be raised here. As we have seen, Nietzsche argued that God is dead—meaning that God has ceased to be a meaningful reality in Western culture. But was this actually good news? Nietzsche himself was far from sure. If God is dead, Nietzsche pointed out, people would transfer their old faith in God to something else. They had to believe in *something*. With precocious foresight, Nietzsche declared that, having lost faith in God, people would now put their trust in barbaric "brotherhoods with the aim of the robbery and exploitation of the non-brothers." For many, this was an alarming prediction—precisely because it *was* predictable—of the rise of the tribalism of the Nazis and other dubious groups. It is as if humanity has to have faith in and be loyal to some individual or group. If God is declared to be out of the running, Nietzsche argues, we turn to other absolutist groups and creeds—such as Adolf Hitler or the Communist Party of the Soviet Union. The elimination of God from Western culture has its darker side, which regrettably has yet to be conceded and explored fully by those who urge it.

Yet liberation embraces more than social and political issues. One of the most important criticisms directed against religion by Sigmund Freud was that it encouraged unhealthy and dysfunctional outlooks on life. Having dismissed religion as an illusion, Freud went on to argue that it was a negative factor in personal development. His views have had a major impact on the practice of health care in the West, especially in the United States. At times, Freud's influence has been such that the elimination of a person's religious beliefs has been seen as a precondition for mental health.

Yet Freud is now a fallen idol, the fall having been all the heavier for its postponement. The toppling of Freud from his seemingly unassailable position in American culture was a slow process. Frank Sulloway's *Freud—Biologist of the Mind* (1979) raised some difficult questions concerning Freud's scientific credentials. Adolf Grünbaum's *Foundations of Psychoanalysis* (1984) drew attention to the many failings and vulnerabilities of his theories. It was left to Frederick Crews, however, in his *Unauthorized Freud* (1998), to popularize a growing body of professional literature that challenged Freud at every level, calling into question the reliability of his original case studies and the integrity of his therapeutic methods, and highlighting the credulity of his followers. Freud, it was argued, had a worrying tendency to convert the accidents of social history into the necessary truths of human nature. The long-overdue outcome was to bring about a collapse of confidence in Freud's judgments concerning religion at the level of popular culture, this conclusion having been reached at least a decade earlier in professional circles.

There is now growing awareness of the importance of spirituality in health care, both as a positive factor in relation to well-being and as an issue to which patients have a right. The major conference "Spirituality and Healing in Medicine," sponsored by Harvard Medical School in 1998, drew public and professional attention as never before to the issue of incorporating spirituality into professional medicine. It was there reported that 86 percent of Americans as a whole, 99 percent of family physicians, and 94 percent of HMO professionals now believe that prayer, meditation, and other spiritual and religious practices exercise a major positive role within the healing process.

Atheist writers, such as Kevin Courcey, generally dismiss this as superstitious nonsense. Yet these viewpoints are grounded in a growing body of empirical evidence that has established a positive correlation between spirituality and health, especially in relation to how patients cope with illness and subsequently recover from it. Without in any way offering a judgment on the truth of patients' religious beliefs, this evidence points unequivocally to the health benefits of faith. It does not exclude the possibility that such beliefs are indeed "superstitious nonsense"—but that was not the object of the investigations. Whatever the truth of these religious beliefs, they are increasingly regarded as therapeutic by medical practitioners.

The outcome of this is significant. There is now growing pressure from patients and health care professionals for the religious views of patients to be incorporated on a consensual basis into medical treatment, especially in relation to the care of the dying. The simple fact of the matter is that religion matters profoundly to many in the West, who wish—without forcing those views on others—to have them incorporated into the health care they receive. Whatever atheists may feel about this, Christians and other religionists believe that their faith has a positive impact upon their lives, and wish to exercise their freedom in this matter.

One of those positive aspects of religion concerns the creation of community, to which we may now turn.

RELIGION AND THE CREATION OF COMMUNITY

The creation of community has become an increasingly important political issue in many Western cultures, especially when set against the backdrop of a breakdown of social cohesion in recent decades. How can a sense of community, if once lost, be re-created? The question naturally invites a comparison of religious and atheist approaches to the creation and maintenance of a sense of community.

The role of religion in creating and sustaining communal identity has been known for some considerable time, and has become increasingly important since about 1965. One of the most obvious indicators of the ongoing importance of religion is the well-documented tendency of immigrant communities to define themselves in religious terms. Great Britain has seen substantial immigration from the Indian subcontinent. Yet the communities that have arisen within British cities self-define using religious (rather than national) parameters, with places of worship acting as community centers. The British media have learned not to speak of "Indian" communities in Britain, but of Sikh, Hindu, and Muslim communities, and to expect the identities of these communities to be focused on the local gudwara, temple, or mosque.

A similar pattern is found in France, where substantial immigration has taken place from Algeria and other North African countries. Once more, these communities define themselves primarily in religious terms, with the mosques of Paris and Marseilles sustaining the identity of France's five million Muslims. The importance of religion in shaping the identity of this community has forced the French government to reconsider its traditional secularist attitudes and give increasing recognition to the importance of religion in national life.

Christian churches have long been the centers of community life in the West. The more entrepreneurial of American churches have recently begun to develop this role further, seeing the church as an oasis of communal stability in a rapidly changing culture. The August 1996 issue of the *Atlantic Monthly* ran an article by Charles Trueheart entitled "Welcome to the Next Church," which featured some of the more radical and innovative approaches now being adopted in Christian worship and life. A good example of these new approaches is found in the Mariners Church, close to Newport Beach, California, which has recently merged with a neighboring megachurch to become Mariners Southcoast Church. The success of this church, and countless others like it, can be attributed to their recognition of the importance of creating a sense of community identity. People want to belong, not just believe. Such churches see themselves as "islands in the stream," like the monasteries of the Middle Ages, offering safety and community to travelers on the journey of life. Identity is about belonging somewhere. And the community churches see themselves as providing a place where its members belong.

A community church is like small-town America of bygone days, with a population numbered in the low thousands. There is a sense of belonging to a common group, of shared values, and of knowing each other. People don't just *go* to community churches; they see themselves as *belonging* there. "Belonging to Mariners or any other large church conveys membership in a community, with its benefits of friends and solace and purpose, and the deep satisfaction of service to others." At a time when American society appears to be fragmenting, the community churches offer cohesion.

Thus Mariners offers its members a whole range of social activities, all designed to meet needs, offer service, and forge community. On the morning that Trueheart visited the church, he discovered seminars on single parenting, meetings on recovery from alcohol and drug abuse, women's Bible studies, a session on divorce dynamics, and a men's retreat—to mention just a few. As Trueheart notes, these churches "are proving themselves to be breeding grounds for personal renewal and human interconnectedness."

It is important to make this connection with the changing face of America. In a much-cited article published in the November 1994 number of the same *Atlantic Monthly*, management guru Peter Drucker made the following point concerning the "Age of Social Transformation": "The old communities—family, village, parish, and so on—have all but disappeared in the knowledge society. Their place has largely been taken by the new unit of social integration, the organization. Where community was fate, organization is voluntary membership." In the old days, community was defined by where you lived. It was part of the inherited order of things, something that you were born into. Now, it has to be *created*—and the agency that creates this community is increasingly the voluntary organization. Christian churches are strategically placed to create and foster community, where more negative social forces are destroying it in American society as a whole. The community churches have proved especially effective in this role, and have grown immensely in consequence.

But what of atheism? The importance of creating a sense of community was recognized at an early stage in the history of the Soviet Union. Having eliminated religion from the public life of the nation, Soviet planners recognized the importance of creating rituals and events that fostered social cohesion and a sense of identity. These were often deliberately conceived as alternatives to their Christian counterparts. Thus the Saturday just before Easter was celebrated as Communist Saturday. Other holidays in the official Soviet calendar included May Day, Victory Day (May 9), Constitution Day (October 7), and Revolution Day (November 7–8). The Soviet year was thus organized in such a way as to commemorate and affirm the fundamental principles of the government and the events that founded it and preserved it. Additional rituals were devised as counterparts to the Christian rite of baptism and confirmation—for example, the "family event" to mark the birth of a new child, or the ceremony to mark admission to the Communist Party.

As the German sociologist Benno Ennker has shown, the cult of Lenin was developed as a means of ensuring social cohesion and political loyalty throughout the Union (the parallel with the Roman emperor cult of the first century is both remarkable and illuminating). The origins of this development go back to 1924, and can be seen as an attempt to inculcate the idea that Lenin's ideals are immortalized in the ethos of the Soviet Union, with the Communist Party as the guardian of this heritage. Historians have noted the obvious and presumably intentional substitution of secular alternatives for Jesus Christ and his church, the anticipated outcome being that the Russian people would make this switch of allegiance without undue difficulty, and show the same loyalty to the party as they once had to the church. Once invented, these rituals became part of normal Soviet life. Yet their potency derived from their imposition by the state, and the fact that no alternatives were permitted. They were intended to represent and so-lidify the values and beliefs of Marxism-Leninism. With the fall of the Soviet Union, these rituals and cults were replaced by a renewed com-mitment to those of the Russian Orthodox church, or retained with drastic modifications to make them more acceptable in a post-Soviet and postatheist era.

The nearest thing in the West to this Soviet model is found in Canada, which seems to think that a sense of community identity can only be created by eliminating any religious presence in the public arena. Religions create division, right? So the best way of creating so-cial cohesion is to keep them out of the public square. Archbishop Michael Peers used his 2002 New Year sermon, preached in Ottawa Cathedral, to raise doubts about this kind of approach: "Secularism, ac-cording to some contributors to this debate, will bring unity and strength to our country by removing from its life the divisiveness of re-ligion," he noted. "This kind of thing, I think, would prove to be not only a suppression of the pluralist reality, but also a folly of the worst sort for society. If we think we can achieve unity by the suppression of knowledge of, and respect for, religious diversity, then we will never understand our world." Canada prides itself on its multiculturalism, he argued, yet is moving to eliminate references to the faiths that under-pin that culture. "Imagine telling Sikhs and Muslims that their culture is respected in this country but the society has no place for their faith. Faith and culture are intimately connected."

But what of atheism in the United States, where the kind of social and intellectual uniformity demanded and imposed by the Communist Party of the Soviet Union is unthinkable, let alone unrealizable? Here, atheism spawns organizations; it does not create community. To give one example: the state chapters and national convention of American Atheists, coupled with this organization's atheist equivalent of creeds, certainly did something to create a sense of shared identity. Yet the community thus created seems to be based solely on a distaste for religion. It doesn't even have a good organizational base, and lacks charismatic leadership—a fatal weakness, to which we now turn.

INSTITUTIONAL ATHEISM:
A FAILURE OF VISION

One of Franz Kafka's best lines about the apparent futility of life has wider implications: "There is a goal, but no way; and what we call a way is vacillation." You may know where you want to go; getting there is rather more complicated, and demands a compelling vision for the future, as well as good leadership—something Western atheism has lacked since the Second World War. Individual atheist writers and thinkers are more than happy to appear on the nation's chat shows to promote their latest books. But they have failed to communicate a compelling vision of atheism that is capable of drawing large numbers of people and holding them securely.

This comprehensive failure of leadership within their institutions is widely discussed within atheist circles. Howard Thompson, sometime editor of the *Texas Atheist*, is undoubtedly one of the most able and reflective atheists in the United States. In his op-ed piece "Who Speaks for Atheism?," Thompson criticized the movement for its lack of direction: "Atheism in America is poorly defined with little organization. We have less social and cultural infrastructure than even the smallest religious groups . . . Atheism desperately needs effective public voices. We need informed, well-spoken people presenting our material realism in opposition to supernaturalism. We need honest, effective representatives building a positive public image for atheism."

And why has this failed to happen? Thompson lays much of the blame at the feet of Madalyn Murray O'Hair, whom he regards as the movement's greatest liability. To his indignation, her organization has failed to learn from her mistakes, and persists in depicting her as a hero, even a martyr, for the atheist cause. Can't atheists learn from their mistakes?

Atheism has a problem. For thirty years Madalyn O'Hair was the most visible atheist. What Madalyn did and said WAS atheism to the public, and it was nasty. The disappearance of the O'Hairs in September 1995 gave hope that more positive atheist initiatives might develop. That's why atheists should worry about the revival of Madalyn's American Atheists, Inc. under the leadership of Ellen Johnson, who assumed the office of President in a questionable Board of Directors meeting. Ellen Johnson is also a die-hard Madalyn fan who continues to present Madalyn as an atheist heroine. What atheism doesn't need is a continuation of Madalyn's negativity . . . Madalyn's style and limited vision stifled positive atheist growth.

What we find in modern American atheism is one of the great dilemmas of all movements that owe their origins and inspiration to a charismatic founding individual. As time passes, the limitations of the founder become a liability rather than an asset. Madalyn's atheism was crude, anti-intellectual, and homophobic, making even the more zealous fundamentalist Christian seem a model of liberal values.

So what is to be done? For Thompson, the answer is clear: grow leaders. It is something that the Christian churches have been doing for years, and they have rather overwhelmed atheism's somewhat unimpressive attempts to date in this area. In another op-ed piece, "The Unlit Bonfire," Thompson argues that a new dawn lies around the corner—if only the leadership issue can be resolved. "Total victory is the only acceptable goal in a mind-control war because humanity is diminished so long as a single mind remains trapped in superstition by programming or choice." But who will lead them? And can this goal actually be achieved?

The fatal flaw within Thompson's argument, found within many other atheist tracts and publications, is his strident insistence that humanity has been enslaved by supernaturalist superstition. It is merely necessary to educate people, he believes, and these mad ideas will fall away, leaving everyone the better for having lost them. Thompson and his colleagues have not even begun to understand a fundamental fact about religion: people actually like their faith, find it helpful in structuring their lives, and inconveniently believe that it might actually be true. More worrying for Thompson, his alternative to the rich fare of a transcendent faith is "a materialistic culture that frees humanity from superstition." This sounds dull, dated, and gray, about as exciting as a lecture on Bulgarian Marxist dialectics. The failure of atheism to capture the public imagination in the West is a reflection of its failure to articulate a compelling imaginative vision of a godless future, capable of exciting people and making them want to gather together to celebrate and proclaim it.

The same dullness pervades the National Secular Society (founded in 1866), the nearest thing Great Britain has to an atheist network. Its Web site, which I visited late in 2002, was a museum of modernity, untroubled by the awkward rise of postmodernity. You can buy a secular mug with the slogan "Just say no to religion!" Or even better, you can download an official Certificate of De-Baptism (medieval font needed) that lets your friends know that you have rejected the "creeds and all other such superstition" in the name of reason. Rationalism, having quietly died out in most places, still lives on here. Yet Western culture has bypassed this aging little ghetto, having long since recognized the limitations of reason. The Enlightenment lives on for secularists. Atheism is wedded to philosophical modernity, and both are aging gracefully in the cultural equivalent of an old folks' home.

And, for those who find their tracts wearisome, the society thoughtfully provides a religious jokes page, which will interest those who like to fantasize about the size of Adam's penis in the Garden of Eden, or the masturbatory habits of nuns. It's the best bit of the site, with a significantly higher intellectual content than what surrounds it. It's grossly offensive, of course, to Christians and others—but hey, that's part of the game! With arguments of this caliber, it can only be weeks before Britain embraces atheism for its cultural sensitivity and good taste. Here's an example of atheism's winsome arguments:

Q. What's the difference between Jesus and a painting?

A. It only takes one nail to hang a painting.

It makes my friends outside the church cringe with embarrassment. Yet I have the impression this is actually meant to persuade people of the intellectual and cultural superiority of a world without religion. Howard Thompson clearly has a point.

Nevertheless, serious issues are occasionally debated on the Web site, including the question of why secular humanism, with its commitment to atheism, has so singularly failed to capture the public imagination. One obvious answer might be the National Secular Society itself, which exudes a pious tedium, trapped in a time warp of the closing decades of the nineteenth century, that seems almost to have been deliberately designed to alienate potential recruits. This is not mentioned on the site, for some reason. However, one of those to wrestle with the issues—a Dr. Reginald Le Sueur—put his finger unerringly on the real point at issue: "The problem with Humanism as such, is that although rational, secular, and 'true,' it is, in comparison with major religions somewhat wishy-washy, and just plain unexciting. It is difficult to see how it could be otherwise, as it has no great myths and legends, or blood and thunder sermonising, and no eschatology of its own, but only a denial and criticism of that of the religions." Atheism is here recognized as derivative, its attraction residing primarily in what it denies, rather than what it articulates as an alternative. On this showing, secularism is as dull as it comes, making a pallid appeal to the reason and failing to engage the imagination and emotions. A Pentecostal worship experience is going to trump anything atheism can offer by way of the secular equivalent of worship.

So does atheism have a future? I have no doubt that it does. But it does not seem to me to be an especially distinguished or exciting future. Listen to John Updike. "Among the repulsions of atheism for me has been its drastic uninterestingness as an intellectual position." I have to confess that I now share his catatonic sense of utter tedium when I reread some of the atheist works I once found fascinating as a teenager, and now see as simplistic, failing to engage with the complexities of human experience, and seriously out of tune with our postmodern culture.

It is easy to write atheism off as something that need no longer be taken with great seriousness. But that would be a massive misjudgment. In bringing this work to a close, we must appreciate the deadly seriousness of the atheist critique of religion. While it is tempting to see atheism as a philosophy that is receding into the past, the reality is much more complex. Atheism stands in permanent judgment over arrogant, complacent, and superficial Christian churches and leaders. It needs to be heard. In the closing pages of this work, its concerns will be taken seriously and to heart.

The Permanent Significance
of Atheism

The greatest virtue of atheism is its moral seriousness. It is impossible to do anything other than admire the criticisms and passionate demands for justice directed by atheists against the corruptions of—shall we say—the French church of the eighteenth century. An excessive degree of criticism must, of course, be regarded with at least some degree of cynicism: who, after all, is not without their own agendas, which they hope to advance in this way? "Moral indignation," as Marshall McLuhan once said, "is a technique to endow the idiot with dignity." But the moral passion of atheism, especially when set alongside the laziness and complacency of European state churches in the eighteenth century, cannot be dismissed in this way. Some Christian leaders at the time of the French Revolution saw that event as a divine judgment against a failing church. There were certainly some at the time of the French Revolution who believed that God was using the atheist critiques of the church as a means of reforming it, calling it back to more authentic modes of existence.

Paradoxically, history strongly suggests that those who are attracted to atheism are first repelled by theism. What propels people toward atheism is above all a sense of revulsion against the excesses and failures of organized religion. Atheism is ultimately a worldview of fear— a fear, often merited, of what might happen if religious maniacs were to take over the world. The existence and appeal of atheism in the West is thus largely derivative, mirroring the failings of the churches and specific ways of conceiving the Christian faith.

As the critics of Homeric religion made clear, the attractions of a godless world rest upon a sense of revulsion against the god(s). Who wanted to worship or imitate gods such as Zeus and Athene, when they merely immortalized the worst moral failings of human beings? The rejection of the general idea of a god rested on the belief that gods were immoral and capricious. Voltaire held no brief for atheism; nevertheless, he believed that the corruption and arrogance of the French church of his day had done more than anything else to propel its antithesis to the forefront of debate, and give it an appeal that it would otherwise never have possessed.

That same concern remains of fundamental importance to modern atheism. In the end, debates about whether God's existence can be proved remain marginal; it is widely conceded that neither the existence nor nonexistence of God can be demonstrated with anything approaching certainty. The central issue is moral and imaginative. Many individuals continue to find aspects of—for example—the Christian rendering of God to be offensive, in that the Christian God seems to fall short in goodness or wisdom. Setting to one side spurious and fractious forms of atheism, which woodenly reject *any* spiritual dimension to life on a priori grounds, a serious and morally demanding atheism poses a fundamental challenge to concepts of divinity that are seen to be morally defective.

The most fundamental criticisms directed against Christianity have to do with the moral character of its God, and often focus specifically on the issue of eternal punishment. No theological issue posed greater difficulties for Victorian England, as the writings of George Eliot make clear. It was for this reason that Charles Darwin found his faith, surprisingly unchallenged by his views on evolution, to be stretched beyond its modest capacity. Others had similarly serious misgivings. "Eternal punishment must be eternal cruelty—and I do not see how any man, unless he has the brain of an idiot, or the heart of a wild beast, can believe in eternal punishment" (Robert Ingersoll). Despite its opportunistic overstatement, Ingersoll's complaint resonates deeply with many who find an apparent contradiction between their deepest intuitions of fairness and the traditionally conceived Christian God.

Christian apologists cannot hope simply to assert such doctrines as eternal damnation and expect Western culture to nod approvingly. This culture is not predisposed to reject Christian doctrines as a matter of principle; it is taken by surprise by what seems to represent a massive retreat from our culture's most fundamental notions of decency and evenhandedness. Atheism arises mainly through a profound sense that religious ideas and values are at least inferior to, and possibly irreconcilable with, the best moral standards and ideals of human culture.

In its most intense and authentic forms, atheism enters a powerful protest against what it sees to be morally or intellectually inferior visions of reality, or institutions grounded in and proclaiming such visions, precisely because they enslave people, preventing them from achieving their true potential. In their place, atheism offered visions of a larger freedom, allowing humanity to throw aside its chains and enter a new and glorious phase in their history. It is perhaps not surprising that many sympathize with Dostoyevsky's character Ivan Karamazov when he respectfully returns God's ticket, in the face of the suffering, pain, and injustice of the world. Christianity must provide answers—good answers—to such fair questions and never assume that it can recycle yesterday's answers to today's concerns.

But the real significance of atheism has to do with its critique of power and privilege. Whatever their failings—and they are many— atheist organizations are right in challenging the idea that any religious grouping can enjoy special privileges in a democratic society. Such groupings have a right to respect, but cannot expect to have influence beyond their demographically determined limits. When religion becomes the establishment, an abuse of power results that corrupts the worldview. When religion starts getting ideas about power, atheism soars in its appeal.

The converse is, of course, true. The rise of militant Islam in Afghanistan was the direct outcome of the Soviet invasion of that nation in 1979, and its clumsy attempts to support an atheist regime. As Karen Armstrong has repeatedly pointed out in her *Battle for God* (2000), the best way to encourage the rise of religious fundamentalism is to try and impose a secular agenda on people who want to get on with their religious lives. The great secularist attempt to control religion by confining it to a purely private space has failed. More than that; it has backfired by causing a reaction against precisely those goals it hoped to achieve.

Atheism's concerns about the Christian exertion of power, status, and influence resonate with many within the church, who find no such imperative to domination within the New Testament. The assumption of the foundational documents of the Christian church is that Christianity is excluded from the establishment, and thus insulated from the temptations and corruption that power brings in its wake—temptations and corruptions, it may be added, to which institutionalized state atheism has shown itself to be equally vulnerable. For many reflective Christians, the church began to lose its compelling moral and spiritual vision with the conversion of Constantine, the first Christian Roman emperor. A movement that was at its most authentic while powerless and weak now became exposed to forces that compromised its integrity.

Yet it must be noted that Christianity is a dynamic entity, constantly changing in its form as it seeks to relate its foundational heritage in the New Testament to the situations in which it finds itself. The churches possess an inbuilt capacity to reform and renew themselves, learning from past errors and exploring new ways of embodying the gospel vision in the future. As our survey has indicated, atheist criticisms of the church are at their most compelling and persuasive when they are directed against the failings of the institution of the church, particularly in the case of the state churches of Western Europe. But these are only one form of Christian self-expression, determined by historical contingencies—such as the politics of early modern Europe—not by the essentials of the Christian gospel. Such churches are on their way out, to be replaced by more dynamic forms of Christian community with a concern for service rather than status. The dramatic rise of Pentecostalism among the urban poor of Asia, Africa, and Latin America is a telling indication of the new trends within the worldwide Christian movement.

The essential difficulty here is that the classic atheist criticisms of the church do not quite ring true any longer, even in the homelands of the much-derided state churches of Western Europe. The repetition of stale clichés from the golden age of atheism sounds increasingly out of touch with postmodern reality. The rise of atheism in the West was undoubtedly a protest against a corrupted and complacent church; yet paradoxically, it has energized Christianity to reform itself, in ways that seriously erode the credibility of those earlier criticisms. Where atheism criticizes, wise Christians move to reform their ways.

The atheist dilemma is that Christianity is a moving target whose trajectory is capable of being redirected without losing its anchor point in the New Testament. And as the theologian John Henry Newman pointed out, Christianity must listen to such criticisms from outside its bounds precisely because listening may be a way of recapturing its vision of the gospel. A static atheism finds a moving Christianity highly inconvenient.

Some atheists have argued that the phenomenon of globalization can only advance a secularist agenda, eliminating religion from the public arena. If the world is to have a shared future, it can only be by eliminating what divides its nations and peoples—such as religious beliefs. Yet many have pointed out in response that globalization seems to be resulting in a quite different outcome. Far from being secularized, the West is experiencing a new interest in religion. Patterns of immigration mean that Islam and Hinduism are now major living presences in the cities of Western Europe and North America. Pentecostalism is a rapidly growing force, strengthened by the arrival of many Asian and African Christians in the West. The future looks nothing like the godless and religionless world so confidently predicted forty years ago. Political opportunism and cultural sensitivity have led to religious beliefs being treated with new respect. The atheist agenda, once seen as a positive force for progress, is now seen as disrespectful toward cultural diversity. It is a highly significant trend, marking a decisive transition in perceptions.

The attractions of a world without God depend on whether the presence of God is seen as a positive matter. For this reason, the appeal and fortunes of atheism do not entirely lie within its own control. If I am to assess the attraction of the atheist vision, I will need to be able to imagine a world *with* God before coming to any decision. Where religion is seen to oppress, confine, deprive, and limit, atheism may well be seen as offering humanity a larger vision of freedom. But where religion manages to anchor itself in the hearts and minds of ordinary people, is sensitive to their needs and concerns, and offers them a better future, the less credible the atheist critique will appear. Believers need to realize that, strange though it may seem, it is they who will have the greatest impact on atheism's future.

Paradoxically, the future of atheism will be determined by its religious rivals. Those atheists looking for a surefire way to increase their appeal need only to hope (for we cannot reasonably ask them to pray) for harsh, vindictive, and unthinking forms of religion to arise in the West, which will so alienate Westerners that they will rush into godlessness from fear and dislike of its antithesis. When religion is seen as a threat to the people, it will fail; when it is seen as their friend, it will flourish. It is therefore important to note how the American Revolution singularly failed to promote atheism, in that forms of Christianity accustomed to opposing the British religious establishment played a leading role in its success.

In his problematic but fascinating work *The Decline of the West*, Oswald Spengler argued that history showed that cultures came into being for religious reasons. As they exhausted the potential of that spirituality, religion gave way to atheism, before a phase of religious renewal gave them a new sense of direction. Might atheism have run its course, and now give way to religious renewal? The tides of cultural shift have left atheism beached for the time being on the sands of modernity, while Westerners explore a new postmodern interest in the forbidden fruit of spirituality. But will it stay there? Might the tide change once more, and the ship of atheism return to the high seas? Its fate lies with others—with the uncontrollable and unpredictable shifts in Western culture and the equally erratic behavior of religious activists.

Western atheism now finds itself in something of a twilight zone. Once a worldview with a positive view of reality, it seems to have become a permanent pressure group, its defensive agenda dominated by concerns about limiting the growing political influence of religion. But is this the twilight of a sun that has sunk beneath the horizon, to be followed by the darkness and cold of the night? Or is it the twilight of a rising sun, which will bring a new day of new hope, new possibilities—and new influence? We shall have to wait and see.

LIST OF WORKS
CONSULTED

Ablaing van Giessenburg, R. C. 1864. *Le testament de Jean Meslier*. Amsterdam: Meijer.

Abrams, M. H. 1973. *Natural Supernaturalism: Tradition and Revolution in Romantic Literature*. New York: Norton.

Acton, E. 1979. *Alexander Herzen and the Role of the Intellectual Revolutionary*. Cambridge, U.K.: Cambridge University Press.

Allen, B. 1994. "Atheism, Relativism, Enlightenment and Truth." *Studies in Religion—Sciences Religieuses* 23(2): 167–77.

Alston, W. P. 1991. "The Inductive Argument from Evil and the Human Cognitive Condition." *Philosophical Perspectives* 5: 30–67.

Altholz, J. L. 1976. "The Warfare of Conscience with Theology." In *The Mind and Art of Victorian England*, ed. J. L. Altholz, pp. 58–77. Minneapolis: University of Minnesota Press.

Altizer, T. J. J. 1966. *The Gospel of Christian Atheism*. Philadelphia: Westminster.

Ammer, V. 1988. *Gottmenschentum und Menschgottum: Zur Auseinandersetzung von Christentum und Atheismus im russischen Denken*. Munich: Sagner.

Anderson, R. M. 1980. *Vision of the Disinherited: The Making of American Pentecostalism*. Oxford, U.K.: Oxford University Press.

Aner, K. 1964. *Die Theologie der Lessingzeit*. Hildesheim, Germany: Olms.

Angiuli, V. 2000. *Ragione moderna e verità del Cristianésimo: l'Atheismus triumphatus di Tommaso Campanella*. Bari, Italy: Levante.

Ashton, R. 1994. *The German Idea: Four English Writers and the Reception of German Thought, 1800–1860*. London: Libris.

Aston, N. 2001. "Romantic Atheism: Poetry and Freethought, 1780–1830." *European History Quarterly* 31(3): 458–61.

Ault, D. D. 1974. *Visionary Physics: Blake's Response to Newton*. Chicago: University of Chicago Press.

Ayer, A. J. 1946. *Language, Truth and Logic*. London: Gollancz.

Bainbridge, W. S., and R. Stark. 1985. *The Future of Religion: Secularization, Revival, and Cult Formation*. Berkeley: University of California Press.

Barth, H.-M. 1971. *Atheismus und Orthodoxie: Analysen und Modelle christlicher Apologetik im 17. Jahrhundert*. Göttingen: Vandenhoeck & Ruprecht.

Barth, K. 1957. *Die protestantische Theologie im 19. Jahrhundert*. Zurich: Evangelischer Verlag.

Behrens, C. B. A. 1985. *Society, Government and the Enlightenment: The Experiences of Eighteenth-Century France and Prussia*. New York: Harper & Row.

Berman, D. 1988. *A History of Atheism in Britain: From Hobbes to Russell*. London: Croom Helm.

———. 1988. "Nietzsche's Three Phases of Atheism." *History of Philosophy Quarterly* 5: 273–86.

Berriot, F. 1984. *Athéismes et athéistes au XVIe siècle en France*. Lille: Atelier national de reproduction des thèses.

Bertaux, P. 1990. *Hölderlin und die Französische Revolution*. Berlin: Aufbau-Verlag.

Besançon, A. 1981. *The Intellectual Origins of Leninism*. Oxford, U.K.: Blackwell.

Besant, A. W. 1887. *Why I Do Not Believe in God*. London: Freethought Publishing.

Bewell, A. 1989. *Wordsworth and the Enlightenment: Nature, Man and Society in the Experimental Poetry*. New Haven: Yale University Press.

Biagioli, M. 1993. *Galileo, Courtier: The Practice of Science in the Culture of Absolutism*. Chicago: University of Chicago Press.

Bianchi, L. 1996. *Rinascimento e libertinismo: studi su Gabriel Naudé*. Naples: Bibliopolis.

Bigler, R. M. 1972. *The Politics of German Protestantism: The Rise of the Protestant Church Elite in Prussia, 1815–1848*. Berkeley: University of California Press.

Blackwell, R. J. 1991. *Galileo, Bellarmine and the Bible*. Notre Dame, Ind.: University of Notre Dame Press.

Blanning, T. C. W. 1981. "The Enlightenment in Catholic Germany." In *The Enlightenment in National Context*, ed. R. Porter and M. Teich, pp. 118–26. Cambridge, U.K.: Cambridge University Press.

Blind, M. 1886. *Shelley's View of Nature Contrasted with Darwin's*. London: Printed for private distribution.

Blum, J. 1978. *The End of the Old Order in Rural Europe*. Princeton, N.J.: Princeton University Press.

Boggs, C. 1984. *The Two Revolutions: Antonio Gramsci and the Dilemmas of Western Marxism*. Boston: South End Press.

Bolton, B. 1995. *Innocent III: Studies on Papal Authority and Pastoral Care*. Aldershot, U.K.: Variorum.

Bosse, H. 1971. *Marx, Weber, Troeltsch. Religionssoziologie und marxistische Ideologiekritik*. Munich: Kaiser.

Branscombe, P. 1991. *W. A. Mozart, Die Zauberflöte*. Cambridge, U.K.: Cambridge University Press.

Braun, H.-J. 1971. *Ludwig Feuerbachs Lehre vom Menschen*. Stuttgart: Frommann.

Breckman, W. 1999. *Marx, the Young Hegelians, and the Origins of Radical Social Theory*. Cambridge, U.K.: Cambridge University Press.

Bredero, A. H. 1994. *Christendom and Christianity in the Middle Ages: The Relations between Religion, Church, and Society*. Grand Rapids, Mich.: Eerdmans.

Brennan, T. 1992. *The Interpretation of the Flesh: Freud and Femininity*. London: Routledge.

Brigham, L. C. 1994. "The Postmodern Semiotics of 'Prometheus Unbound.'" *Studies in Romanticism* 33: 31–56.

Brooke, J. H. 1992. "Natural Law in the Natural Sciences: The Origins of Modern Atheism?" *Science and Christian Belief* 4: 83–103.

Brotemarkle, D. 1993. *Imagination and Myths in John Keats's Poetry*. San Francisco: Mellen Research University Press.

Brotóns, V. N. 1995. "The Reception of Copernicus in Sixteenth-Century Spain: The Case of Diego de Zúñiga." *Isis* 86: 52–78.

Brown, C. G. 2001. *The Death of Christian Britain: Understanding Secularisation 1800–2000*. London: Routledge.

Brown, F. B. 1986. *The Evolution of Darwin's Religious Views*. Macon, Ga.: Mercer University Press.

Buchbinder, R. 1976. *Bibelzitate, Bibelanspielungen, Bibelparodien, theologische Vergleiche und Analogien bei Marx und Engels*. Berlin: Schmidt.

Buckley, M. J. 1987. *At the Origins of Modern Atheism*. New Haven: Yale University Press.

Burgess, R. 2001. "The Case for Atheism—Notes and Comments (Regarding Ludovic Kennedy's Quarrel with the Christian Religion)." *Heythrop Journal—A Quarterly Review of Philosophy and Theology* 42(1): 66–70.

Burns, C. D. 1947. *The First Europe: A Study of the Establishment of Medieval Christendom*. London: Allen & Unwin.

Butler, M. 1982. *Romantics, Rebels and Reactionaries: English Literature and Its Background, 1760–1830*. New York: Oxford University Press.

Camille, M. 1989. *The Gothic Idol: Ideology and Image-Making in Medieval Art*. Cambridge, U.K.: Cambridge University Press.

Cantelli, G. 1969. *Teologià e ateismo: Saggio sul pensiero filosòfico e religioso di Pierre Bayle*. Florence: La Nuova Italia.

Carnell, J. F. 1986. "Newton of the Grassblade? Darwin and the Problem of Organic Teleology." *Isis* 77: 405–21.

Carpenter, M. W. 1986. *George Eliot and the Landscape of Time: Narrative Form and Protestant Apocalyptic History*. Chapel Hill: University of North Carolina Press.

Carr, K. L. 1992. *The Banalization of Nihilism: Twentieth-Century Responses to Meaninglessness*. Albany: State University of New York Press.

Carroll, W. E. 1997. "Galileo, Science and the Bible." *Acta Philosophica* 6: 5–37.

Cashdollar, C. D. 1989. *The Transformation of Theology, 1830–1890: Positivism and Protestant Thought in Britain and America*. Princeton, N.J.: Princeton University Press.

Chadwick, O. 1975. *The Secularization of the European Mind in the Nineteenth Century*. Cambridge, U.K.: Cambridge University Press.

———. 1981. *The Victorian Church*. London: A. & C. Black.

Chartier, R. 1991. *Les origines culturelles de la Révolution française*. Paris: Seuil.

Christensen, C. C. 1979. *Art and the Reformation in Germany*. Detroit: Wayne State University Press.

Churchill, J. 2000. "Suspicion and Faith: The Religious Uses of Modern Atheism." *International Journal for Philosophy of Religion* 47(3): 183–85.

Clay, J. S. 1989. *The Politics of Olympus: Form and Meaning in the Major Homeric Hymns*. Princeton, N.J.: Princeton University Press.

Cobb, R. 1987. *The People's Armies: The* armées révolutionnaires: *Instrument of the*

Terror in the Departments April 1793 to Floréal Year II. New Haven: Yale University Press.

Colwell, F. S. 1996. "Figures in a Promethean Landscape." *Keats-Shelley Journal* 45: 118–31.

Conradi, P. 2001. *Iris Murdoch: A Life*. London: HarperCollins.

———. 2001. *The Saint and the Artist: A Study of the Fiction of Iris Murdoch*. London: HarperCollins.

Copleston, F. 1991. "Ayer and World Views." In *A. J. Ayer: Memorial Essays*, ed. A. P. Griffiths, pp. 63–75. Cambridge, U.K.: Cambridge University Press.

Courtois, S. 1999. *The Black Book of Communism: Crimes, Terror, Repression*. Cambridge, Mass.: Harvard University Press.

Cox, H. 1965. *The Secular City: Secularization and Urbanization in Theological Perspective*. New York: Macmillan.

———. 1996. *Fire from Heaven: The Rise of Pentecostal Spirituality and the Reshaping of Religion in the Twenty-First Century*. London: Cassell.

Crews, F., ed. 1998. *Unauthorized Freud: Doubters Confront a Legend*. New York: Penguin.

Cunningham, C. 2002. *Genealogy of Nihilism: Philosophies of Nothing and the Difference of Theology*. London: Routledge.

Curran, S. 1990. "The Political Prometheus." In *Spirits of Fire: English Romantic Writers and Contemporary Historical Methods*, ed. G. A. Rosso and D. P. Watkins, pp. 260–80. Madison, N.J.: Fairleigh Dickinson University Press.

Dahlke, S. 2001. " 'Godless Communists': Atheism and Society in Soviet Russia, 1917–1932." *Jahrbucher für Geschichte Osteuropas* 49(2): 284–85.

Dahm, H. 1991. "The Problem of Atheism in Recent Soviet Publications." *Studies in Soviet Thought* 41(2): 85–126.

Davenport-Hines, R. 2002. *The Pursuit of Oblivion: A Social History of Drugs*. London: Phoenix.

Davie, G. 1994. *Religion in Britain since 1945: Believing without Belonging*. Oxford, U.K.: Blackwell.

———. 2000. *Religion in Modern Europe: A Memory Mutates*. Oxford, U.K.: Oxford University Press.

———. 2002. *Europe: The Exceptional Case. Parameters of Faith in the Modern World*. London: Darton, Longman & Todd.

Dawkins, R. 1986. *The Blind Watchmaker: Why the Evidence of Evolution Reveals a Universe without Design*. New York: W. W. Norton.

———. 1989. *The Selfish Gene*. New York: Oxford University Press.

———. 1998. *Unweaving the Rainbow: Science, Delusion and the Appetite for Wonder*. Boston: Houghton Mifflin.

DeLaura, D. J. 1969. *Hebrew and Hellene in Victorian England: Newman, Arnold, and Pater*. Austin: University of Texas Press.

Dempster, M. W., B. D. Klaus, et al. 1999. *The Globalization of Pentecostalism: A Religion Made to Travel*. Carlisle, U.K.: Regnum Books International.

Di Giovanni, G. 1989. "From Jacobi's Philosophical Novel to Fichte's Idealism: Some Comments on the 1798–99 'Atheism Dispute.' " *Journal of the History of Philosophy* 27(1): 75–100.

Dijksterhuis, E. J. 1986. *The Mechanization of the World Picture: Pythagoras to Newton*. Princeton, N.J.: Princeton University Press.

Dodd, V. A. 1990. *George Eliot: An Intellectual Life*. Basingstoke, U.K.: Macmillan.

Doyle, W. 1992. *The Old European Order, 1660–1800*. Oxford, U.K.: Oxford University Press.

———. 1999. *Origins of the French Revolution*. Oxford, U.K.: Oxford University Press.

Duchemin, J. 1974. *Prométhée: Histoire du mythe, de ses origines orientales à ses incarnations modernes*. Paris: Les Belles Lettres.

Duffy, E. 1992. *The Stripping of the Altars: Traditional Religion in England c.1400–c.1580*. New Haven: Yale University Press.

Dupré, L. 1999. "On the Intellectual Sources of Modern Atheism." *International Journal for Philosophy of Religion* 45(1): 1–11.

Dyson, F. 1995. "The Scientist as Rebel." In *Nature's Imagination: The Frontiers of Scientific Vision*, ed. J. Cornwell, pp. 1–11. Oxford, U.K.: Oxford University Press.

Eliade, M. 1967. "Cultural Fashions and the History of Religions." In *The History of Religions: Essays in the Problem of Understanding*, ed. J. M. Kitagawa, pp. 21–38. Chicago: University of Chicago Press.

Ennker, B. 1997. *Die Anfänge des Leninkults in der Sowjetunion*. Cologne: Böhlau.

Epshtein, M. 1999. "Post-Atheism: From Apophatic Theology to 'Minimal Religion.'" In *Russian Postmodernism: New Perspectives on Post-Soviet Culture*, ed. M. Epshtein, S. Vladiv-Glover, and A. Genis, pp. 345–93. Oxford, U.K.: Berhhahn.

Fahr, W. 1969. *Theous nomizein: Zum Problem der Anfänge des Atheismus bei den Griechen*. Hildesheim, Germany: Olms.

Fastenrath, H. 1993. *Ein Abriss atheistischer Grundpositionen: Feuerbach, Marx, Nietzsche, Sartre*. Stuttgart: Klett.

Figes, O. 1997. *A People's Tragedy: A History of the Russian Revolution*. New York: Viking.

Foa, A. 1980. *Ateismo e magia: Il declino della concezione magica nel "Dictionnaire" di Pierre Bayle*. Rome: Ateneo.

Force, J. E. 1990. "The Breakdown of the Newtonian Synthesis of Science and Religion: Hume, Newton and the Royal Society." In *Essays on the Context, Nature and Influence of Isaac Newton's Theology*, ed. R. H. Popkin and J. E. Force, pp. 143–63. Dordrecht: Kluwer Academic Publishers.

Frank, J. 2002. *Dostoevsky: The Mantle of the Prophet, 1871–1881*. Princeton, N.J.: Princeton University Press.

Friesen, S. J. 1993. *Twice Neokoros: Ephesus, Asia, and the Cult of the Flavian Imperial Family*. Leiden: Brill.

Fromm, E. 1966. *Marx's Concept of Man*. New York: Ungar.

Fukuyama, F. 1992. *The End of History and the Last Man*. New York: Free Press.

Fyfe, A. 1997. "The Reception of William Paley's *Natural Theology* in the University of Cambridge." *British Journal for the History of Science* 30: 321–35.

Gagliardo, J. G. 1991. *Germany under the Old Regime, 1600–1790*. London: Longman.

Garrard, G. 1994. "Rousseau, Maistre, and the Counter-Enlightenment." *History of Political Thought* 15: 97–120.

Garrison, J. W. 1987. "Newton and the Relation of Mathematics to Natural Philosophy." *Journal of the History of Ideas* 48: 609–27.

Gascoigne, J. 1988. "From Bentley to the Victorians: The Rise and Fall of British Newtonian Natural Theology." *Science in Context* 2: 219–56.

Gay, P. 1968. *Deism*. Princeton, N.J.: Van Nostrand.

———. 1979. *The Dilemma of Democratic Socialism: Eduard Bernstein's Challenge to Marx*. New York: Octagon Books.

———. 1987. *A Godless Jew: Freud, Atheism, and the Making of Psychoanalysis*. New Haven: Yale University Press.

Gerth, H. H. 1935. *Die sozialgeschichtliche Lage der bürgerlichen Intelligenz um die Wende des 18. Jahrhunderts: Ein Beitrag zur Soziologie des deutschen Frühliberalismus*. Berlin: VDI Verlag.

Getty, J. A., and O. V. Naumov. 1999. *The Road to Terror: Stalin and the Self-Destruction of the Bolsheviks, 1932–1939*. New Haven: Yale University Press.

Gibson, I. 1978. *The English Vice: Beating, Sex, and Shame in Victorian England and After*. London: Duckworth.

Gide, A. 1930. *Le Prométhée mal enchaîné*. Paris: Gallimard.

Gildin, H. 1997. "Deja Jew All Over Again: Dannhauser on Leo Strauss and Atheism." *Interpretation: A Journal of Political Philosophy* 25(1): 125–33.

Gillespie, M. A. 1995. *Nihilism before Nietzsche*. Chicago: University of Chicago Press.

Gillespie, N. C. 1979. *Charles Darwin and the Problem of Creation*. Chicago: University of Chicago Press.

———. 1990. "Divine Design and the Industrial Revolution: William Paley's Abortive Reform of Natural Theology." *Isis* 81: 214–29.

Gioia, G. 1983. *Ateismo e trascendenza: Dio e la sua assenza*. Palermo: Enchiridion.

Glicksberg, C. I. 1966. *Modern Literature and the Death of God*. The Hague: Martinus Nijhoff.

Gliozzo, C. A. 1971. "The Philosophes and Religion: Intellectual Origins of the De-Christianization Movement in the French Revolution." *Church History* 40: 273–83.

Good, J. A. 2001. "Rational Mothers and Infidel Gentlemen: Gender and American Atheism, 1865–1915." *Journal of Church and State* 43(3): 619–20.

Gorman, M. J. 1996. "A Matter of Faith? Christoph Scheiner, Jesuit Censorship and the Trial of Galileo." *Perspectives on Science* 4: 283–320.

Gottlieb, R. S. 1987. *History and Subjectivity: The Transformation of Marxist Theory*. Philadelphia: Temple University Press.

Gould, S. J. 1989. *Wonderful Life: The Burgess Shale and the Nature of History*. New York: Norton.

———. 1992. "Impeaching a Self-Appointed Judge." *Scientific American* 267(1): 118–21.

Gould, S. J., and N. Eldredge. 1977. "Punctuated Equilibria: The Tempo and Mode of Evolution Reconsidered." *Paleobiology* 3: 115–51.

Groth, B. 1986. *Sowjetischer Atheismus and Theologie im Gespräch*. Frankfurt am Main: Knecht.

Grünbaum, A. 1984. *The Foundations of Psychoanalysis: A Philosophical Critique*. Berkeley: University of California Press.

Gullace, G. 1985. *Il Candide nel pensiero di Voltaire*. Naples: Società editrice napoletana.

Halbig, C. 2001. "Arguing for Atheism." *Zeitschrift für Philosophische Forschung* 55(2): 277–96.

Hall, A. R. 1996. *Isaac Newton: Adventurer in Thought*. Cambridge, U.K.: Cambridge University Press.

Hanratty, G. 1988. "The Origin and Development of Mystical Atheism." *Neue Zeitschrift für Systematische Theologie und Religionsphilosophie* 30(1): 1–17.

Harvey, V. A. 1995. *Feuerbach and the Interpretation of Religion*. Cambridge, U.K.: Cambridge University Press.

Hasselhorn, M. 1958. *Der altwürttembergische Pfarrstand im 18. Jahrhundert*. Stuttgart: Kohlhammer.

Hastings, A. 1986. *A History of English Christianity 1920–1985*. London: Collins.

Hauerwas, S. 1996. "Murdochian Muddles: Can We Get Through Them If God Does Not Exist?" In *Iris Murdoch and the Search for Human Goodness*, ed. M. Antonaccio and W. Schweiker, pp. 190–208. Chicago: University of Chicago Press.

Heitsch, E. 1994. *Xenophanes und die Anfänge kritischen Denkens*. Stuttgart: Franz Steiner.

Herrin, J. 1987. *The Formation of Christendom*. Princeton, N.J.: Princeton University Press.

Hill, C. 1997. *The Intellectual Origins of the English Revolution*. Oxford, U.K.: Clarendon.

Hoffmann, A. 2000. *Mit Gott einfach fertig: Untersuchungen zu Theorie und Praxis des Atheismus im Marxismus-Leninismus der Deutschen Demokratischen Republik*. Leipzig: Benno-Verlag.

Holmes, L. M. 2000. " 'Godless Communists': Atheism and Society in Soviet Russia, 1917–1932." *Slavic Review* 59(4): 911–12.

Höltgen, K. J. 1984. *The Reformation of Images and Some Jacobean Writers on Art*. Tübingen: Max Niemeyer.

Hoolsema, D. 2000. "Romantic Atheism: Poetry and Freethought, 1780–1830." *Religion & Literature* 32(3): 117–21.

Hughes, K. 1999. *George Eliot: The Last Victorian*. London: Fourth Estate.

Hurth, E. 1996. "When 'Man Makes God': Feuerbachian Atheism in New England." *ESQ: A Journal of the American Renaissance* 42(4): 254–89.

Husband, W. 1998. "Soviet Atheism and Russian Orthodox Strategies of Resistance, 1917–1932." *Journal of Modern History* 70: 74–107.

Hüsser, H. 1993. *Nature ohne Gott: Aspekte und Probleme von Ludwig Feuerbachs Naturverständnis*. Würzburg: Konigshausen & Neumann.

Huxley, A. 1937. *Ends and Means: An Inquiry into the Nature of Ideals and into Methods Employed for their Realization*. New York: Harper.

Huxley, T. H. 1860. "The Origin of Species." *Westminster Review* 17: 541–70.

Idema, H. 1990. *Freud, Religion, and the Roaring Twenties: A Psychoanalytic Theory of Secularization in Three Novelists: Anderson, Hemingway, and Fitzgerald*. Savage, Md.: Rowman & Littlefield.

Jay, E. 1979. *The Religion of the Heart: Anglican Evangelicalism and the Nineteenth-Century Novel*. Oxford, U.K.: Clarendon.

Johnson, P. 1988. *Intellectuals*. London: Weidenfeld and Nicolson.

Jones, E. 1953. *Sigmund Freud: Life and Work*. London: Hogarth Press.

Jugurtha, L. 1985. *Keats and Nature*. New York: Peter Lang.

Jüngel, E. 1982. *Gott als Geheimnis der Welt: Zur Begründung der Theologie des Gekreuzigten im Streit zwischen Theismus und Atheismus*. Tübingen: J. C. B. Mohr.

Kaiser, C. B. 1986. "Calvin, Copernicus and Castellio." *Calvin Theological Journal* 21: 5–31.

Kaiser, J.-C. 1981. *Arbeiterbewegung und organisierte Religionskritik: Proletarische Freidenkerverbände in Kaiserreich und Weimarer Republik*. Stuttgart: Klett-Cotta.

Kampits, P. 1968. *Der Mythos vom Menschen: Zum Atheismus und Humanismus Albert Camus*. Salzburg: Müller.

Kasper, J. J. 1906. *La révolution religieuse d'après Edgar Quinet*. Paris: Davy.

Keane, J. 1994. "Religion and Liberty—Tom Paine's Attack on Revolutionary Atheism." *Times Literary Supplement* (4741): 13–14.

Kegel, M. 1908. *Bruno Bauers Übergang der Hegelschen Rechten zum Radikalismus*. Leipzig: Quelle & Meyer.

Kennedy, E. 1994. "The French Revolution and the Genesis of a Religion of Man." In *Modernity and Religion*, ed. R. McInerny, pp. 61–88. Notre Dame, Ind.: University of Notre Dame Press.

Keulman, K. 2000. "Western Atheism: A Short History." *Journal of Church and State* 42(3): 577–79.

Keynes, R. 2001. *Annie's Box: Charles Darwin, His Daughter and Human Evolution*. London: Fourth Estate.

Kleiner, S. A. 1981. "Problem Solving and Discovery in the Growth of Darwin's Theories of Evolution." *Synthese* 62: 119–62.

———. 1988. "The Logic of Discovery and Darwin's Pre-Malthusian Researches." *Biology and Philosophy* 3: 293–315.

Knoepflmacher, U. C. 1970. *Religious Humanism and the Victorian Novel: George Eliot, Walter Pater, and Samuel Butler*. Princeton, N.J.: Princeton University Press.

Koch, H. G. 1963. *Neue Erde ohne Himmel: Der Kampf des Atheismus gegen das Christentum in der "DDR"—Modell einer weltweiten Auseinandersetzung*. Stuttgart: Quell-Verlag.

Koch, L. 1971. *Bruno Bauers "kritische Kritik": Beitrag zum Problem eines humanistischen Atheismus*. Stuttgart: Kohlhammer.

Kors, A. C. 1990. *Atheism in France, 1650–1729*. Princeton, N.J.: Princeton University Press.

———. 1993. "Skepticism and the Problem of Atheism in Early Modern France." In *Scepticism and Irreligion in the Seventeenth and Eighteenth Centuries*, ed. R. H. Popkin and A. Vanderjagt, pp. 185–215. Leiden: Brill.

Köster, U. 1972. *Literarischer Radikalismus: Zeitbewusstsein und Geschichtsphilosophie in der Entwicklung vom jungen Deutschland zur Hegelschen Linken*. Frankfurt: Athenaum Verlag.

Kristeller, P. O. 1968. "The Myth of Renaissance Atheism and the French Tradition of Free Thought." *Journal of the History of Philosophy* 6: 233–43.

Küng, H. 1979. *Freud and the Problem of God*. New Haven: Yale University Press.

Lackey, M. 1998. "The Gender of Atheism in Virginia Woolf's 'A Simple Melody.'" *Studies in Short Fiction* 35(1): 49–63.

———. 2000. "Atheism and Sadism: Nietzsche and Woolf on Post-God Discourse." *Philosophy and Literature* 24(2): 346–63.

Landes, D. S. 1969. *The Unbound Prometheus: Technological Change and Industrial Development in Western Europe from 1750 to the Present*. Cambridge, U.K.: Cambridge University Press.

Landow, G. P. 1980. *Victorian Types, Victorian Shadows: Biblical Typology in Victorian Literature, Art, and Thought*. Boston: Routledge & Kegan Paul.

———. 1982. *Images of Crisis: Literary Iconology, 1750 to the Present*. London: Routledge & Kegan Paul.

Lane, C. 1981. *The Rites of Rulers: Ritual in Industrial Society—The Soviet Case*. Cambridge, U.K.: Cambridge University Press.

Larson, E. J., and L. Witham. 1997. "Scientists Are Still Keeping the Faith." *Nature* 386: 435–36.

Lebrun, R. A. 1988. *Joseph de Maistre: An Intellectual Militant*. Montreal: McGill–Queen's University Press.

Lecourt, D. 1996. *Prométhée, Faust, Frankenstein: Fondements imaginaires de l'éthique*. Paris: Synthelabo.

Lefkowitz, M. R. 1989. "Impiety and Atheism in Euripides' Dramas." *Classical Quarterly* 39(1): 70–82.

Lehmann, H. 1969. *Pietismus und weltliche Ordnung in Württemberg vom 17. bis zum 20. Jahrhundert*. Stuttgart: Kohlhammer.

Leith, J. A. 1979. "Les trois apothéoses de Voltaire." *Annales historiques de la Révolution française* 236: 161–209.

Lendle, O. 1957. *Die "Pandorasage" bei Hesiod: Textkritische und motivgeschichtliche Untersuchungen*. Würzburg: Triltsch.

Leuba, J. H. 1916. *The Belief in God and Immortality: A Psychological, Anthropological and Statistical Study*. Boston: Sherman, French.

Levitt, N. 1999. *Prometheus Bedeviled: Science and the Contradictions of Contemporary Culture*. New Brunswick, N.J.: Rutgers University Press.

Ley, H. 1966. *Geschichte der Aufklärung und des Atheismus*. Berlin: Deutscher Verlag der Wissenschaften.

Lienhard, F. 2001. "Atheism." *Études Theologiques et Religieuses* 76(3): 462–63.

Lightman, B. V. 1987. *The Origins of Agnosticism: Victorian Unbelief and the Limits of Knowledge*. Baltimore: Johns Hopkins University Press.

Lindberg, D. C., and R. L. Numbers. 1984. "Beyond War and Peace: A Reappraisal of the Encounter between Christianity and Science." *Church History* 55: 338–54.

Livingstone, D. N. 1987. *Darwin's Forgotten Defenders: The Encounter between Evangelical Theology and Evolutionary Thought*. Grand Rapids, Mich.: Eerdmans.

———. 1992. "Darwinism and Calvinism: The Belfast-Princeton Connection." *Isis* 83: 408–28.

Lloyd-Jones, H. 1983. *The Justice of Zeus*. Berkeley: University of California Press.

Locke, D. 1980. *A Fantasy of Reason: The Life and Thought of William Godwin*. London: Routledge & Kegan Paul.

Loetscher, L. A. 1983. *Facing the Enlightenment and Pietism: Archibald Alexander and the Founding of Princeton Theological Seminary*. Westport, Conn.: Greenwood.

Lokke, K. E. 2001. " 'The Mild Dominion of the Moon': Charlotte Smith and the Politics of Transcendence." In *Rebellious Hearts: British Women Writers and the French Revolution*, ed. A. Craciun and K. E. Lokke, pp. 85–106. Albany: State University of New York Press.

Lucas, C. 1990. *La structure de la Terreur: L'exemple de Javogues et du département de la Loire*. Saint-Étienne: Centre interdisciplinaire d'études et de recherches sur l'expression contemporaine.

Lund, R. D. 1989. "Strange Complicities: Atheism and Conspiracy in a 'Tale of a Tub.' " *Eighteenth-Century Life* 13(3): 34–58.

Lynch, W. F. 1975. *Christ and Apollo: The Dimensions of the Literary Imagination*. New York: New American Library.

MacCulloch, D. 2003. *Reformation: Europe's House Divided, 1490–1700*. London: Allen Lane.

MacKinnon, D. M. 1991. "Ayer's Attack on Metaphysics." In *A. J. Ayer: Memorial Essays*, ed. A. P. Griffiths, pp. 49–61. Cambridge, U.K.: Cambridge University Press.

Manent, P. 1977. *Naissances de la politique moderne: Machiavel, Hobbes, Rousseau*. Paris: Payot.

———. 1994. *La cité de l'homme*. Paris: Fayard.

Manuel, F. E. 1974. *The Religion of Isaac Newton*. Oxford, U.K.: Clarendon.

Marcus, S. 1969. *The Other Victorians: A Study of Sexuality and Pornography in Mid-Nineteenth Century England*. London: Transworld.

Martin, D. 1997. *Does Christianity Cause War?* Oxford, U.K.: Clarendon.

Marwick, A. 1999. *The Sixties: Cultural Revolution in Britain, France, Italy, and the United States, c.1958–c.1974*. Oxford, U.K.: Oxford University Press.

Mayer, A. J. 2002. *The Furies: Violence and Terror in the French and Russian Revolutions*. Princeton, N.J.: Princeton University Press.

McGovern, A. F. 1986. "Marx's Atheism Revisited." *Journal of Ecumenical Studies* 23(1): 113–18.

McGrath, A. E. 2001. *Christian Theology: An Introduction*. Oxford, U.K.: Blackwell.

McKown, D. B. 1975. *The Classical Marxist Critiques of Religion: Marx, Engels, Lenin, Kautsky*. The Hague: Martinus Nijhoff.

McLachlan, H. 1941. *The Religious Opinions of Milton, Locke, and Newton*. Manchester, U.K.: Manchester University Press.

McLellan, D. 1969. *The Young Hegelians and Karl Marx*. London: Macmillan.

McManners, J. 1998. *The Church in Eighteenth-Century France*. Oxford, U.K.: Clarendon.

Mee, J. 1992. *Dangerous Enthusiasm: William Blake and the Culture of Radicalism in the 1790s*. Oxford, U.K.: Clarendon.

Miccoli, P. 1971. *Il problema del male e dell'ateismo in Albert Camus*. Alba, Italy: Edizioni paoline.

Michael, J. 2000. *Anxious Intellects: Academic Professionals, Public Intellectuals, and Enlightenment Values*. Durham, N.C.: Duke University Press.

Milosz, C. 1998. "The Discreet Charm of Nihilism." *New York Review of Books* 45(18) (November 19): 17–18.

Monod, J. 1997. *Chance and Necessity: An Essay on the Natural Philosophy of Modern Biology*. London: Penguin.

Moore, J. R. 1995. *The Darwin Legend*. London: Hodder & Stoughton.

Moss, J. D. 1993. *Novelties in the Heavens: Rhetoric and Science in the Copernican Controversy*. Chicago: University of Chicago Press.

Murdoch, I. 1992. *Metaphysics as a Guide to Morals*. London: Penguin.

Murphy, H. R. 1955. "The Ethical Revolt against Christian Orthodoxy in Early Victorian England." *American Historical Review* 60: 800–17.

Nagy, G. 1999. *The Best of the Achaeans: Concepts of the Hero in Archaic Greek Poetry*. Baltimore: Johns Hopkins University Press.

Neusner, J. 1995. *Judaism after the Death of "The Death of God."* Atlanta: Scholars Press.

Newell, W. L. 1986. *The Secular Magi: Marx, Freud, and Nietzsche on Religion*. New York: Pilgrim Press.

Nussbaum, M. C. 2001. *Upheavals of Thought: The Intelligence of Emotions*. Cambridge, U.K.: Cambridge University Press.

Obbink, D. 1989. "The Atheism of Epicurus." *Greek, Roman and Byzantine Studies* 30(2): 187–223.

O'Connor, D. 1990. "On Failing to Resolve Theism-versus-Atheism Empirically." *Religious Studies* 26: 91–103.

Ogletree, T. W. 1966. *The "Death of God" Controversy*. London: SCM Press.

O'Higgins, J. 1970. *Anthony Collins: The Man and His Works*. The Hague: Martinus Nijhoff.

———. 1971. "Hume and the Deists." *Journal of Theological Studies* 22: 479–501.

Ollman, B. 1977. *Alienation: Marx's Conception of Man in Capitalist Society*. Cambridge, U.K.: Cambridge University Press.

Onnasch, E. O. 2000. "Origins of Atheism. Studies in the Critique of Metaphysics and Religion in the 17th and 18th Centuries." *Tijdschrift voor Filosofie* 62(1): 174–75.

Otto, W. F. 1954. *The Homeric Gods: The Spiritual Significance of Greek Religion*. New York: Pantheon.

Pailin, D. 2000. "Should Herbert of Cherbury be regarded as a 'Deist'?" *Journal of Theological Studies* 51: 113–49.

Palmer, D. W. 1983. "Atheism, Apologetic and Negative Theology in the Greek Apologists of the Second Century." *Vigiliae Christianae* 37: 234–59.

Peckham, M. 1985. "Cultural Transcendence: The Task of the Romantics." In *English and German Romanticism: Cross-Currents and Controversies*, ed. J. Pipkin, pp. 35–57. Heidelberg: Winter.

Pedersen, O. 1983. *Galileo and the Council of Trent*. Vatican City: Specolo Vaticana.

Peikoff, L. 1993. *Objectivism: The Philosophy of Ayn Rand*. New York: Penguin.

Penglase, C. 1994. *Greek Myths and Mesopotamia: Parallels and Influence in the Homeric Hymns and Hesiod*. London: Routledge.

Peterfreund, S. 1987. "An Early Response to Shelley's *The Necessity of Atheism*." *Keats-Shelley Journal* 36: 26–31.

Plekhanov, G. V. 1969. *Fundamental Problems of Marxism*. New York: International Publishers.

Poland, B. C. 1957. *French Protestantism and the French Revolution: A Study in Church and State, Thought and Religion, 1685–1815*. Princeton, N.J.: Princeton University Press.

Porter, J. E., and D. L. McLaren, eds. 2000. *Star Trek and Sacred Ground: Explorations of Star Trek, Religion and American Culture*. Albany: State University of New York Press.

Pospielovsky, D. V. 1987. *A History of Marxist-Leninist Atheism and Soviet Anti-Religious Policies*. New York: St. Martin's Press.

Post, W. 1969. *Kritik der Religion bei Karl Marx*. Munich: Kösel.

Preus, S. J. 1987. *Explaining Religion: Criticism and Theory from Bodin to Freud*. New Haven: Yale University Press.

Price, S. R. F. 1984. *Rituals and Power: The Roman Imperial Cult in Asia Minor*. Cambridge, U.K.: Cambridge University Press.

Priestman, M. 1999. *Romantic Atheism: Poetry and Freethought, 1780–1830*. Cambridge, U.K.: Cambridge University Press.

Prignitz, C. 1976. *Friedrich Hölderlin: Die Entwicklung seines politischen Denkens unter dem Einfluss der französischen Revolution*. Hamburg: Helmut Buske.

Radar, M. 1979. *Marx's Interpretation of History*. New York: Oxford University Press.

Rawidowicz, S. 1964. *Ludwig Feuerbachs Philosophie: Ursprung and Schicksal*. Berlin: Walter de Gruyter.

Read, C. 1979. *Religion, Revolution and the Russian Intelligentsia, 1900–1912: The Vekhi Debate and Its Intellectual Background*. London: Macmillan.

Ricoeur, P. 1966. "The Atheism of Freudian Psychoanalysis." *Concilium* 6: 31–37.

———. 1970. *Freud and Philosophy: An Essay on Interpretation*. New Haven: Yale University Press.

Rizzuto, A. M. 1979. *The Birth of the Living God: A Psychoanalytic Study*. Chicago: University of Chicago Press.

Roe, N. 1992. *The Politics of Nature: Wordsworth and Some Contemporaries*. New York: St. Martin's.

Rogers, B. 1999. *A. J. Ayer: A Life*. London: Chatto & Windus.

Rosen, E. 1960. "Calvin's Attitude towards Copernicus." *Journal of the History of Ideas* 21: 431–41.

Rosen, Z. 1977. *Bruno Bauer and Karl Marx: The Influence of Bruno Bauer on Marx's Thought*. The Hague: Martinus Nijhoff.

Roth, R. A. 1991. "Nietzsche's Use of Atheism." *International Philosophical Quarterly* 31(1): 51–64.

Rowe, W. L. 1979. "The Problem of Evil and Some Varieties of Atheism." *American Philosophical Quarterly* 16: 335–41.

Rowell, G. 1974. *Hell and the Victorians: A Study of the Nineteenth-Century Theological Controversies concerning Eternal Punishment and the Future Life*. Oxford, U.K.: Clarendon.

Ruse, M. 1975. "Darwin's Debt to Philosophy: An Examination of the Influence of the Philosophical Ideas of John F. Herschel and William Whewell on the Development of Charles Darwin's Theory of Evolution." *Studies in the History and Philosophy of Science* 66: 159–81.

———. 1996. *Monad to Man: The Concept of Progress in Evolutionary Biology*. Cambridge, Mass.: Harvard University Press.

Russell, C. A. 1989. "The Conflict Metaphor and Its Social Origins." *Science and Christian Faith* 1: 3–26.

Ryan, R. M. 1997. *The Romantic Reformation: Religious Politics in English Literature, 1789–1824*. Cambridge, U.K.: Cambridge University Press.

Schama, S. 1989. *Citizens: A Chronicle of the French Revolution*. London: Viking.

Scharff, R. C. 1995. *Comte after Positivism*. Cambridge, U.K.: Cambridge University Press.

Schlingensiepen-Pogge, A. 1967. *Das Sozialethos der lutherischen Aufklärungstheologie am Vorabend der Industriellen Revolution*. Göttingen: Musterschmidt.

Schmidt, A. 1971. *The Concept of Nature in Marx*. London: New Left Books.

Schoedel, W. R. 1973. "Christian 'Atheism' and the Peace of the Roman Empire." *Church History* 42: 309–19.

Schott, U. 1973. *Die Jugendentwicklung Ludwig Feuerbachs bis zum Fakultätswechsel 1825: ein Beitrag zur Genese der Feuerbachschen Religionskritik*. Göttingen: Vandenhoeck und Ruprecht.

Schröder, W. 1998. *Ursprünge des Atheismus: Untersuchungen zur Metaphysik und Religionskritik des 17. und 18. Jahrhunderts*. Stuttgart–Bad Cannstatt: Frommann-Holzboog.

Schuffenhauer, W. 1972. *Feuerbach und der junge Marx: Zur Entstehungsgeschichte der marxistischen Weltanschauung*. Berlin: Deutscher Verlag der Wissenschaften VEB.

Schweitzer, A. 1954. *The Quest of the Historical Jesus*. London: A. & C. Black.

Sciabarra, C. M. 1995. *Ayn Rand: The Russian Radical*. University Park: Pennsylvania State University Press.

Scudo, F. M., and M. Acanforo. 1985. "Darwin and Russian Evolutionary Biology." In *The Darwinian Heritage*, ed. D. Kohn, pp. 731–52. Princeton, N.J.: Princeton University Press.

Sécher, R. 1988. *Le génocide franco-français: La Vendée-Vengé*. Paris: Presses universitaires de France.

———. 1991. *Juifs et Vendéens: d'un génocide à l'autre*. Paris: Olivier Orban.

Segal, C. 1990. *Lucretius on Death and Anxiety: Poetry and Philosophy in De rerum natura*. Princeton, N.J.: Princeton University Press.

Ségur, L.-P. 1826. *Mémoires, ou Souvenirs et anecdotes*. Paris: Eymery.

Senge, A. 1985. *Marxismus als atheistische Weltanschauung: Zum Stellenwert des Atheismus im Gefüge marxistischen Denkens*. Paderborn: Schoningh.

Shlapentokh, D. 1996. *The French Revolution in Russian Intellectual Life, 1865–1905*. Westport, Conn.: Praeger.

Shlapentokh, V. 1990. *Soviet Intellectuals and Political Power*. Princeton, N.J.: Princeton University Press.

Smart, J. J. C., and J. J. Haldane. 2003. *Atheism and Theism*. Oxford, U.K.: Blackwell.

Smith, J. C. 2002. *Sensuous Worship: Jesuits and the Art of the Early Catholic Reformation in Germany*. Princeton, N.J.: Princeton University Press.

Smith, Q. 1991. "Atheism, Theism and Big Bang Cosmology." *Australasian Journal of Philosophy* 69: 48–66.

Spengler, O. 1926. *The Decline of the West: Form and Actuality*. London: Allen & Unwin.

Stannard, D. E. 1980. *Shrinking History: On Freud and the Failure of Psychohistory*. New York: Oxford University Press.

Stark, R. 2001. *One True God: Historical Consequences of Monotheism*. Princeton, N.J.: Princeton University Press.

———. 2003. *For the Glory of God: How Monotheism Led to Reformations, Science, Witch-Hunts, and the End of Slavery*. Princeton, N.J.: Princeton University Press.

Stewart, L. 1996. "Seeing through the Scholium: Religion and Reading Newton in the Eighteenth Century." *History of Science* 34: 123–65.

Stoeffler, F. E. 1965. *The Rise of Evangelical Pietism*. Leiden: Brill.

Strier, R. 2000. "William Shakespeare and the Skeptics (Investigations into Supernatural Intervention and Renaissance 'Atheism')." *Religion & Literature* 32(2): 171–96.

Sullivan, R. E. 1982. *John Toland and the Deist Controversy: A Study in Adaptations*. Cambridge, Mass.: Harvard University Press.

Sulloway, F. J. 1979. *Freud, Biologist of the Mind: Beyond the Psychoanalytic Legend*. New York: Basic Books.

Sutherland, D. 1985. *France 1789–1815: Revolution and Counterrevolution*. London: Fontana.

Sydenham, M. J. 1999. *Léonard Bourdon: The Career of a Revolutionary, 1754–1807*. Waterloo, Ontario: Wilfrid Laurier University Press.

Tackett, T. 1986. *Religion, Revolution, and Regional Culture in Eighteenth-Century France: The Ecclesiastical Oath of 1791*. Princeton, N.J.: Princeton University Press.

Talbot, J. H. 1989. *The Nature of Aesthetic Experience in Wordsworth*. New York: Peter Lang.

Taylor, A. 1992. *Annie Besant: A Biography*. Oxford, U.K.: Oxford University Press.

Taylor, C. 2002. "Modern Social Imaginaries." *Public Culture* 14: 91–123.

Teixidor, J. 1977. *The Pagan God: Popular Religion in the Greco-Roman Near East*. Princeton, N.J.: Princeton University Press.

Teodorovich, N. A. 1970. *Religion und Atheismus in der UdSSR: Dokumente und Berichte*. Munich: Claudius.

Thompson, E. P. 1993. *Witness against the Beast: William Blake and the Moral Law*. Cambridge, U.K.: Cambridge University Press.

Thwaite, A. 2002. *Glimpses of the Wonderful: The Life of Philip Henry Gosse 1810–1888*. London: Faber and Faber.

Till, N. 1993. *Mozart and the Enlightenment: Truth, Virtue and Beauty in Mozart's Operas*. New York: Norton.

Todes, D. P. 1989. *Darwin without Malthus: The Struggle for Existence in Russian Evolutionary Thought*. Oxford, U.K.: Oxford University Press.

Toulmin, S. 1990. *Cosmopolis: The Hidden Agenda of Modernity*. New York: Free Press.

Touraine, A. 1992. *Critique de la modernité*. Paris: Fayard.

Tourpe, E. 2000. "Introduction to Modern Atheism." *Revue Philosophique de Louvain* 98(1): 107–33.

Tracy, D. 1996. "Iris Murdoch and the Many Faces of Platonism." In *Iris Murdoch and the Search for Human Goodness*, ed. M. Antonaccio and W. Schweiker, pp. 54–75. Chicago: University of Chicago Press.

Traill, D. A. 1996. *Schliemann of Troy: Treasure and Deceit*. London: Penguin.

Trevor-Roper, H. R. 1967. "The Religious Origins of the Enlightenment." In *Religion, the Reformation and Social Change*, pp. 193–236. London: Macmillan.

Trott, N. 1990. "The Coleridge Circle and the 'Answer to Godwin.'" *Review of English Studies* 41: 212–29.

Trousson, R. 1976. *Le thème de Prométhée dans la littérature européenne*. Geneva: Droz.

Tuck, R. 1992. "The 'Christian Atheism' of Thomas Hobbes." In *Atheism from the Reformation to the Enlightenment*, ed. M. Hunter and D. Wootton, pp. 102–20. Oxford, U.K.: Clarendon.

Tucker, R. C. 1970. *The Marxian Revolutionary Idea*. London: Allen & Unwin.

Turner, D. 1995. *The Darkness of God: Negativity in Christian Mysticism*. Cambridge, U.K.: Cambridge University Press.

———. 2002. *How to Be an Atheist: An Inaugural Lecture Given in the University of Cambridge*. Cambridge, U.K.: Cambridge University Press.

Turner, F. M. 1978. "The Victorian Conflict between Science and Religion: A Professional Dimension." *Isis* 69: 356–76.

Turner, J. 1985. *Without God, Without Creed: The Origins of Unbelief in America*. Baltimore: Johns Hopkins University Press.

Vallin, P. 1986. "Les 'Soirées' de Joseph de Maistre: Une création théologique originale." *Recherches des Science Religieuses* 74: 341–62.

van Herik, J. 1982. *Freud on Femininity and Faith*. Berkeley: University of California Press.

Van Kley, D. K. 1996. *The Religious Origins of the French Revolution: From Calvin to the Civil Constitution, 1560–1791*. New Haven: Yale University Press.

Vattimo, G. 1988. *The End of Modernity: Nihilism and Hermeneutics in Postmodern Culture*. Cambridge, U.K.: Polity Press.

Verona, L. 1975. *Jean Meslier: Prêtre athée, socialiste révolutionnaire*. Milan: Cisalpino-Goliardica.

Vidler, A. R. 1990. *The Church in an Age of Revolution: 1789 to the Present Day*. Harmondsworth, U.K.: Penguin.

Volf, M. 1989. "God, Freedom, and Grace: Reflections on the Essentiality of Atheism for Marx and Marxism." *Neue Zeitschrift für Systematische Theologie und Religionsphilosophie* 31(2): 213–29.

Volkov, D. 2001. "After Atheism: Religion and Ethnicity in Russia and Central Asia." *Journal for the Scientific Study of Religion* 40(3): 551–52.

Vovelle, M. 1994. "1789–1917: The Game of Analogies." In *The French Revolution and the Creation of Modern Political Culture*, ed. K. Baker, pp. 349–78. Oxford, U.K.: Pergamon.

Wackenheim, C. 1963. *La faillite de la religion d'après Karl Marx*. Paris: Presses universitaires de France.

Wade, I. O. 1971. *The Intellectual Origins of the French Enlightenment*. Princeton, N.J.: Princeton University Press.

Walker, M. 1998. *German Home Towns: Community, State, and General Estate, 1648–1871*. Ithaca, N.Y.: Cornell University Press.

Walsh, J. J. 1991. "On Christian Atheism: Pagan Hostility to Christianity in the 1st-Century and 2nd-Century." *Vigiliae Christianae* 45(3): 255–77.

Wangermann, E. 1981. "Reform Catholicism and Political Radicalism in the Austrian Enlightenment." In *The Enlightenment in National Context*, ed. R. Porter and M. Teich, pp. 141–63. Cambridge, U.K.: Cambridge University Press.

Wartofsky, M. 1982. *Feuerbach*. Cambridge, U.K.: Cambridge University Press.

Waser, R. 1994. *Autonomie des Selbstbewusstseins: eine Untersuchung zum Verhältnis von Bruno Bauer und Karl Marx (1835–1843)*. Tübingen: Francke.

Watts, F. 1997. "Are Science and Religion in Conflict?" *Zygon* 32: 125–38.

Weber, M. 1930. *The Protestant Ethic and the Spirit of Capitalism*. London: Allen & Unwin.

Wedeman, A. H. 1987. *The East Wind Subsides: Chinese Foreign Policy and the Origins of the Cultural Revolution*. Washington, D.C.: Washington Institute Press.

Weger, K.-H. 1979. *Religionskritik von der Aufklärung bis zur Gegenwart: Autoren-Lexikon von Adorno bis Wittgenstein*. Freiburg im Breisgau: Herder.

Weiner, D. R. 2000. *Models of Nature: Ecology, Conservation and Cultural Revolution in Soviet Russia*. Pittsburgh: University of Pittsburgh Press.

Westman, R. S. 1975. "The Melanchthon Circle, Rheticus and the Wittenberg Interpretation of the Copernican Theory." *Isis* 66: 165–93.

———. 1975. "Three Responses to the Copernican Theory: Johannes Praetorius, Tycho Brahe, and Michael Maestlin." In *The Copernican Achievement*, ed. R. S. Westman, pp. 285–345. London: University of California Press.

———. 1990. "Proof, Poetics and Patronage: Copernicus' Preface to *De Revolution-*

ibus." In *Reappraisals of the Scientific Revolution*, ed. D. C. Lindberg and R. S. Westman, pp. 167–205. Cambridge, U.K.: Cambridge University Press.

Wetherly, P. 1992. *Marx's Theory of History: The Contemporary Debate*. Aldershot, U.K.: Avebury.

Whaley, J. 1981. "The Protestant Enlightenment in Germany."In *The Enlightenment in National Context*, ed. R. Porter and M. Teich, pp. 106–17. Cambridge, U.K.: Cambridge University Press.

Wheen, F. 1999. *Karl Marx*. London: Fourth Estate.

White, J. D. 1996. *Karl Marx and the Intellectual Origins of Dialectical Materialism*. New York: St. Martin's.

White, R. 1980. "Calvin and Copernicus: The Problem Reconsidered." *Calvin Theological Journal* 15: 233–43.

Whitman, C. H. 1958. *Homer and the Heroic Tradition*. Cambridge, Mass.: Harvard University Press.

Wielema, M. R. 2001. "Unbelief and Atheism in Early Modern Europe." *Tijdschrift voor Geschiedenis* 114(3): 332–53.

Wilhelm, U. 1995. *Der deutsche Frühliberalismus von den Anfängen bis 1789*. Frankfurt am Main: Peter Lang.

Willis, W. W. 1987. *Theism, Atheism and the Doctrine of the Trinity: The Trinitarian Theologies of Karl Barth and Jürgen Moltmann in Response to Protest Atheism*. Atlanta: Scholars Press.

Wilson, A. N. 1999. *God's Funeral*. London: John Murray.

Wilson, C. A. 1975. "Rheticus, Ravetz and the 'Necessity' of Copernicus' Innovation." In *The Copernican Achievement*, ed. R. S. Westman, pp. 17–39. Berkeley: University of California Press.

Winter, B. 2001. "Naming the Oppressor, Not Punishing the Oppressed: Atheism and Feminist Legitimacy." *Journal of Women's History* 13(1): 53–57.

Wisan, W. L. 1986. "Galileo and God's Creation." *Isis* 77: 473–86.

Wolfe, T. 2000. "The Great Relearning." In *Hooking Up*, pp. 140–45. London: Jonathan Cape.

Wolff, R. L. 1977. *Gains and Losses: Novels of Faith and Doubt in Victorian England*. London: John Murray.

Wolfson, S. J. 2000. "Charlotte Smith's *Emigrants*: Forging Connections at the Borders of a Female Tradition." *Huntington Library Quarterly* 63: 509–46.

Wood, J. 1999. "The Sickness unto Life." *New Republic* (November 8, 1999), 89–96.

Wordsworth, J. 1982. *William Wordsworth: The Borders of Vision*. Oxford, U.K.: Oxford University Press.

Wright, T. R. 1986. *The Religion of Humanity: The Impact of Comtean Positivism on Victorian Britain*. Cambridge, U.K.: Cambridge University Press.

Young, R. 1969. "Malthus and the Evolutionists: The Common Context of Biological and Social Theory." *Past and Present* 43: 109–45.

Young, R. M. 1971. "Darwin's Metaphor: Does Nature Select?" *Monist* 55: 442–503.

———. 1993. "Darwin's Metaphor and the Philosophy of Science." *Science as Culture* 16: 375–403.

Zacharias, R. 1996. *A Shattered Visage: The Real Face of Atheism*. London: Hodder & Stoughton.

INDEX